# COUNTRY BOYS

# COUNTRY BOYS

## Masculinity and Rural Life

Foreword by Carolyn Sachs

Photographs by Cynthia Vagnetti

edited by

HUGH CAMPBELL

MICHAEL MAYERFELD BELL

MARGARET FINNEY

The Pennsylvania State University Press
University Park, Pennsylvania

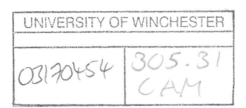
**Library of Congress Cataloging-in-Publication Data**

Country boys : masculinity and rural life / edited by Hugh Campbell,
Michael Mayerfeld Bell, Margaret Finney ; photographs by Cynthia Vagnetti.
   p.  cm.—(Rural studies series)
Includes bibliographical references and index.
ISBN 0-271-02874-2 (cloth : alk. paper)
ISBN 0-271-02875-0 (pbk. : alk. paper)
1. Rural men.
2. Masculinity.
3. Country life.
I. Campbell, Hugh, 1964– .
II. Bell, Michael, 1957– .
III. Finney, Margaret, 1967– .
IV. Rural studies series (University Park, Pa.)

HQ1090.C69   2006
305.3109173′4—dc22
2005035395

To the memory of our friend and colleague
*Robin Law*

# Contents

# Foreword

*Carolyn Sachs*

From New Zealand pubs to Iowa farms, *Country Boys* provides compelling evidence that rural masculinity matters. In a time of postmodernism and hyperurbanism, this book may seem anachronistic, but its editors and authors make a compelling argument about the centrality of representations and practices of rural masculinities for a broader understanding of culture and society. Rural men are real men. They hunt in the wilderness, operate large machinery, get dirty, and drink beer. Such representations and idealizations abound in the media, even though the every day lives of these men tell a different story. A major strength of this book is its ability to go back and forth between the representations and realities of rural masculinities. Few studies of this subject have been conducted and *Country Boys* makes a significant contribution to the field, beginning to define the field of rural masculinities while at the same time setting the research agenda for the future.

The notion of multiple masculinities runs through the chapters, suggesting that rural masculinity is neither set in stone nor frozen in time. Based on the framework of hegemonic masculinities, *Country Boys* show how rural masculinities are socially constructed, historically situated, invisible, and multiple. Crossing oceans from the United States to New Zealand to Ireland, the authors reveal a multitude of rural masculinities; there are many different ways to be a "country boy." Most of the chapters focus on particular sites (such as bars and pubs, sporting events, workplaces, and businesses) where masculinities are constructed and reinforced. Through this strategy, the book clearly illustrates Michael Kimmel and Abby Ferber's claim that manhood is proved in public spaces, in the eyes of other men. But as Peggy Bartlett's chapter on Georgia farms reveals, masculinity is also played out in the private sphere of one's emotional life and family. Many of the chapters reveal how the enactment of privileged masculinities enables most men to dominate women and some men to dominate other men. And as the editors convincingly argue, the contemporary hegemonic version of masculinity is based on the symbolic consumption and production of rural men. Ideas, images, and representations of rural men influence all masculinities. This argument becomes all the more credible through the fascinating ethnographic studies in which we hear the voices of Georgia farmers, rural militia members, and Irish men in pubs.

Several intriguing chapters attempt to untangle the complicated relationships between sexuality, the body, and masculinities. Rural spaces are seen as both safe havens for erotic love between men and also as the last bastions of uncontested heteronormativity. Written before the release of *Brokeback Mountain*, the 2006 film about two gay cowboys, Michael Bell's chapter on cowboy love reminds us that rural masculinities also include rural gay masculinities. From the chapter's representations of rural homosexuals, we learn what it means to be gay in cowboy country. Rural gay masculinity is often represented as natural, manly, and rough in contrast with hyperurban representations of gay men. Rural spaces are often portrayed as idyllic locations for male homosexuality, but the realities of being gay in cowboy country involve exclusion as well as violence, as the case of Matthew Shepard so clearly illustrates.

One of the strengths of this collection is its emphasis that rural masculinities are changing and these changes occur in multiple directions. As Berit Brandth and Marit S. Haugen point out, masculinities are multiple but always defined as superior to femininities. However, the hierarchy of masculinities in which some dominate others also suggests the possibilities for change. Although rural men may symbolically represent real men, these same versions of hegemonic masculinity fail rural and working-class men. Rural men with SUV's, chainsaws, large tractors, and beer glasses capture the public imagination on TV advertisements, but these men are increasingly distanced from the wealthy, highly educated, elite men who run corporations and government. As farming, forestry, and other traditional rural male occupations decline, rural men may symbolically represent real men but, in practice, they struggle to maintain their masculinities. Efforts to preserve their masculinity also affects rural men's health as they engage in unhealthy behaviors such as drinking too much, working too hard, and denying stress as well as other emotions.

The chapters in the book show that the threat to rural masculinities may bring both disturbing and promising visions. For example, the society-wide impact of the marginalization of rural men as militia men becomes all too clear in Chapter 7. These militia members are seeking to reclaim their manhood—specifically white, rural masculinities—through asserting a superior moral claim over women, blacks, Jews, and gays. Here, violence is the response to threatened rural masculinities. Controlled aggression and violence, in the form of military training, are also constructed in the countryside. Chapter 13 focuses on how rural spaces are the sites where military masculinities are taught to soldiers. But these hegemonic masculinities are in flux, as several chapters reveal that there are openings for change in hegemonic masculinities.

The editors are optimistic that emerging rural masculinities may become sources of empowerment *with* others rather than sources of power *over* others. Men farmers in rural Iowa and Georgia are rejecting industrial agriculture's emphasis on control over nature, large machinery, and strong chemicals and constructing a new type of farming masculinity based on sustainability, working with nature, and collaborating with other farmers. Despite the images of physically strong, outdoorsy men as real men, several chapters show that men with power tend to be those with managerial skill rather than physical strength and prowess.

*Country Boys* contributes to the exciting scholarly field of masculinity studies and to studies of rural places. Through its tour of pubs, military trainings, and farms, the book successfully convinces the reader of the centrality of rural masculinities for understanding contemporary global and local cultures. It charts new theoretical territory on to how and where the representations and realities of masculinities are constructed. Theoretical issues on embodiment, sexuality, and gender performance in rural sites are addressed and the need for more research at these intersections is made clear. Across borders of the United States, New Zealand, and Europe, intersections between class, sexuality, gender, and locality often reinforce particular forms of hegemonic rural masculinities that leave little space for women and other less dominant men. But we are left with a sense of hope, convinced that rural masculinities are shifting and that this shift may create less exclusive rural spaces and multiple possibilities for performing masculinity.

# Masculinity and Rural Life: An Introduction

*Hugh Campbell, Michael Mayerfeld Bell, and Margaret Finney*

In case you thought this book was of limited relevance to your life, let us point out that, as we write, country boys rule the world.

This may seem a large claim to make concerning what might at first blush seem a topic of interest only to specialists. "Blush" may also be the apt word for describing the embarrassed reaction those who research rural masculinity often get when describing their work to others ("You're studying *what?*"). But there will be no blush on President George Bush's face as he faces the cameras at the next photo opportunity at his Crawford, Texas, ranch. Wearing his boots and Stetson, posing with his horses, leaning on the rail of his cattle yards, clearing brush, and striding out across his land, Bush uses the imagery of rural life to portray not just a persona of authority and control but a *masculine* persona of authority and control. Here in the wilds of the Texas plains, Bush radiates a sense of primeval masculine power, a deep authenticity of leadership that can be counted on when the going gets tough. It has helped make Bush at times wildly popular (pun intended).

Bush is not the only male leader who has tried to use the imagery of rural life to give an impression of power and toughness. Bush's rival in the hotly contested 2000 American presidential race, Al Gore, famously tried to "reinvent" himself as an "alpha male" after Bush gained the presidency. Rather than posing as an alpha male cowboy, however, Gore began appearing at photo opportunities with the thick beard and red-and-black-checkered shirt of the stereotypical woodsman. Possibly Gore and his advisers felt that the cowboy role was already taken. Possibly they felt that the woodsman would be a more sympathetic image for environmentalists, for the political left in America, and for other elements of Gore's constituency. Whatever the reason, both Bush and Gore sought symbolic power through the imagery of country boys—a contest of the cowboy versus the woodsman. And then, in the equally contentious 2004 presidential election, Bush's new rival, John Kerry, sought to portray another kind of rural alpha male: that of the warrior hero, battle-tested in the watery wilds of the Vietnam jungle, gun in hand. Kerry also sought to renew that image during the campaign, taking time out for a carefully photographed pheasant shoot, decked out in an orange hunting vest, gun in hand once more. Indeed, even the whole notion of "alpha males," a concept drawn from zoological studies of wolf packs, is based on our imagined idea that the true natures we encounter in the rural primeval, where the wolf packs run and howl, are authentically masculine.

Country boys not only rule the world politically. Take the way advertisements for a vast range of products make their pitch through rural masculine poses. Perhaps most widely recognized is the lonely profile of the Marlboro man, tough and independent on his horse in the badlands of the American west. suv and truck advertisements similarly place their products in the rocky and the rough, calling on the symbolic power of the venerable rural myth of rugged individualism. Such advertisements not only suggest that the vehicle's owner personally gains this rugged power and reputation, but also make a symbolic claim for the reliability and toughness of the product itself. As one of the chapters in this book shows, beer advertisements also routinely use rural settings and rural activities to pitch this conventionally male drink. Real men don't drink latte. They drink beer, smoke Marlboros, and ride their suvs through mud and up mountains, to the acclaim of women and the envy of other men. Real men are rural men: this cultural idea wields not only enormous political power but enormous economic power.

But rural masculinity is not only an image. Clearly, it is also part of the lived experience of the half of the world that still lives in rural areas—even in the developed world roughly one-fourth of the population still resides in rural areas. We quite deliberately say "half of the world" and "one-fourth of the developed world" and not just the men living there, because rural masculinity is equally an aspect of the lives of men and women. One does not have to be male to experience masculinity. The way rural men conduct their lives has a huge impact on how rural women live *their* lives, for gender is a relational matter. Notions of what are appropriate actions for men are often conceived in contrast to what is deemed appropriate for women, and vice versa. (Imagine Hillary Clinton, Elizabeth Dole, Nancy Pelosi, Condoleezza Rice, or another of the leading women of American politics in a cowboy hat or hunting vest, facing the cameras.) By extension, we can see that the constraints that men experience in their lives and the ways they operate within them will in turn shape the constraints that women experience and their ways of operating, and once again vice versa. For both men and women, therefore, rural masculinity constitutes not only a relational *ideology* but also a relational set of *social practices*.

This book explores rural masculinity (or what we prefer to term *rural masculinities,* as we explain later) in both senses: that is, as something we imagine and as something we live. We say "we" meaning everyone, male and female, rural and urban. Whether it is the rural man gutting it out into the night on his tractor, the rural woman bringing him his dinner out in the field so he can keep on going, the urban man off on a hunting or a fishing trip with his weekend buddies, or the urban woman left behind to chase the kids, images and experiences of rural masculinity shape all of our lives. Rural masculinity shapes people's employment chances, their recreation choices, their buying habits, their voting preferences, and their daily interactions with women and men.

With the hope that we might encourage more freedom in those chances, and more informed reflection in those choices, habits, preferences, and interactions, we offer this book.

## Seeing Rural Masculinities

So far, we've talked about easily recognizable images of rural masculinity: cowboys, woodsmen, farmers, hunters. But, however recognizable they may be, images work—perhaps paradoxically—by making some aspects visible while at the same time making others invisible. Everything that an image shows excludes that which is not shown. This exclusion is not necessarily a matter of calculated manipulation, although it may often be. A photograph, a sentence, a thought: there are practical limits to what these can include, and thus every inclusion depends on exclusion, even when we intend no manipulation. So too with constructions of rural masculinity. Every image of rural masculinity renders some aspects of life visible, while obscuring those other aspects that contradict the message being created in the visible world. Since not everything can be included, choices need to be made—choices that, frankly, provide many opportunities for cultural mischief. Obscuring becomes ignoring, which slides easily into concealing and deliberately distorting. Every image of rural masculinity is thus a partial vision of our gendered world—generally (and perhaps unavoidably) partial in both senses of the word, even when this is not our intention.

Some of the most important and sociologically interesting country boys are the invisible and obscured ones we do not easily recognize. Take, for example, homosexuals, who are virtually absent from our thoughts about the rural. In the same way, the rural is typically absent from our thoughts about homosexuality, which has a strongly urban cast in our imagination. In her celebrated short story "Brokeback Mountain," now a celebrated movie, Annie Proulx points out that this lack of recognition is not a simple oversight or a mere matter of the inherent exclusion of any specific inclusion in an image.[1] She tells the story of two young cowboys who spend half their lives as lovers, meeting sporadically at remote mountain locations even as they both get married and raise families. But to be a "homosexual" and a "cowboy" is to live a dangerous contradiction between the visible and acceptable rural masculinity of the cowboy and the invisible rural world of homosexual masculinity. The potential hazards of this contradiction mean that the two protagonists must live carefully guarded double lives, for when the invisible becomes visible the response can be violent. When one of the lovers—Jack—fails to respond to the annual invitation to slip away into the mountains, his partner, Ennis, rings Jack's wife:

> [S]he said in a level voice yes, Jack was pumping up a flat on the truck out on a back road when the tire blew up. The bead was damaged somehow and the force of the explosion slammed the rim into his face, broke his nose and jaw and knocked him unconscious on his back. By the time someone came along he had drowned in his own blood.
>
> No, he thought, they got him with the tire iron.[2]

The potential violence of visibility and invisibility is not just a topic for fiction. "Brokeback Mountain" was published in October 1998, the same month that a young gay man, Matthew Shepard, was savagely beaten on a back road in Wyoming and, like Jack, left to die. Matthew Shepard—again like Jack—was killed for transgressing the sexual order of one version of rural masculinity: the version that dictates that country boys are resolutely heterosexual. Being a gay country boy can be very dangerous indeed.

But even the most familiar and accepted country boys have their invisible sides. A common and celebrated icon of the rural masculine is that of the farmer struggling to survive against all odds, heroically staving off the bankers and the weather through plowing, planting, and harvesting for days on end without sleep. In these narratives, the farm survives against the odds because of a tough kind of farming masculinity that endures—and goes on enduring—hardship. Embedded beneath the surface of these narratives are also the stories of the family members who must live with this version of farming masculinity, and who accommodate and support this lonely drama on the prairies. It is the man who typically claims the title "farmer," even on a family farm where the "farm wife" and the "farm kids" labor both in the fields and in the home on tasks essential to the farm enterprise: feeding livestock, driving grain wagons to the elevator, balancing the books, washing the clothes and dishes, cooking the food, and acting as reserve drivers. Nonetheless, every farm typically has only one "farmer."

Then there are the small-town patriarchs: the local mayors, the chairs of the chambers of commerce, leaders of the Elks and the Shriners and the local sports clubs, the pillars of the local church. Here we encounter images of rural masculinity that are perhaps less celebrated in the wider culture but are no less central to the sense many rural people have of the appropriate conduct of rural men. Here too we encounter as many invisibilities as visibilities: aspects of masculinity actively constructed out of the materials of rural life to become cultural clothing that presents the man, baring and obscuring as it drapes his contours. For example, as with the family farm, no local polity, chamber of commerce, Elks' club, or church could survive without the support of family members. And yet there is only one mayor, one chair of the chamber of commerce, one Grand Exalted Ruler of the Benevolent and Protective Order of the Elks, and one church deacon, and they are nearly always men.

In other words, rural life is typically highly patriarchal. We are even tempted to suggest that it is typically more patriarchal than urban life, although this assessment cannot be a matter of precise measurement. Indeed, part of the allure of rural masculine imagery may be the sense of greater power that it grants both rural and urban men, but again, this allure is something that can only be suggested, not rigorously affirmed. Perhaps this indefiniteness constitutes yet another aspect of the power of rural masculinity. In an age where—thankfully—the justice of patriarchy is under much greater scrutiny than in the past, overt declarations of masculine prerogative are increasingly difficult to sustain ideologically—even among men themselves, eager for a "new man" self-image. Patriarchy has long gained its power through a complex mixture of the visible and the invisible, both among the wielders of its authority and those who submit to that authority. In this, the authors of this volume certainly see no change.

The growing uneasiness with patriarchy, including rural patriarchy, leads us to an important complexity in rural masculinity: its imagery is by no means always positive. Often our imagined country boys are dangerous and depraved, wandering around with a shotgun, wearing long underwear and a straw hat, slurping moonshine and chasing nice urban white-water rafters, like the now legendary villains of the movie *Deliverance*. Or they may be ignorant rubes, the slow-witted and six-fingered left behind by those with the get up and go who got up and went, off to the civilized life of the city, the kind of menacing folk who form the shadowy and sexually depraved mob inhabiting a whole genre of American horror films.[3] Or they may be yobs and yahoos, crass good old boys who actually see a cowboy hat, a Confederate flag, or a woodsman's coat as symbols worthy of admiration. While Bush, Gore, and Kerry may have sought some political gain through their display of rural imagery, we cannot ignore the fact that the press in the United States often ridicules these all too obvious masculine pretensions. Take the scorn heaped on Gore's "alpha male" reinvention, or the constant lambasting of Bush's cowboy-hat masculinity in political cartoons. One well-known political cartoon series, *Doonesbury*, used to go so far as to portray Bush solely with a cowboy hat, bodiless, floating in the air, reducing Bush to this icon of rural masculinity. Still others respond that such ridicule is a sign of a liberal elitism out of touch with the dreams of common people. These complexities should come as no surprise to us. Symbols of power, whether rural or urban, male or female, are nearly always contested, for contestation is what power is all about.

Obviously, all these images of rural masculinity—positive and negative, visible and invisible—are not without practical consequence. When we speak of power, we speak of the consequences for the organization of social life. Rural masculine imagery commonly supports social practices that advantage some men over other men, and men as a whole over women as a whole, whether that imagery is positive or negative in tone. Rural masculinity matters.

But here too we need to note an important complexity. While rural masculinity commonly advantages its practitioners, it can also have negative effects, particularly for rural men. In this regard, let us review some empirical evidence. In this volume, Will Courtenay demonstrates that rural men are more likely to start drinking at a young age than their urban counterparts, and are more likely to drive while drunk. They are exposed to more risks than the average person, especially those who engage in two of the riskiest of occupations, mining and farming. They also take more risks, perhaps in part because of a tough-guy vision of masculinity, which leads to poor health behavior like refusing to use sun-block lotion. Rural men have smaller social networks, seek help for medical issues (especially mental health issues) more slowly than urban men, and are more susceptible to suicide. With fewer resources and job prospects and less education and political power, rural men are perhaps more easily seduced by "hypermasculine" behavior. The hypermasculine swagger of rural masculinity can also have negative consequences for urban men when they engage in its risky ways. Again, rural masculinity matters.

And if it matters, we would be wise to learn to see it more readily—both its practices and its imagery. To that end, we (the editors) have organized this book into three main sections: *practices, representations,* and *changes.*

There is no clear line between social practices and the images with which we represent them, as we hope we have already shown. Each shapes the other in a kind of continuous dialogue. The authors of the chapters to follow continually endeavor to show these interconnections and continuities. But they do typically start at one moment or other in the dialogue, going from practices to representations or representations to practices, or at least implying this movement. In the section on practices, the authors more characteristically begin in what rural masculinity leads us to do, or "practice." By contrast, in the section on representations, the authors enter the analysis of rural masculinity from its imagery and ideology and proceed from there to interactions with practices.

The good news, we believe, is that these interactions are not necessarily static. If one is persuaded, as are the authors of this volume, that rural masculinity is not always beneficial in its current manifestations, learning to see rural masculinity more clearly may also enable us to see beyond it. This is the business of the final section of the book, two short reflections and refractions on the potential for changes in rural masculinity, its practices and representations.

## Studying Masculinities

To help our authors in this task, we would like to review some key issues in the way in which sociologists understand both *masculinity* and the *rural*. These are, after all, the two key terms that describe the subject of this book. If our goal is to see rural masculinity more clearly, we would also do well to turn a magnifying glass on the masculine and the rural themselves. As we shall see, both terms embody the interaction of representation and practice in social life. In this section we take up how sociologists have envisioned masculinity and, most important, why sociologists today prefer to speak (although it sounds awkward to say) not only of masculinity but of *masculinities*.

In order to view the interplay of visibility and invisibility in the imagery of rural masculinity, we need first to contend with a deeper issue: the general invisibility of masculinity as a whole, both in everyday life and in academic inquiry—what Donna Harraway calls the "god-trick" of men being everywhere and yet invisible, omnipresent yet unnoticed. When we talk about social life, and identify some things as *normal,* or *the norm* for human behavior, how many times are we actually talking about what *men* do? Robin Law et al. use the example of the way we talk about "politicians" and "women politicians."[4] We ask, for instance, when we will have the first "woman" president or prime minister, or the first "black" president or prime minister. Obviously, the male version of a politician is linguistically (and socially) unmarked, while the female or black politician is clearly marked—and therefore signaled as not normal. In this way, masculinity (and white masculinity at that) has often hidden itself from our eyes using the disguise of "the norm."

As early the 1950s, however, writers both in and outside academia began to see men as *men.* On the one hand, there were those who saw men as *a problem,* associated with rising feminist concerns. Another, however, saw men as *having problems,* as experiencing identity difficulties in response to social changes.[5] The "organization man," to use the terminology of the time, was in trouble.

From this point, and in loose parallel with these concerns, two distinct academic approaches to masculinity emerged. One stream saw the study of masculinity as an adjunct to feminist analysis of gendered power in society. The other stream adopted an "insider" stance, looking at men's individual experiences in order to analyze the "crisis" of masculine identity through changes in men's work, culture, and politics. While both these approaches aimed to emancipate men from their academic and social invisibility, the first, more feminist approach typically analyzed gender relations in a way that made it difficult to position men, along with women, as oppressed by patriarchy. By contrast, the second approach tended to look at problems of gender less relationally, and thus as unique to either men or women at various times. According to this second approach, men were equally—although inevitably differently—"co-victims" of gender.

Academic research into masculinities matured in 1987 with the sudden publication of several key studies.[6] These studies clearly illustrated the two distinct directions of masculinities research, with some authors concentrating on the critical analysis of masculinities as part of the wider feminist critique of gender relations,[7] and others focusing on men as "co-victims" in their own right.[8] There was, however, some basic common ground.

Most important, all these researchers emphasized the idea that masculinity was not an essentialist biological or psychological state and did not reside in a single "sex role" that was in "crisis." The idea of sex roles created an impression that people's gender was something that, in the normal course of life, people grew into—unconsciously choosing one of a small variety on offer. Social theory thus tended to emphasize those occasional situations where something went "wrong" and "role socialization" had not taken place in the way that was expected. Moreover, the idea of "sex roles" seemed to imply that men and women had to adopt particular practices in order for society to function properly: society required men and women to enact masculinity and femininity with the assumption that change would be hazardous for all of us. Both streams of research argued that this "functionalist" view was more of a political position than an accurate account of social dynamics.

In contrast, both of these more recent research streams replaced the idea of the male sex role with the understanding that masculinity was "socially constructed" in different social and historical spaces. That is, they argued that masculinity has never been an unchanging monolith writ in biological and social necessity. Rather, they said, masculinity is as various and as variable as society itself. Consequently, these studies suggested, if we wanted to understand masculinity, we had to understand the changing social contexts in which particular *representations* and *practices* of masculinity emerge.

One useful way of approaching the social construction of masculinities is the concept of *hegemonic masculinity*. This idea—originally attributed to Tim Carrigan et al.[9] but most consistently associated with the body of work by Australian sociologist Raewyn Connell—has helped to unify many of the theories behind the study of masculinity in the 1980s and 1990s. By hegemonic masculinity, sociologists mean understanding masculinity as a critical partner to feminist analyses of power, looking at why and how some forms of masculinity become dominant in a particular society. Connell provides a simple definition of the term: "Hegemonic masculinity is not a fixed character type, always and everywhere the same. It is, rather, the masculinity that occupies the hegemonic position in a given pattern of gender relations."[10] Hegemonic masculinity is, therefore, the version of masculinity that is considered legitimate, "natural," or unquestionable in a particular set of gender relations.

By moving toward hegemony theory, Connell shifts the focus of analysis away from *men* as a social group and toward *masculinities*. Not all men enact the same constellation of masculine ideas and practices, nor does any one man enact the same constellation at all times. For example, men commonly vary in their sexuality, both across society and across the course of their own individual lives. Not every man presents himself as a tough guy, and even those who do may at times shuck the cowboy hat and take off the boots, literally and metaphorically. While men as a group tend to experience a higher social dividend of power and reward than women, certain social conditions typically reward specific masculinities over others. In fact, even men who usually do not themselves enact these dominant masculinities will still benefit from the patriarchal society dominant masculinities reflect and support. Thus the enactment of privileged masculinities will enable most men to dominate over most women, and some men to dominate over some other men.[11]

Hegemonic masculinity theorists argue, however, that this most approved or privileged masculinity is typically not something we see as such. Because of its legitimacy, hegemonic masculinity comes to be seen as natural, and thus is largely unnoticed and invisible even as we strive to enact its practices and representations. Because of its relative invisibility, hegemonic masculinity becomes difficult to contest openly, thus reinforcing its hegemonic power, because all other gender relationships and dynamics must "fit in" around this dominant norm.

In other words, masculinities exist in complex power relations with each other, and with various constructions of femininity. Thus, Connell argues, the term "hegemonic masculinity" is deceptively simple, as there is no single hegemonic masculinity, separate and apart.[12] Rather, hegemonic power relations actually involve a range of masculinities whose interactions empower some over others. Indeed, their interactions help constitute them to begin with. The tough guy and the sissy, for example, cannot exist without each other. One wins on the playground, but both can win the longer game in life because of how they conceptually support the value of male power. In more formal theoretical language, Connell suggests that we can distinguish at the very least hegemonic, complicit, subordinate, and marginalized masculinities within this range of relationships.

There is something of a grab-bag character to the theory of hegemonic masculinity, as Connell herself has noted.[13] Rather than a single overarching theory, hegemonic masculinity is more a popular conceptual hook upon which theorists hang related ideas about masculinity. Law et al. identify four key ideas researchers usually associate with the theory:

- the socially constructed basis of masculinity;
- the role of history in constructing masculinities;
- the continuing invisibility of masculinity; and
- the idea of plural or multiple masculinities.[14]

We would also add a fifth:

- the interaction between representations and practices of masculinity in all its multiple and relational forms.

Many of the chapters of this book have made at least some use of this framework, even while proposing other theoretical approaches. For example, the chapter by Gregory Peter et al. (which includes one of us) distinguishes between "dialogic" and "monologic" forms of masculinity—in brief, a masculinity that sees itself relationally versus one that does not. Peter et al. in part situate this idea within hegemonic masculinity theory's notion of plural masculinities. Peter et al. also share the view that all masculinities are socially constructed and relational—even in the case of monologic masculinity, which, ironically, finds its power through denying its constructed and relational character.

Pierre Bourdieu, the famous French social theorist, offered an account of masculinity in one of his last books that also fits well with hegemonic masculinity.[15] In that study, Bourdieu used the idea of *doxa* as a way of describing a certain orthodoxy that emerges around masculinity. Doxa is the end result of many processes and practices that eventually create an established and accepted set of behaviors that signify masculinity or femininity. Doxa is what people in a particular social situation come to accept as the normal, natural, and accepted version of masculinity or femininity in their lives. While Bourdieu fits the pieces together differently, there is a clear similarity here to the idea of hegemonic masculinity. Of course, both Bourdieu and the hegemony theorists do not think that the story begins or ends at that point. Every version of masculine doxa has not only been constructed through quite specific historical and social processes, but will be continually transformed and contested as time goes by.

Other researchers, including Connell, are increasingly emphasizing the place of the body and performance in hegemonic masculinity. In a 1995 book, Connell examines how we "act out" or "advertise" our gender through "body reflexive practices," or behaviors in which our body's physical attributes and activities become an active component in gendering us as human subjects. Jo Little's chapter in the present volume also extends our understanding of masculinities to the practices and performances of the body. She examines the active construction of rural men and women as embodied participants in an unquestioned heterosexual world. A lot of cultural work goes into making us, and our bodies, "unscary" in heterosexual life.

Theorists of masculinity, again including Connell, have also explored "poststructuralism" as an approach to hegemonic masculinities. Poststructuralist theories emphasize that meanings or definitions are indeterminate: we cannot simply "read" one unchanging meaning into behaviors or issues. Rather, our experiences are made up of a constant series of intersections between power, gender, individuality, society, ideology, and material practices. If we look at men and masculinities through a poststructuralist lens, therefore, we need to consider that the experience of "being a man" is often complex, ambiguous, fluid, and self-contradictory. Poststructuralism thus questions our accepted public definitions of categories, even the very category "gender." As a theoretical standpoint, post-structuralism has been taken up both by mainstream scholars such as Connell[16] and also by researchers interested in feminist analysis, media studies, and queer theory.[17]

Only recently seen as a marginal field of study at best, research on masculinities has now spread far and wide through the social science and liberal arts disciplines, including sociology,[18] history,[19] art history,[20] anthropology,[21] and media studies.[22] Masculinity has emerged as an important aspect of "white studies," postcolonial analysis, and literary criticism. If it is not quite there yet, masculinity research is certainly on the cusp of becoming "mainstream."

But this overview of masculinities research provides only half the theoretical agenda we need to understand country boys. We have looked at the "boys"; now we need to look at the "country."

## Studying the Rural

How do we study the rural? This question frustrates rural sociologists and geographers, because while we all use the term "rural" with a fair degree of certainty about what we mean, establishing exactly what conceptual evidence we base that "fair degree of certainty" upon is actually quite difficult.[23]

In its most practical sense, "rural" refers to those particular spaces that are not metropolitan. In other words, "rural" has immediate meaning as the opposite of "urban" and "metropolitan." Folk who are rural dwellers are folk who live outside the city. But how do we decide where the city stops and where rural life begins? This separation is becoming especially difficult as the boundaries around cities become blurred by the increasing numbers of "city people" who settle in semirural surroundings. Therefore, can we just decide that you are rural or urban by where you live? Not so easily.

Sociologists used to apply the ideas of the classical social theorist Ferdinand Tönnies to distinguish between urban and rural. In 1887 Tönnies suggested that there are two basic configurations of social life, what he termed *Gemeinschaft* and *Gesellschaft*. *Gemeinschaft* (which is the German word for "community") is the web of sentimental ties that connect people one to the other, while *Gesellschaft* (which is the German word for "society") are the ties of material interest that link us.[24] Tönnies stressed that the two forms of connection interact and can be found together in all social contexts, although in some contexts one or the other will usually be more salient. In the mid-twentieth century, sociologists who missed Tönnies's emphasis on the interactive character of *Gemeinschaft* and *Gesellschaft* proposed that the two could be mapped spatially onto rural and urban life, respectively.[25] The more rural, the more *Gemeinschaft*-like life was likely to be; the more urban, the more *Gesellschaft*-like.

Thus was born the now infamous "rural-urban continuum" theory in rural sociology. Despite strong initial support, the concept of the rural-urban continuum faltered in the 1960s, as academics began to question whether the continuum held up in reality. After all, weren't there plenty of "urban villages" in city neighborhoods that had all the same qualities of so-called rural life?[26] Since then, probably no idea has been or continues to be more criticized in the pages of rural sociology.[27]

A second line of academic argument aimed to distinguish the urban and the rural through demographic and geographic means. In this argument, geographical areas that experienced population densities below a certain level were rural, while any population densities above the line were urban. While this was a simple idea, in practice it proved a little abstract. Did small rural towns of 999 inhabitants really become small urban towns with an increase to 1,000 inhabitants? Furthermore, how could academics make international comparisons when countries like Canada and New Zealand administratively demarcated the differences between rural and urban towns at populations of 1,000, while the United Kingdom used 10,000, the United Nations 20,000, Japan 30,000, and the United States 50,000?[28]

Subsequently, researchers looked at defining the rural through the existence of particular industries, such as agriculture. The most popular images of rural life often involve some level of agricultural activity—when we think of a "rural" scene, for instance, we often think of a farm landscape. Several rural sociologists in the 1980s, therefore, began thinking less about the distinctiveness of rural society and more about the distinctiveness of the extensive industries in rural areas: farming, fishing, forestry, and (later) tourism.[29] While this approach began to tell us a lot about the sociology of agriculture (and other industries), many felt that the "economically driven" definition of the rural left out more than it included.

The early 1990s saw a significant change in the way academics understood the rural. Yes, rural society might have interesting characteristics; yes, rural folk might live in lower-density areas of population; yes, they might work in industries like farming and forestry—but all these academic attempts to fit certain things inside the word "rural" were clearly less than useful. Why not turn around and stop trying to identify a single object called "the rural" and look at the *variety* of ways in which the word (and concept) "rural" is used by both academics and the general public in our social lives.[30] In many ways this "turnaround" paralleled the shift within masculinity theory from examining the objective category called "men" to engaging with the many subjective ideas and practices making up different "masculinities." Likewise, in rural research this "cultural turn" changed the emphasis of study from trying to define the one "real" rural to trying to understand multiple *rurals*.

This new approach recognizes the different narratives that create meaning when we use the term "rural." To start with, Michael Bell and Andy Pratt point out that the long debates among rural sociologists and geographers about "the meaning of rural" are debates held entirely among academics.[31] These academic arguments about the rural hold little meaning in terms of the different ways lay people use the term "rural." In the 1980s, some academics categorized these different conceptions about the rural in terms of a distinction between the subjective rural "myths" of laypeople and the objective rural "facts" of academics.[32] In their words, "beyond the popular images there is an objective rural America."[33] By the 1990s, however, newer debates—such as the one between Jonathan Murdoch, Pratt, and Chris Philo—showed that cultural approaches to sociology were breaking down this distinction between objective "fact" and subjective "myth." If people act according to a variety of particular discourses about what is rural, then their subjective ideas are just as important as objective "facts" or evidence about their lives.[34]

Because researchers were now looking at ideas and conceptions *of* the rural as well as facts *about* the rural, new approaches to discourses of rurality also extended from how people define the rural to how people act out the rural.[35] As a result, sociologists now stress the importance of the ways in which media and advertising represent the rural, as well as the ways in which tourists, incomers, and exurban weekend residents practice the rural through their enactment of a symbolically desirable lifestyle—a kind of symbolic consumption of the rural.

Through these overviews we can see that while the rural and the masculine are distinct areas of study, there are some important similarities in their theoretical development. Specifically, the transition from studying men to studying masculinities is very similar to the transition from attempting to objectively define the "real" rural to analyzing multiple discourses of rurality. If we now combine these two areas of study, we can identify the important issues and concerns of the practices and representations of "rural masculinity" itself.

## Key Sites of Rural Masculinities

The previous sections show that there is nothing entirely straightforward about trying to analyze either the masculine or the rural. Rather, we must situate rural masculinities in specific historical, symbolic, and spatial contexts. This does not mean, however, that we cannot locate some important commonalities or significant sites that reappear across a variety of rural masculinities. Initially, we want to identify nine sites in which rural masculinities operate or become important, although this is certainly not an exhaustive list.[36]

### At the Household Level

Rural industry is often firmly based in the family or household. In particular, farming involves important household dynamics, and these dynamics—including the division of labor, the division of wealth, cultural legitimacy, decision-making processes, and raising the next generation of farmers—are strongly influenced by gender. While, since the mid-1980s, there has been a great deal of rural sociology and geography focused on women in farm households, male farmers and farming masculinities have, until recently, slipped past us—a clear example of masculinity, as the sociological norm, being invisible. While Kristi Anne Stølen produced the first ethnographic account specifically directed at masculinity in farm households,[37] only in the past few years has much published work engaged ethnographically with masculinities in farm households.[38]

### In the Politics of Farming

The very activity of farming itself is not something that we can accept as a natural, normal, or uncontested feature of our lives. How we farm is,

therefore, subject to its own politics. This is particularly important for issues such as conflicts between intensive and extensive systems, leasehold
versus freehold, contracting versus cooperatives, and the relationship between conventional and alternative agriculture. Peter et al. provide clear
evidence that the way in which farmers construct their masculinity has
implications for how they approach sustainability issues in farming.[39] At
the level of industry politics, Ruth Liepins showed how farmer representatives are overwhelmingly portrayed through a specific construction of masculinity.[40] These two articles indicate that from the paddock to the
boardroom, the politics of farming is influenced by rural masculinities.

## At the Level of Small Communities

Small-town and agricultural-community politics is strongly influenced by
gender. Little and Jones provided a case study showing how a seemingly
mundane political process—the competitive funding of development projects for small towns in England—was actually deeply (and unconsciously)
influenced by the "masculinity" of the proposals and presentations.[41]
While invisible to the participants, a particular version of rural masculinity, Little and Jones argued, was being privileged in these processes. This
case study is just one example of the way in which power, politics, and
influence intersect significantly with gender in rural communities. In the
later chapters of this collection we revisit research on the influence of masculinity on power in small towns, and look at some specific examples in
detail.

## In the Restructuring of Rural Industry

Since the mid-1980s, many rural sociologists and geographers have examined the impact of changes in rural industries like agriculture, fishing,
forestry, and tourism.[42] We suggest that rural masculinities have a role in
how and where these impacts occur. Berit Brandth and Marit Haugen, for
instance, discuss the importance of changing work structures in Norwegian farming and forestry, and how these have influenced (and been influenced by) particular rural masculinities.[43] They argue that these forms
of restructuring the industry are at the heart of changing definitions of
what constitutes the hegemonic version of masculinity in these industries.
Again, little other work has been done in this important area, although

clearly these impacts are wide-ranging and influence many areas of rural experience.

### In the Spatial Politics of Migration

Another important issue in rural communities is who leaves and who stays behind. Many rural communities demonstrate a form of spatial politics in which one key act of resistance to power structures is simply to leave town. Because those who oppose oppressive or unjust power structures remove themselves from the community, these "unbalanced" structures continue to receive an abnormally high degree of consent from those remaining. In this collection, Caitríona Ní Laoire and Shaun Fielding, David Bell, and Hugh Campbell, address the importance of out-migration for the sexual and gender order of rural communities, and for the institutional structures of such communities.[44]

### In the Embodied Experience of Masculinities

In this collection, Jo Little provides an excellent introduction to the issue of masculinity, embodiment, and the rural.[45] She argues that the body has emerged as an important part of recent theoretical examinations of gender and sexuality. Rather than adhere to traditional concepts of the mind/body split—which suggests that what we think and why we act are more important than the body, which we simply drag through social life as a passive object—we need to study the physically embodied experience of gendered, sexual people. Her examples provide compelling reasons for seeing the rural as both constructed *by* and helping *to* construct our embodied experience of gender and sexuality. In many different rural sites and industries this embodiment is clearly demonstrated by the mutual construction of masculinity and technical skills.[46]

### Through Association with "Nature"

As we have seen, there has been, and continues to be, complex academic struggle over how to define the term "rural." Equally complex debate swirls around the concept of "nature." To make matters more complicated, the two terms undeniably have a vague but companionable relationship. Many people think of nature as being spatially located somewhere "out there" (looking out from the city) and point in the same direction they might point if they were asked where "the rural" was located. In several chapters in this volume, the authors interrogate the association of masculinity with the "natural" qualities of rural space and highlight how this association can legitimate and authorize some gender identities.

## Through the Symbolic Life of the Rural

In a previous work, Campbell and Bell suggested that traditionally most rural sociology has stuck firmly to empirical and structural sociological reasoning.[47] From the outset, however, work on rural masculinities has emphasized a more cultural approach. Many chapters in this volume support our observations, as they work from the study of masculine practice to the use of the rural as a symbolic realm, and vice versa. To use the terminology we introduced earlier, such work moves beyond studying masculinity as something that occupies rural space, and toward understanding masculinities as behaviors and attitudes that "produce" and "consume" the rural. In this volume, therefore, rather than tacking on such ideas as afterthoughts to the "real" rural sociology of masculinity, we argue that the study of rural masculinities often shows exactly how rural sociology can escape from its traditional boundaries and begin to contribute to the wider analysis of masculinities.

## Through the Symbolic Life of the Masculine

In other words, what all of the chapters of this book imply is that rural masculinity is not some tinkling adornment on the main animal of masculinity itself. Rather, they suggest that masculinity is, in considerable measure, constructed out of rural masculinity. The "real man" of many currently hegemonic forms of masculinity is, as we noted, a rural man. Although we are used to seeing the rural as the weaker partner in the rural/urban dichotomy, the studies presented here together suggest that rural masculinity is central to the power of masculinities in rural and urban places alike—to its symbolic representations and thus to its practices, and back to its symbolic representations again.

## The Ubiquity of Rural Masculinity

Rural masculinity, then, is neither only rural nor only about men and masculinity. It is everywhere, a part of all our lives: male and female, rural and urban, masculine and feminine, heterosexual and homosexual, young and old, rich and poor, developed world and developing world. Turn on the television, and there it is, in the advertisements and in the shows. Open the paper, and there it is, right on the front page in the manly looks of the country boys who, as we write, rule the world. Go out on the street, and there it is in the suv in your neighbor's driveway, and perhaps in your own. Go out in the countryside, and there it is again, rugged and wild at times, at other times nurturing, but always, in our imagination, natural and free. Rural masculinity is something we think and something we do, something we represent and something we practice. Rural masculinity is something we live.

But rural masculinity is also something we can change. We know this because, for all its ubiquity, rural masculinity is always a contested assemblage of rural masculinities in the plural, as variable as they are widespread. We know rural masculinity can vary because it does vary. We know it can change because it does change.

But again, for all its ubiquity, we have seldom seen rural masculinity. It is the proverbial fish swimming in water it scarcely considers. The goal of this book is to present some intellectual tools for the consideration of this water. For example, as our list of suggestions above indicates, at present rural masculinity stands as a topic of study primarily in terms of the Western world, a focus largely reflected by our chapters. Clearly, however, rural masculinities are not the sole preserve of the West. As well, they are deeply inflected by race and ethnicity, as Kimmel and Ferber, Courtenay, and Lobao specifically suggest. The plurality of rural masculinities finds expression along a myriad of other axes of social experience as well, as yet scarcely researched. Given the aim of this volume—to make visible previously unrecognized, "taken-for-granted" performances of the rural and the masculine—we envisage further studies will take up some of the "invisible" areas implied in this collection: African American, Native American, Hispanic, Asian, Aboriginal, Maori New Zealander, Pacific Rim, mainland European masculinities, and more; the impact of the rural masculine and the masculine rural on lesbian farmers; the role of the handicapped "on the land"; ethics of animal husbandry; and the part children play learning, supporting, or rejecting specific gendered "performances" of rural masculinity, to name only a few. This is an incomplete list, as it must be: not all the manifold expressions and consequences of rural masculinities are yet visible even to the researchers who have tried to investigate them.

May the clouds soon lift. We—the editors and the authors of the chapters to come—believe the very act of consideration and recognition will change, at least in some small way, both rural masculinity and the broader dynamics of gender it helps constitute. At least this is our hope. For, although rural masculinity is always contested, at present it is not contested nearly enough.

## NOTES

1. Proulx (1999).

2. Ibid., 311.

3. Clover (1992).

4. Law, Campbell, and Schick (1999).

5. Savran (1998).

6. In the United States, Brod (1987); Kaufman (1987); Kimmel (1987); in Australia, Connell (1987); and in New Zealand, Phillips (1987).

7. Connell (1987, 1995a); Hearn (1987); Kimmel (1987).

8. Brod (1994); Brod and Kaufman (1994); Kaufman (1987). The co-victim narrative in academia was very mild compared to the sudden emergence of the new men's movement in the United States. Leading proponents of an antifeminist men's movement included Robert Bly (1990), Sam Keen (1991), and Warren Farrell (1994). Clatterbaugh (1997) provides a useful critique of the ideological agenda of the wider men's movement.

9. Carrigan, Connell, and Lee (1985).

10. Connell (1995a, 74).

11. Law, Campbell, and Schick (1999, 25–27).

12. Connell (1995a).

13. Ibid.

14. Law, Campbell, and Schick (1999).

15. Bourdieu (2001).

16. See also Craig (1992); Hanke (1992).

17. Boyd (1996); Edwards (1997); Jackson (1991); Perchuk and Posner (1995); Pfeil (1995); Segal (1990).

18. Connell (1995a).

19. Roper and Tosh (1991).

20. Perchuk and Posner (1995).

21. Cornwall and Lindisfarne (1994).

22. Craig (1992).

23. Marsden, Lowe, and Whatmore (1990).

24. Tönnies (1887/1957).

25. The classic work in this misguided vein is Loomis and Beegle (1950). See M. Bell (1992, 1998b) for details.

26. Gans (1962); Pahl (1964).

27. Friedland (2002).

28. G. Lewis (1979, 21–22).

29. Marsden, Lowe, and Whatmore (1990).

30. Philo (1992, 1993); Murdoch and Pratt (1993, 1994); Jones (1995); Halfacree (1995); Pratt (1996).

31. M. Bell (1992); Pratt (1996).

32. For example, Dillman and Hobbs (1982).

33. Ibid., 2.

34. M. Bell (1992); Halfacree (1995).

35. Mormont (1990).

36. See also Little (2002b).

37. Stolen (1995).

38. Bryant (1999); Peter et al. (2000); Saugeres (2002a, 2002b); Barlett and Conger (2004); Bell et al. (2004).

39. Peter et al. (2000).

40. Liepins (2000).

41. Little and Jones (2000).

42. Marsden, Lowe, and Whatmore (1990).

43. Brandth (1995); Brandth and Haugen (2000).

44. See also Ní Laoire (2001).

45. See also Little (2002b).

46. Brandth (1995); Brandth and Haugen (Chapter 12 in this volume); Quam-Wickham (1999).

47. Campbell and Bell (2000).

# PART 1
## Practices

Masculinity is not something that is just "there," a Mount Everest in the social landscape of rural life. Masculinity is something that is done: something we *practice*—something we do and something we do over and over again, trying to get it right, as we best understand that rightness. As we practice masculinity, however, we inevitably shape it to the specific local contexts in which we find ourselves. Masculinity is indeed there in the landscape of rural life, but because we practice and shape it, it is far from an unchanging monolith.

This first section of the book traces the local embeddedness of the variable practices of rural masculinity. Here we have chosen and arranged the chapters to provide examples of how particular versions of masculinity vary within different rural spaces, and the ways in which these rural masculinities emerge and change. We also present these chapters as ways of engaging rural masculinity with three long-standing concerns of rural sociology: farming, small towns and communities, and broad rural processes.

Some of these chapters deal directly with the first of these concerns: industries that are peculiar to rural space. In particular, the agriculture industry strongly conditions—and is conditioned by—different versions of masculinity. For example, Greg Peter et al. examine Iowa as an example of how the transition to sustainable agriculture in the United States is intimately bound up with the conflicts and power relations between versions of farming masculinity. Here, the masculinity associated with intensive, industrial farming contrasts with that seeking a more open engagement with other points of view and ways of farming. This latter style tends to be characteristic of farmers working toward sustainable agriculture. Extending this example, Peggy Barlett demonstrates that these conflicts between industrial and sustainable agriculture—and their close association to different styles of masculinity—are also manifest in other farming states across the United States. She then elaborates on an agrarian version of farming masculinity that presents a provocative contrast to industrial and sustainable versions of farming masculinity.

The second area of interest to rural sociology is the way in which gender operates in rural small towns and communities. Three chapters in the book focus specifically on gender relations in small communities and identify particular styles of masculinity that—in the same way that certain masculinities are privileged in farming—become powerful in these communities. These chapters identify particular sites in rural society—businesses, sporting activities, and pubs and bars—as important places in which masculinities develop and are reinforced. Sharon Bird examines business owners in a small, rural American town to trace how a particular paternalistic version of masculinity emerges within these businesses, becomes embedded, and then becomes powerful in establishing the entire gender order of such small towns. In a similar study, Hugh Campbell shows that small-town businesses and local pubs become closely related sites in which hegemonic masculinity is created. In his study of small-town New Zealand, pubs and workplaces become key sites where an equally powerful masculinity embeds its dominance in community life. In response, many young women choose to leave town and never return—thus undermining a key potential area of resistance to men's power. Similar themes also emerge in Catríona Ní Laoire and Shaun Fielding's study of two villages in England and Ireland. Again, a dominant form of masculinity becomes "rooted" in these communities—a masculinity that, despite cultural differences, has a strong resemblance to that described by both Bird and Campbell. Ní Laoire and Fielding also show how this rooted masculinity is challenged, undermined, and even partly formed by "routed" masculinities—masculinities that tend to draw young men away from these villages and promote rural out-migration.

The final area of interest to rural sociology is the way in which broader rural processes influence gender in general, and masculinity in particular. Working in this area, Michael Kimmel and Abby Ferber describe the emergence of a whole social movement of militias and separatists in the rural United States, and show how one commonality between these militias is the way they construct a particular definition of masculinity. This form of masculinity is a masculinity wounded but still proud; a masculinity patriotic and resistant to the incursions of "liberal, feminized" America; a masculinity prepared to resort to violence to defend itself. Finally in this section, Will Courtenay explores how broad social processes encourage rural men to engage in masculine practices that undermine their physical health. As Courtenay shows, rural men are more likely to suffer from a range of adverse health outcomes in their lives that can be causally related to the kinds of work rural men undertake, the social structure of rural life, and the particular risky behaviors that have been accepted as normal and natural for rural men to engage in.

Collectively, these chapters show that the different ways of "being a country boy" have an important bearing both on power in rural society and on how rural people establish their sense of self and other. They also show that the "mountain" of masculinity is a human creation, and as such—and however much we may imagine it otherwise—inevitably subject to constant change and variation in the face of the geology of the social.

# 2 Cultivating Dialogue: Sustainable Agriculture and Masculinities

*Gregory Peter, Michael Mayerfeld Bell, Susan Jarnagin, and Donna Bauer*

It is a typical late spring morning in the Iowa heartland—a sunny day in the high 60s is forecast, a welcome respite from the last two weeks of rain. Snapping off the weather channel, Kyle Jenson[1] bolts out the kitchen door, straps on his boots, and hurriedly feeds and checks the hogs. With only a two-day window before the next rain, he is itching to fire up his John Deere 8780 tractor and set up his new no-till drill for planting soybeans in his back sixty, a field he and his father at one time plowed with horses. Kyle's wife, Wendy, is already folding laundry, paying the bills, and planning "dinner" (the middle meal of the day for many rural Iowans). She is also getting ready to go to work at her off-farm job in the afternoon, but she will hold off on dinner and going to work until Kyle is ready to take a break. Knowing Kyle will be hungry and tired when he gets back in, Wendy fixes a solid meal: porkburgers, pork and beans, and bread and butter, with milk to top it off. She is eager to hear how far he gets this morning, how wet the ground is, and how well the equipment is holding up. At this time of year Wendy always worries about Kyle pushing to do all the planting by himself—often well past dark—only stopping for the one meal and to refill his planter with seed.

This spring scene plays out all over Iowa. The division of labor on the typical Iowa farm is gendered: men do most of the outdoor work, and women support their hectic schedules by providing meals at odd hours, doing chores, running the household, running for tractor parts, and work-

We are grateful to all the collaborators on this project, including the members of the sustainable agriculture group Practical Farmers of Iowa (PFI) and their families and neighbors; our academic neighbors; our families; the editors of *Rural Sociology*; and the editors of this book. Many thanks also to the audience at the Rural Sociological Society and Agriculture and Human Values meetings, where we first presented these ideas. Funding for this research came from the North Central Sustainable Agriculture Research and Education Program of the USDA.

ing at off-farm jobs—not to mention taking care of the children and doing everything else the men do not have time for. But although women play an integral role in Iowa agriculture, it is the men who most often claim the identity of "farmer."

Beginning in 1995, we set out to understand the social conditions of sustainable agriculture in Iowa through a participatory qualitative study of farm households that are members of Practical Farmers of Iowa (PFI), Iowa's principal sustainable agriculture group, and their non-PFI neighbors.[2] In this chapter, we report on one dimension of these conditions: the connection between ideologies of masculinity and the transition to sustainable agriculture. We argue that most male farmers' conventional masculinity hinders the transition from industrial to sustainable agriculture. By extension, the success of the sustainable agriculture movement depends, in part, on providing a social and an ecological arena in which men may discover and perform different masculinities.

Kyle Jenson's masculine performance, described in the opening vignette, represents what we call *monologic masculinity,* a single-voiced, conventional masculinity with rigid expectations and strictly negotiated performances that clearly differentiate between men's and women's work. Monologic masculinity also limits the range of topics deemed appropriate for men and women to discuss, regulates a specific definition of what constitutes work and success, and recognizes precise boundaries of manhood—including, in farming, appropriate relationships to farming processes, the environment, and animals.

A different scenario, however, is becoming more prevalent in Iowa among male PFI farmers. *Dialogic masculinity* presents a broader, more open, multivoiced understanding of what it is to be a man. Dialogic masculinity allows people more scope to talk about making mistakes, to express emotions, to accept change and criticism, to embrace a less controlling attitude toward machines and the environment, and to experiment with different measures of work and success.

The distinction between monologic and dialogic masculinity is an analytical tool, not a dichotomy. No rigid boundary separates the two; they are what Max Weber once called "ideal types."[3] Kyle Jenson is not purely monologic; no one is. Each male farmer experiences a constant tension between monologic and dialogic masculinity. But overall, those farmers in our study who practice industrial agriculture (capital intensive, low management, and low environment and community commitment) exhibited a more monologic masculinity, while those farmers who lean more toward sustainability (less capital intensive, higher management, and higher environmental and community commitment) exhibited a more dialogic masculinity.[4]

Of course, ideas of masculinity have a close association with ideas of femininity, and one might reasonably ask why we emphasize masculinity in this chapter. Is not everything already about men?

Perhaps our first answer to this important question is that, given this close association, we could not have done this research had there not already been studies of rural and farm *women*.[5] We are grateful to previous researchers for creating a space for this study of masculinities within agriculture. Moreover, our research is not simply a study of *men;* gender is socially organized, socially constructed, and negotiated in everyday interaction, so it involves both women and men.[6] As Berit Brandth puts it, "Femininity exists only in relation to masculinity and vice versa."[7] To study masculinity is to study a central factor in the lives of both rural men and rural women. Through this study, we can then offer some analytic tools necessary for critiquing the current expressions of masculinity in agriculture.

## Dialogue and Masculinities

There is not one masculinity in agriculture (or in any other field of human endeavor) but many *masculinities.* Most researchers in the sociology of masculinity agree, and Raewyn Connell has perhaps most forcefully argued, that masculinity is a social construction. Therefore, it is a product of the multiple social contexts and structures that do the constructing.[8] Masculinity, then, is as variable as social and environmental contexts themselves.

Building from the Russian social theorist Mikhail Bakhtin, we can apply the distinction between monologic and dialogic modes of behavior to social contexts themselves, so we examine monologic social conditions and dialogic social conditions. In the former, we tend more to speak and act without acknowledging others—their words, their wishes, indeed sometimes their very presence—in anything more than a superficial and objectified way.[9] We conceive of the world as divided along precise, rigid, and generally hierarchical boundaries, a separateness of individual actors and discrete categories. In dialogic conditions, however, social actors seek to *take each other into account.*[10] We maintain an openness to others' concerns and views; we envision our place in social life as an interactive part of the constantly changing whole; and we regard our categories and language with a similarly open and interactive outlook.

Bakhtin suggests understanding the distinction between the two types dialogically. Any one social situation is likely to have both monologic and dialogic elements, just as we in our own lives from time to time lean more one way or the other depending on our social histories, interactions, social structures, and cultures. Indeed, pure monologue is not possible. By the same token, pure dialogue is unlikely, and perhaps impossible. Bakhtin suggests, however, that a preponderance of monologue is more common in many spheres of social life.[11]

We extend his work here as a device for understanding the culture of masculinity—or, more precisely, the cultures of masculinities—in an agroecology context. Just as social life has its monologic and dialogic sides, so does masculinity. We are not claiming that the distinction between monologic masculinity and dialogic masculinity describes all features of masculinities. However, our fieldwork suggests that this distinction describes many of the differences in the masculine ideologies of more industrially inclined farmers and those of more sustainably inclined farmers in Iowa. The sustainable agriculture movement is more strongly dialogic not only in the social conditions it promotes but also in the social lives of those attracted to it. It emphasizes a less individualistic, less categorical, less homogeneous approach to farming than more traditional models, and thus a more interactive and holistic outlook. At least in its rhetoric, sustainable agriculture emphasizes a way of farming that attends to and takes into account the needs of others in society and the physical environment.

In other words, sustainable agriculture is dialogic not only in masculinities but also in the interaction between farmers and the environment.[12] Industrial agriculture, on the other hand, is more monologic in masculinities as well as in other areas.[13]

The sustainable agriculture movement consequently provides farm men with an ecologically grounded arena for discovering and performing a more dialogic masculinity. As Erving Goffman and Judith Butler suggest, gender is a performance that requires an audience and the assistance of other persons on and off stage.[14] While the metaphor of performance is a useful analytic device, focusing only on the performers potentially obscures the social structures and power relations involved in the drama of social life (as many have complained of a Goffmanesque analysis).[15] Performances generally involve other players, stagehands, and an audience, but these people may not be willingly involved in the performance of masculinity, particularly as the masculine actor is often both the scriptwriter and the theater paymaster, ensuring a production that meets his performance standards.

It is also important to note that the masculine actor may not himself perform altogether willingly; while he may have considerable power, he rarely has complete control over the script or the theater payroll. *Structures of performance* shape every social act. Farming is an infamously uncertain source of livelihood and thus of social identity, and farm men often find that their financial worth and sense of self-worth hangs in precarious balance. Consequently, performing masculinities within agri(culture) becomes a constant struggle, regardless of whether men conceive of masculinity in more monological or more dialogical terms.

## The Gendered Landscape of Fieldwork in Iowa

Qualitative research methodologies have been criticized for using "top-down" approaches in which the academic researcher is the sole authority behind the representation of the evidence.[16] In response, many methodologists are calling for more reflexive and participatory approaches that involve the researched in the process of research, gaining the benefit of the perspectives of both those inside and those outside the research subject.[17]

With these critiques in mind, we triangulated our fieldwork with a four-person team composed of both "insiders" and "outsiders." Each member of the research team brought to the project different levels of familiarity with Iowa, with agriculture, and with PFI. Both Susan Jarnagin and Donna Bauer have long associations with PFI, Jarnagin as the spouse of a PFI founder and longtime PFI employee, and Bauer as a PFI board member and farmer. In contrast, Michael Bell and Gregory Peter were relative newcomers to Iowa agriculture and rural life. Our team also represented insiders and outsiders with regard to masculinity: two men and two women.

Since it emerged in 1985 during the midst of the 1980s farm crisis, PFI has developed into Iowa's principal farmer-based sustainable agriculture organization. Membership in 2005 stood at about 750 members, about half of whom farm. One distinctive and pioneering feature of the group is

its focus on "on-farm research," in which farmers do their own scientific trials, often in collaboration with university researchers. PFI sponsors annual field days at member farms that participate in the trials, and these field days have been an important means of promoting sustainable agriculture in Iowa and the state's universities. PFI provides the organizational structure for exchanging information through regional and statewide meetings, a quarterly newsletter, and a network connecting sustainable farmers throughout the state. The group also works on a range of projects in the development of food systems, such as alternative forms of marketing, consumer education, and connecting local food with local chefs.

As a team, we conducted taped interviews with 108 individuals from thirty-five PFI households and thirty-four non-PFI households. The bulk of the initial interviews were conducted in the spring and summer of 1996. Follow-up interviewing and participation with farmers continued until 2003. We often asked to interview men and women together in their homes, but sometimes gate-keeping by the male farmer kept the interview to only one participant from the farm family. Every participant also gave us a farm tour that sometimes developed into a neighborhood or community tour.[18]

Beyond the taped interviews, we came to know the farm households in more informal ways, through farm stays of varying lengths. We ironed, cooked, ran errands, got groceries, and evaluated antiques. We helped bale hay, plant beans, slaughter chickens, fix refrigerators, repair jammed augers and planter wheels, feed horses, and chase down escaped livestock. We ate meals, watched television, took care of children, played the fiddle, shot basketballs, visited neighbors, and sometimes spent the night on participating farms. We also regularly attended PFI meetings and field days.

Iowa has more prime agricultural soil than any other state in the United States and the highest percentage of land under cultivation. First the plow, then mechanization, then hybrid seed corn transformed the prairie into a prime agricultural landscape and then into a highly industrialized, commercialized, and internationally recognized commodity. Agriculture is Iowa's principal industry and primary source of regional identity, as the current state slogan suggests ("Iowa, Fields of Opportunities"). To maximize industrial fields of opportunity in Iowa, most historical fencerows were taken out. A more metaphorical fence, however, was constructed in their place—a fence that still separates farm families from their neighbors. Monologue is the fence. If sustainable agriculture is to have an effect on farming, it has to succeed here on the home front of agricultural industrialization—and of conventional agricultural masculinity.

## Gender and Farm Talk

As in other male-dominated professions, the language of agriculture is highly gendered. We consistently heard male and female farmers in Iowa using gendered terminology when discussing agriculture. Danny, a recent graduate in agronomy from Iowa State University and a non-PFI farmer, is comfortable using this kind of language. Danny farms with his father, Dan, growing hundreds of acres of corn for a seed company. His mother, Sarah, does not consider herself a farmer but is actively involved in "the business." Greg interviewed Danny (who still dressed like a college student), Dan (who wore work overalls and a feed cap), and Sarah (who wore dress slacks and a blouse), in their newly remodeled farm kitchen. They talked a bit about family and student life; Greg then asked Danny to describe the difference between "conventional" and "sustainable" agriculture. Danny replied: "Conventional farming to me is you take that plow out there and black her up. Like over there in that field [pointing to a field recently plowed by a seed company]. You black her up and you know that's the way it was done maybe thirty to forty years ago." The pronouns Danny uses refer to the land as female and as something "you" control; "you black her up." His father agreed and continued the line of thought: "Seed companies are out there for their own self and they don't care who they rape, including the land." To these men, then, there are farmers who "rape" the earth, and there are those that treat the land the way "she" should be treated. While Sarah participated in the rest of the interview, she did not use the same language that Danny and Dan used. Overall, we found that women generally refrained from using this kind of language.[19]

Kay and Jerry, an older non-PFI couple, followed a similar linguistic pattern when Sue interviewed them at the small place they have farmed for many years. Sue asked Jerry why he liked to farm, a question he immediately warmed to. "I've done a great many things in my years, but I've always left one foot solidly on the ground as a farmer," he said. "As I've said once before, all things come from the ground. So if all [other] things go sour, we can live off the land."

Kay also warmed to the topic (although she later told Sue she does not consider herself a farmer). "A real farmer," said Kay, "can't wait to get out in spring to turn that ol' sod and smell that soil, just like a gardener."

Jerry took up the conversation again, but with a significant shift of metaphor: "It gives you a feeling that you're going to impregnate this earth, and I'm going to harvest it next fall."

For Kay, a real farmer is like a gardener, appreciating the gender-neutral sensuousness of sod and smell. But for Dan, Danny, and Jerry, the imagery of farming is about impregnating and sometimes even raping a female land—metaphors that culturally support male dominance in agriculture and over the environment in general—even when they contest patterns of dominance, as Dan and Danny did. Not only is the land female, and often violently controlled, but the "farmer" is almost always male.

Although women in the study usually did not use gendered imagery to describe farm practices, they did typically use gendered categories of farming identity. We often asked the couples we interviewed if the woman on the farm was a "farmer." Despite their extensive participation in agricultural production, few women considered themselves "farmers" or were considered "farmers" by men.[20] Take the case of Diana, who puts in twenty hours a week, sometimes more, working with her husband on their farm. Mike asked if she would consider herself a farmer.

"I wouldn't mind it," Diana replied. "I just don't consider that I do enough farm work to be a farmer."

"Part-time farmer?" Mike asked.

"Part-time farmer, I suppose. But once again Frank's in charge. He's the farmer. I'm the helper. I'm the homemaker and farm hand."

Through interviews, farm stays, and return visits, we discovered that in Iowa most farm women "help" on the farm, just as some men "help" in the home. With women as "helpers," the category of farmer remains the exclusive domain of men's work not only in the eyes of the community but within the family as well.


## "A Guy Can't Be Afraid of Getting Dirty"

Greg was reintroduced to the social and environmental performances of masculinities early one spring morning by Leonard, an older non-PFI farmer with a small hog confinement operation. Expecting a tour of Leonard's farm plus some hands-on farming experience, Greg came dressed in clean but faded jeans, a T-shirt, work boots, and an Iowa State University baseball cap. Leonard, dressed in work overalls and a well-worn seed cap, evidently regarded Greg's appearance as too scrubbed and collegiate for a farmer—or so the subsequent dramatics suggest. The tour eventually led to the farrowing house of Leonard's hog confinement operation. After showing Greg the feeding equipment, Leonard walked over to the manure pit, unzipped, and urinated into the pit. "Being a farmer, I'm more comfortable pissin' out here than inside," he told Greg, nodding back toward the house.

Later, when they entered another part of the building, Leonard yelled, "Pigs out!" A mother sow had knocked open the door on her confinement pen and six piglets had escaped, falling into the manure pit below. Leonard jumped into action. Partly out of a concern for the animals, and partly out of concern for creating a favorable impression, Greg jumped in with him. Greg's job was to grab the manure-spattered blade of a spade and poke the wooden handle down through the steel grating to guide the drowning piglets to the side of the pit, where Leonard had a little wire lasso attached to a stick. Leonard snagged a piglet leg with the lasso, hauled the piglet squealing onto the concrete floor, and then went back for another. In the end, two of the six piglets survived the ordeal. Leonard looked approvingly at Greg, who was now properly soiled; and after a futile attempt at washing up with a hose, Leonard offered him a ride in his truck to see the rest of his farm. (Previously Leonard had not planned to give Greg the whole tour of the farm.) He told Greg in the truck that "a guy can't be afraid of getting dirty."

These performances by both Leonard and Greg were homosocial statements of the sharply bounded monologic masculinity we often encountered in the fieldwork. Several cultural oppositions underlay their performance—dirtiness versus cleanliness; outside versus inside; danger versus safety; farmer versus nonfarmer; and male versus female. Initially, Greg seemed to play the counterrole of the less masculine man. Through his successfully performed rite of passage, however, he managed to cross the boundary into manly manhood, becoming a man among men who are not afraid of getting dirty, of relieving themselves outdoors, or of performing dangerous and unpleasant tasks.

When the monologic male denies himself bodily comforts in this way, he reinforces not only his view of himself but also his view of others. Greg and Leonard enacted this denial of the other (the feminine, the indoor, and the sanitized) homosocially, but farmers in our study also enacted it in heterosocial situations. Ron, a younger non-PFI farmer, manages thousands of acres and is well known in his community for his huge tractors, sixty-foot-wide planter, and punishing work schedule. He seemed to take pride in telling Donna, during an interview with him and his wife, Nancy, how during planting season he and his hired men work "around the clock."

Donna asked, "So does that mean one person puts in a shift of ten hours?"

"No," Ron replied. "It means one person puts in a shift of about forty-eight hours."

"Go till you drop?" Donna offered.

"Pretty much," he said laughing. "We just hope when a guy drops you hit your head, and it brings you around so you can get back up and go some more."

It seemed to Donna an expression Ron had used before (perhaps also in the presence of men). With it, Ron presents the heterosocial image of a manly man who relishes hard work and is able to deny himself bodily comfort—and is also monologically capable of denying others' comfort. Monologic ascetic denial also involves not eating while working. While helping non-PFI farmers, both Mike and Greg participated in this monologic approach to work—long periods on the tractor or the combine without food or drink. They were being culturally introduced to the manly world of "hard work." As an agricultural television advertisement in Iowa from the fall of 1997 proudly proclaimed, "farmers invented hard work." Most male farmers in our study, PFI and non-PFI alike, relished this image and its accompanying rituals.

Male PFI farmers, however, more frequently enacted dialogic moderation and concern for the comfort of others in work situations. For example, one afternoon, Greg was riding on the wheel well of a 1967 John Deere tractor cultivating soybeans with John, a younger PFI farmer with a small farm. They had already been out for a few hours and John (querying whether Greg had to be anywhere) asked, "What's your time frame like?" It was about 5:30 P.M., not late. Greg did actually need to get home to his family but remained monologically noncommittal. John said, "I tell you what Greg, I need to go home and get something to eat. I really haven't eaten that much today." On the surface, there is nothing surprising about such a comment. But Greg had the distinct feeling that John was kindly giving him a face-saving excuse to go home, by saying that he, John, was the one who needed to stop. Although enacted against a monologic cultural background in which face needed to be saved, this interchange manifested the communal orientation of dialogic masculinity—a greater concern about others' needs and feelings, like being hungry and tired.

## Controlling Nature and a Not-So-Silent Spring

Farm men's fascination with big machines that control the environment is a well-known aspect of rural culture. Indeed, as Brandth notes: "The masculinization of farming became particularly marked after the mechanization of agriculture."[21] Male farmers do the overwhelming majority of outdoor fieldwork, the work that everyone can see and that other men homosocially seldom fail to notice even when sliding precariously down a loose gravel road in an old pickup truck. Both PFI and non-PFI men in our study often expressed fascination with heavy outdoor machinery. But PFI farmers also expressed reservations about the cultural implications of the "big iron" mentality, as one PFI farmer derisively described it. Instead, PFI men often described the value of a less controlling orientation to the land and to animals—a more dialogic approach.

Take, for example, Ted, a PFI member who is moving away from standard corn and beans row-crop agriculture on his small farm. He told Mike that he has trouble talking with farmers who are mostly interested in machinery and owning thousands of acres: "I feel uncomfortable getting in with the other crowd, so to speak, because mainly what they talk about is machinery. The new this. The new that. How many acres I'm farming or, you know, this or that or whatever. You know, I couldn't care less. I don't have any interest in that stuff."

But this sort of outlook toward machines can isolate farm men from their neighbors, and thus an important feature of PFI is that it provides social, structural, and cultural support for this less mechanized masculinity—a place for different kinds of conversations. As Frank, another PFI member, puts it: "PFI is the one farm organization that I belong to that I really have lively interest in. . . . They aren't going big. They aren't excited by the big machinery and the big new stuff."

PFI farmers are not oblivious to the monologic attractions of "going big" and enjoying more control over nature, as John, a third PFI farmer, explained: "I always look forward to cultivating because it's that control thing—it's controlling nature. You get out there with your machinery, and you cut up those weeds with that machinery, and it feels good." He continued: "You see the end result immediately. When you plant, it's weeks before you see what you planted; here, it's instant gratification." Although John clearly enjoys cultivating, he is also self-conscious about "controlling nature." He admits he enjoys it but wishes he could overcome "that control thing."

In a culture dominated by a monologic orientation, it is often difficult to maintain a dialogic masculinity. A farmer who lets go of the "big iron" mentality also lets go of a well-established cultural repertoire of self-esteem—and power. The subject of machinery safety and chemicals came up in the conversation between John, his father, Harold, Roger, and Greg. Harold brought up *Silent Spring* (the landmark text on chemical environmental degradation) and said of author Rachel Carson: "There may be something to what she said in *Silent Spring*; it may not be silent, but it sure is happening."

Mike observed similar reactions when he went out to work with George, an older PFI farmer with a corn and soybean operation in southwest Iowa. When Mike arrived, George and his twelve-year-old son, Thomas, were changing the planter over from corn to beans. This required unbolting the corn seed wheels and rebolting the bean ones. George was reluctant to let Mike help at first because the corn seed was "treated." Mike was looking at the planter wheels, which still carried a fair bit of grain stained purple from antifungal treatment. George looked over at Mike and said, "I've got enough of this stuff under my skin already; we don't need to spread it around." He then talked about how next year the companies were going to come out with some antifungal treatment that was not so bad for people, which he thought was a good thing: "They're starting to realize that they've got to pay attention to the health of the farmer too." While George represents dialogic masculinity in many other areas, he has a more monologic approach when handling chemicals (wearing protective clothing when working on the farm is "unmanly"). After working on the planter, however, George did make sure afterward that everyone went to wash up at an external hose (not an inside sink) where he had a bar of soap waiting. While George himself had taken the worst job—cleaning out the "boxes" of the remaining corn seed, which required quite a bit of contact with the treated seed—he focused particularly on his son: "Now Thomas, make sure you wash up good," he insisted. On the one hand, George was being very sensitive to the health impact of treated seed and protecting his son and guest from it. On the other, his comment that he already had "enough of this stuff under my skin" showed his own willingness to handle such risks, lest there be any question about it.

Ron, the go-til-you-drop farmer, has a strong opinion about chemical use and environmentalists. When interviewed, he told Mike that "in the environmental business people are pushing things. I'm afraid down the road if things don't straighten around, they're going to push us out of using chemicals . . . you can't farm that way. Our productivity, it'll go to crap." There was no fear of chemicals here, no ambivalence or categorical complexity that the acceptance of multiple voices encourages. And although no farmer expressed it explicitly, we could not help at times hearing monologic echoes of concern for virility and masculine control in the focus on productivity typical of Ron and other non-PFI farmers.

On the other side of the fence, more sustainable farmers are excited about using fewer chemicals and increasing safety on their farms. Safety, for instance, came up in Greg's interview with Joan and Mark Hilson. Joan picked up on it first, saying that another favorable aspect of sustainable farming was that "our eight-year-old can be involved. He's out there moving fences with him. I don't know if you can say that about crop farming. How many kids are involved [in that]? And now you know these herbicides and chemicals are dangerous stuff. Your kids can't be involved in that; and you don't want your kids around there." Mark then chimed in with: "Well, that's exciting and before the grass thing [rotational grazing] I would have told him, 'don't even bother thinking about farming.' Now, I see there is a way he can get into it if he wants to down the road—that's the great thing."

## Husbands and Husbandry

While big machines and strong chemicals in Iowa monologically define masculinity, certain types of livestock (such as raising broiler hens) are more monologically associated with femininity, at least stereotypically. Sustainable agriculture of the sort promoted by PFI, however, usually depends on incorporating these types of livestock into the farm operation, as well as diversifying production and adding value. The "big iron" view of farming is thus culturally incompatible with the ideology of sustainability—or so PFI members Jim and Jerilyn (mainly Jim) explained to Mike. Jim and Jerilyn are a middle-aged couple who run a small diversified farm with several crops in addition to the usual corn and soybeans, as well as three different livestock operations.

"I think having animals around humbles a person," Jim began. "I think it humbles you because . . ."

"You got to go out and scoop poop," interjected Jerilyn.

"And you know sometimes they die," continued Jim. "Sometimes [even if you] do everything right, there'll be some other factor come in like a weather change. Or something will make them sick. Where cash grain tends to be more 'blow black smoke with big power' and 'cover a wide swath.' It's more of a power trip or image of authority: 'I can do this because I've got 400 horsepower under the tractor, and I can make sixty feet black.' Or something like that. It's more of a machinery-dominating thing. Where having animals, you don't dominate them the way you dominate land. Animals are much more humbling because they're just harder—harder to control."

Jim and Jerilyn support a different masculine performance here, a masculinity that is distinctive in appreciating the humbling lack of control brought by animals and the livestock business—a lack of control that Jim dialogically feels he does not need to deny.[22]

## Enhancing Dialogue

Although male PFI farmers expressed ambivalence about giving up environmental and social control, they were more willing than non-PFI farmers to do so. In this section we discuss the greater social openness of PFI men, especially with regard to dialogue within the family, the community, and the environment.

To begin, it is important to note the infamously uncertain character of farming. As Carl, a non-PFI member who used to grow seed corn, explained to Mike: "[In] the business of farming . . . a person has to be very optimistic. You wouldn't dare get into farming if you weren't an optimist because you have everything thrown at you. The markets which you have no control over. You got Mother Nature which you have no control over. You have insects you have no control over. What the government does you have no control over. There's so many factors out there that the farmer has no control over."

This struggle to survive in farming is in part a cultural struggle between masculinities and sustainability. Farmers who are less in control of their resource management, less productive, and less successful may present less masculine selves than other farmers. One defensive response to agriculture's uncertain structures of masculine performance, therefore, is to assert a rigid, oppositional, and socially controlling masculinity—a strongly monologic masculinity.

Although PFI men may also attempt the hierarchical satisfactions of monologic control, we were often struck in our fieldwork by their struggle to perform a more socially open masculinity. One example is John, a PFI farmer discussed earlier, who with his family recently participated in a holistic management (HM) workshop. HM is a decision-making approach that has become very popular among PFI members and others in the sustainable agriculture movement. HM provides farmers with a decision-making template that takes into account the social, economic, and environmental implications of farm practices, based on each family member's values and goals. Central to the HM approach, then, is collective decision making within the family. In other words, HM promotes a multivoiced, dialogic masculinity.

As John explained to Greg: "Well, one thing, by trying to use it [HM] you realize, boy, you got to learn how to cooperate with people. That's a big part of it. Learning cooperation even within the family. Getting everybody tuned into the goals. Well, I'll point out to you that we just did that two weeks ago. We made our own family goal. We sat around for two hours one Sunday night with the kids and we said, 'Well what do we want this family to be like, and what do we want to do?'"

It is interesting to note that John said "even within the family," indicating his view that family cooperation is unusual. In making this observation, John is trying to redefine his masculinity within the family context, as are many PFI men.[23]

PFI provides an important social support structure for this more dialogic masculinity. Among the places where we saw this support was in one of PFI's "Shared Visions" community-building groups. Mike regularly visited a Shared Visions group that focused each meeting on how to improve the farm practices of a different couple in the group. The frank, friendly criticism of the group had been a particular challenge for male participants, but also a great relief. It is hard to keep up a constant façade of control, especially in difficult times where simple mistakes can cost dearly. As one middle-aged farmer, Brad, remarked during a meeting: "You know, you feel like a fish out of water, flopping around. And this Shared Visions group helped me through that a bit."

Sharon, usually rather shy and awkward in the group, burst into the conversation. "I just want to say," she said, looking across the room at Brad, "what you said about being a fish out of water—that was a hard thing, especially for a man, to say. That says a lot about what's good about this group. That we can say these things." By reinforcing Brad's openness to expressing his feelings to the group, she is also reinforcing dialogic masculinity and communality within the group.

An important element of admitting lack of control in farming is a dialogic openness to admitting mistakes that others can learn from. Brian, a PFI member, explained to Mike the difference he finds between PFI members and other farmers:

> People will share. They're willing to talk about their successes and their failures. They like to share with people. [With other organizations] you hear about the successes but nobody ever wants to talk about their failures. Even the neighbor down the road. You can go down there, and he might let you know about his success. . . . The simple fact [is] that he'd like to boost his ego up a little bit. But he'll never tell you about that mistake he made back on the back forty which nobody ever would see.

PFI men often described to us the importance of sharing ideas, providing emotional support, sharing labor, and other forms of community building. While non-PFI men were not necessarily silent on these topics, most did not emphasize them to the same degree as PFI men—and certainly not to the degree that Jim did when he went so far as to praise lack of control as a positive benefit of livestock farming. With livestock, he explained: "You're more dependent on a feed dealer. You're dependent more on a veterinarian. You're dependent more on your plumber, your electrician. You're dependent more on people. You work with a lot more people in livestock production than you do in cash grain."

In these and other ways, PFI men present a more socially open masculine performance. They are not always so dialogic, nor are non-PFI men completely monologic. But part of what many PFI men find attractive about their organization's structure and culture is the support it gives them to be more dialogic and still just as masculine as the guy standing in the field next door.

## Back Across the Fence?

On the whole, Iowa farm families still maintain traditional gender roles and masculine identities. However, the transition to sustainable agriculture seems to be accompanied by changes in masculinity. Specifically, we see a shift from monologic to dialogic masculinity, as the oppositional character of monologic masculinity fits poorly with sustainable agriculture's emphasis on openness to social and environmental change. But cultural opportunities for social change exist even within monologic structures of performance: as Bakhtin optimistically points out, there is no such thing as a pure monologue. Moreover, most of the PFI and non-PFI farm men in our study showed a dialogic side—some, of course, more than others. Men with a more dialogic conception of their masculinity appear to support and be supported by an organization like PFI. As Anthony Giddens put it, a "duality of structure" is at work here, with dialogic masculinity working in consort with its organizational structures.[24]

We also suggest that for men, the struggle to survive in farming is simultaneously a struggle to cultivate an ecological dialogue between masculinities and sustainability. This is no less true for male sustainable farmers than it is for male industrial farmers. In fact, for these men, accepting a less polarized masculinity may be an essential element in the future viability of sustainable agriculture. Practical farmers need a practical identity. They need an identity with flexible boundaries and one that opens up (agri)cultural space for other voices and other ways of farming—including the voices of the environment and of animals.

Women's voices in farming are also of particular sociological importance. While we still cannot describe women's voices in PFI as being as loud as men's, they are certainly increasing in volume. As we write, three of the group's ten elected and two ex-officio board members are women. These include two of PFI's three officers: the treasurer and the group's first woman president—both of whom are self-described farmers. The growth of community-supported agriculture and interest in direct marketing, areas of agriculture with greater female representation, has also given women more prominence in the group. Outside PFI, women have played a central role in developing the sustainable agriculture movement at all levels: national, regional, on- and off-farm, and in-home. Across the state and country, women are better represented and more prominent in sustainable agricultural organizations than in industrial agricultural organizations. For example, as we write, twenty-six men and no women sit on the board of directors of the aptly named Iowa Cattlemen's Association—the state's main beef commodity association, and a bastion of industrial agriculture.

Our analysis of PFI suggests this is not accidental. Dialogic masculinity opens up the conversation—not only between women and men but also between men and men, and between men, women, and the land. In one male farmer's words, this type of group "has brought us back across the fence." Yes . . . and no. While we share this farmer's optimism, the development of dialogic masculinity, like sustainable agriculture itself, is still in its early stages. Men and women need to cultivate deeper dialogic relations with each other and the earth. In other words, we are still *coming* back across the fence—but that is nevertheless welcome news indeed.

NOTES

1. All names used in this article are pseudonyms and all inessential farm characteristics and physical attributes have been changed to maintain strict confidentiality.

2. The results of the full study can be found in Bell et al. (2004).

3. Weber (1978).

4. Theoretically it is important to note that not only does sustainable ideology lead to more dialogic masculinity, but dialogic masculine identities are more drawn toward sustainable practices. For more on our distinctions between industrial and sustainable agriculture, see Bell et al. (2004).

5. Chiappe and Flora (1998); Meares (1997); Knobloch (1996); Brandth (1994a); Barlett (1993); Fink (1987).

6. Connell (1995a); Kessler and McKenna (1978).

7. Brandth (1994a, 130).

8. Connell (1995a).

9. Bakhtin (1981, 1986).

10. M. Bell (1998a).

11. Bakhtin's work is explicitly normative—Bakhtin thinks monologue is bad. As such, his approach fits into a style of theory we might term *moral postmodernism*—social theory that abandons the modernist faith in the possibility of and the necessity for a separation of social science and values. Increasingly, critical and applied sociologists have been writing about the need for this abandonment, which in part accounts for the increasing popularity of a Bakhtinian approach. See Seidman (1994); Levine

(1995); M. Bell (1995); Warner and England (1995).

12. M. Bell (1998c, 4).

13. For more on this argument, see Bell et al. (2004).

14. Goffman (1959, 1979); Butler (1993). Also, Kimmel (1996) points out the commonly homosocial context of its performance. That is, men frequently direct their masculine performances with other men in mind. Masculinity may also be what, in parallel, we term heterosocial: performed with an audience of women in mind. It may also be both, in varying degrees. In any event, as Chodorow (1978) has argued, men in both their homosocial and heterosocial performances typically conceive masculinity as not feminine, a categorical opposition we regard as culturally monologic.

15. We are indebted to Jacqueline Litt, our colleague at Iowa State University, for this observation. A recommended resource on this issue is Reynolds (1990), chapter 9.

16. Clough (1992); Van Maanan (1988); Clifford (1986).

17. M. Bell (1998a); Gaventa (1993).

18. The interviews ranged in length from one hour to five and a half hours, and used what we call *co-structured* procedures—that is, they were open not only to the directions the researchers wanted to take but to the directions the participants wanted to take. This participatory technique increased the likelihood that the content of our interviews reflected more than the researchers' preconceptions.

19. For more ecofeminist analysis of agriculture, see Knobloch (1996).

20. This was the case when we interviewed couples jointly and separately.

21. Brandth (1994a, 131).

22. Reflexively Mike noted that Jim dominated this conversation, as he did most of the interview.

23. The reality may be that John used the occasion for "getting everybody tuned" in to his goals; we were not able to interview other family members on this point. But our impression is that he was making a concerted effort to be more open to others' opinions and less controlling.

24. Giddens (1984).

# 3 Three Visions of Masculine Success on American Farms

*Peggy F. Barlett*

Mack, a Georgia farmer in his late fifties, is talking proudly of his lifetime's success. He sits in a vinyl recliner in the living room of his modest brick home, surrounded by fields of corn, soybeans, and peanuts. The living room tables are covered with doilies and a large console television backs onto a wall decorated with family pictures. The floor is linoleum, with a rag rug. "I couldn't get no start when I was young—I would have loved to have bought land before, but I was just a poor boy. What we got, we dug up—we slaved for it." Mack's wife has always had a job in town, and her income has been valuable in the family's quest to own and operate an independent farm. But Mack resists the view of his neighbors that a "good job in town" is better than farming: "If you've got a job today, you've got nothing. If you have a farm, you've got something; and we've still got it!"[1]

Not far away, another farmer, Richard, stands beside the picture window in his architecturally designed home that would fit in an affluent suburb. Upholstered sofas furnish the carpeted room. He is also proud of his life's work and loves farming, but his definition of success emphasizes the financial aspects of the farm business and his family's lifestyle: "Farmers used to be second-class citizens and people in town would look down on us—as peasants, as people who don't have air conditioning in their homes. But today, homes in the country are furnished the same, and we eat the same or maybe even better." Richard's farm has seen considerable entrepreneurial expansion: "I've had the initiative, ambition, and guts to tackle things. And I'm not afraid of debt." Providing an income high enough that

This chapter is a revised version of Barlett and Conger (2004). The Georgia research reported here was funded by the National Science Foundation (BNS8121459 and BNS8618159) and the National Geographic Society. The opinions, findings, conclusions, and recommendations expressed here do not represent the official views of the National Science Foundation. Special thanks go to the farmers of Dodge County, Peter Brown, Sonya Salamon, and Paul Rosenblatt.

his wife can be a full-time homemaker has been important to Richard's sense that he has been a success.

These two snapshots of Georgia farmers highlight two perspectives of masculine success. On the surface, we might think that these farmers have contrasting visions because Mack belongs to a less affluent socioeconomic group than Richard, and in fact Richard's farmstead and farm income are several times larger than Mack's. But participant observation and interviews with fifty-eight full-time farmers in Dodge County, Georgia (a random sample of half the farms in one of Georgia's largest farming counties), revealed that full-time farmers of all levels of education, farm size, and wealth can embrace either definition of masculine success: the *agrarian* definition, which values farm life, family partnership, and continuity on the land; or the *industrial* definition, which sees farming as the means to gain an appropriate standard of living, business opportunities, and a lifestyle in which the husband is the provider, the wife the homemaker.

My long-term anthropological fieldwork among Georgia farmers found substantial variability in notions of masculine success, even within one rural county and one occupational group. Studies in Georgia, Iowa, and Illinois show that over the past hundred years, political and economic change in American society, and especially in the Southeast, has created a context in which divergent ideologies emerged. This chapter focuses on two important dimensions of masculine agricultural success, which are in turn central to the moral economy of farming families: the way men judge their success on the farm and the way they view their wives' work off the farm. Views about personal success are connected to contrasting patterns of farm management style, and thus this chapter explores the interlinked dimensions of *work, livelihood,* and *marital partnership.* These ideals of success are not equally easy to fulfill and, as the hard times of the 1980s and 1990s show, the *industrial* ideal defines a man as a failure far more easily than the *agrarian* ideal does.

However, other ideals are possible. In my conclusion, I explore an emerging "third-wave" definition of masculine success in the Midwest: the *sustainable* agriculture ideal (building on the work of Gregory Peter and his colleagues in the previous chapter in this volume). When rural sociologists in Illinois and Iowa set out to explore how farmers adopt alternative agricultural methods, they found older visions of masculinity altering alongside a new paradigm of systems thinking and sustainability. On some farms, in other words, an alternative, sustainability-oriented farmer is increasingly becoming a new version of masculine agricultural success.

## Masculinity, Difference, and American Farms

Since the 1990s, researchers have stressed that gender is not monolithic and unchanging but rather varies by place, time, and social position.[2] Several writers have similarly recognized race, class, and ethnicity as central dimensions of variation in gender ideology and practice,[3] and recent work on masculinity has also recognized the importance of difference and variation by race or class or other dimensions of power within a complex society.[4] Studies that draw attention to differing norms of masculinity within one occupational group are rarer,[5] although recent work in rural sociology emphasizes the multiple constructions of rural masculinity.[6]

This exploration of comparative masculinities focuses on male commercial family farm operators in Georgia, Illinois, and Iowa, and on one dimension of the ideology of masculinity—the criteria of personal success. The two ideal types of masculine success found among the Georgia farmers—agrarian and industrial—cut across ethnic and class lines, and their contrasts are echoed in other regions of the United States.[7] Farmers vary in the extent to which they articulate these perspectives, and some men embrace dimensions of both, but most express personal goals or values that largely conform to one or the other of the two ideal types sketched in the following sections.

Clearly, "masculinity" itself is a complex term, particularly in relation to farming. Peter and his colleagues define masculinity as "the behavior, practices, and conversations deemed culturally appropriate for men" and link ideologies and values to behavioral practices in the private and semi-public work arena of the farm.[8] Michael Kimmel, on the other hand, argues that manhood has to be proved in the public sphere, in the eyes of other men.[9] Even so, some dimensions of masculine performance are intensely private. While, for some, male success is proved "in the market-place," for others it may also be proved in the home or extended family. It may be linked to the competitive gaze of other males, but it may also be linked to an audience of women.[10] And what about failure? While public disparagement from peers (male or female) can cause great distress, for many men a private failure to live up to an internalized conception of the masculine ideal may be even more painful.

On most American farms, male success or failure is played out in the interrelated circles of household, family, farm, and marriage. While some of these circles involve only "homosocial enactments" of masculinity, in which "men define their masculinity, not as much in relation to women, but in relation to each other,"[11] many of these circles are closely involved with the feminine. As Matthew Gutmann argues,[12] in these areas men's notions of masculinity must be connected to women's notions, reactions, and identities. In turn, marital partnerships (and, indeed, heterosexual marriage itself) significantly affect masculine notions of success. While space restrictions prevent me from fully discussing the important role of marriage in farming life, later in the chapter examples of how different farm men react when their wives enter the public marketplace are evidence of interrelated gender roles within the farming family.[13]

Life histories of contemporary Dodge County farmers suggest that most now settle into a notion of their life's goals and expectations between late adolescence and the early years of marriage. Evidence suggests that for these men, concepts of masculinity and femininity—and masculine and feminine success—also develop early. Men identify their fathers as the strongest influence on their views of masculinity and adult achievement, but other family members, peers, and neighbors, together with experiences in school and jobs, and the powerful messages of the mass media also contribute. As in any social group, these men are also influenced by their personal desire for upward mobility, their status consciousness, their perception of certain gender ideologies having a status value, and by the surrounding set of opportunities and economic conditions to which they must adapt, especially in adolescence and early adulthood. If and when they marry, their wives' expectations and values, together with the couple's early experiences in marriage, are also important.[14] All these factors contribute to the specific models of behavior and management that Dodge County farmers value as ideals of masculine and agricultural success.

Masculinity, therefore, has many dimensions: internalized masculine ideals; psychological experiences of masculinity; and public and private enactments of masculinity. As Arlie Hochschild notes, even for a single individual these different versions of masculinity may not be compatible (or "congruent") with each other.[15] My analysis of agrarian and industrial models of masculinity in Dodge County—a site at which family, farm, and marriage are particularly strongly interrelated—takes this potential incompatibility into account by exploring the intersection of all three dimensions of gender: values, behavior, and emotional response.

## Masculine Commonalities Among Farmers

For many, the "all-American farmer" provides a popular and accessible folk model of masculinity. Farming has many elements associated with the masculine: working outdoors, performing strenuous physical labor, handling large animals and heavy machinery, bargaining with suppliers and buyers, and engaging in the financial calculations of long-term investments and annual profits. Agricultural life thus embodies rugged outdoor work together with the skillful manipulation of machines and nature, all in the context of geographic and social stability.[16] Of course, women can also do any of these things, and some women on American farms do all of them. But such elements of farming life are usually associated with a masculine self, and this persistent association in part explains why it is often hard for girls to aspire to be farm operators.[17]

Older Dodge County farmers, who chose their occupation during the Great Depression, point out that in the 1930s "farming was all there was." The economic boom after World War II, however, meant that many rural people left farming to take up white-collar jobs, a choice in keeping with the southern elite's historic disdain for manual labor.[18] In the later decades of the twentieth century this demographic changed again: many "modern" young men love farming, and its masculine qualities are part of that attraction. Farming is not only connected to a "tough image" of trucks, guns, and dogs, but farm boys also develop adult competencies early: driving trucks before age sixteen is common, and some boys are given their own tractors, their own animals, or even their own small fields to practice on. Farm boys value the respect of peers and family that comes with doing an adult's work: "Boys are proud of what they can accomplish on the farm," explained one mother, although, one farmer added, "you'd never talk about it out loud." Similar opportunities to demonstrate maturity are not available to most nonfarm young men.

Farming today is tied intimately to knowledge of engines and machine repair, and such machinery management is especially associated with male gender. On the farm, endless conversations revolve around the equipment one owns or aspires to own, the irritations of breakdowns and repairs, and production feats with machinery.[19] Farming takes place outdoors and is connected to the masculine realms of dirt, mud, and manure, realms integral to the identity of "farmer." "A guy can't be afraid of getting dirty," one Iowa farmer pointed out succinctly.[20] "Farming is dirty work," agree many Georgia men and women, although most argue this does not make it "a lower-class type of work."

Some "tough guy" aspects of Georgia farm life may be specific to the region. The macho use of machinery and the youthful bravado of "driving up and down the roads" observed in Georgia are not aspects of masculinity seen in all farming regions of the country.[21] Such "toughness" suggests that these southern farmers locate themselves in a tradition that resists the (feminized) domestication of "the evangelical life"[22] and post–Civil War temperance, preferring the "drinking, brawling, hunting, swearing, and dueling" tradition.[23] By comparison, different historical models operate in the Midwest, where the agrarian tradition often draws on German or Scandinavian roots. However, for most farmers from the Georgian coastal plain, like their fellow farmers throughout America, pride in accomplishment, hard work, and expertise join with the accouterments of big machines, technology, and business acumen to create a common ground of masculinity in American farming.[24]

## The Historical Context of Variation in Masculine Ideals

How have the ideals, values, and ideologies of masculine success changed over the past two hundred years?[25] In particular, how has the emergence of capitalism affected ideals of masculine achievement? In general, increasingly capitalist economies see population movement from rural settlements to industrial cities. In the process, male success rests less on values of "honest toil," a sense of productive craft, stalwart loyalty, and contributions to the community and more on values of individual achievement, material possessions, entrepreneurial success, and competitiveness.[26] Kimmel labels these two contrasting ideals of male success "the heroic artisan" and the "the self-made man."[27] The "heroic artisan" ideal reflects the rural and small-town context of a predominantly agricultural economy and the household-based models of production[28] that characterized the livelihood of most families before the Civil War.[29] In comparison, the "self-made man" emerges with modern industrial capitalism: his means of earning a living no longer revolve around the household unit but reflect more mobile, urban, and commercial occupations.

Studies show that contemporary American farmers still model themselves on these two contrasting masculine ideals: the self-employed agrarian artisan (rural farmer, blacksmith, or carpenter) and the upwardly mobile entrepreneurial businessman (town-dwelling storekeeper, factory owner, or itinerant salesman).[30] Sonya Salamon's work echoes these two images of American masculinity, and she differentiates "yeomen" and "entrepreneurs" among Illinois farmers. Salamon and others suggest that a man's status as yeoman or entrepreneur may link to ethnic background: yeoman were more likely to be German Catholic or Irish, while entrepreneurs were typically British or German Protestant. While I found no patterns in values or management practices by ethnic background, religious affiliation, social class background, or race in my Georgia research, contrasting images of masculinity are seen in the "cautious" or "ambitious" management styles.[31] Historians of western American settlement and capitalist agriculture describe parallel distinctions between the entrepreneurial "bonanza farmer" and the family-oriented homesteader in other areas.[32] In South Dakota in the 1950s, for instance, Scott McNall and Sally McNall describe farmers with more than a thousand acres as having an identity as "business persons," a notable contrast to the traditional farmers in the area, who saw farming as "a way of life."[33] John Bennett's work in Canada also notes that family farmers with a more agrarian ethic resisted the agricultural extension service's attempts to promote economic rationality and business orientation in farming,[34] while Gerry Walker notes some similar contrasts in Illinois.[35]

Where did ideals of success come from? Historical evidence from Dodge County, Georgia, suggests that industrial notions of success moved into the county with the advent of Yankee railroad builders in the late 1800s.[36] From then on, the economic center gradually shifted from agricultural production, based on pioneer homesteaders, to the capitalistic production of lumber and turpentine and, later, large-scale agriculture. Throughout the early decades of the twentieth century, the loss of an independent yeomanry and the transition to cotton tenancy heightened the clash of settler/farmer values with townsfolk values.[37] Economic and social changes also meant changes in gender relations. By the Depression years, national media, together with the agricultural extension service, supported

urban ideals of a male breadwinner and female homemaker. Farming families seeking an improved standard of living and increased respectability
in the post–World War II era, therefore, had to choose between adopting
a more industrial definition of personal success or holding onto agrarian
ideals. Industrial values might be accorded higher status among townsfolk,
but with limited opportunities to fulfill such ideals, they understandably
were not always attractive to rural men and women. Many families still
preferred the more equal marital partnership embodied in agrarian ideals,
and believed that farm operation was better served by this moral
economy.[38]

By the 1980s, when research in Dodge County began,[39] the rural economy had been transformed by the New Deal and post–World War II prosperity to a structure of commercial row-crop and livestock farms, similar
in technological sophistication to midwestern agriculture. Important acre-
ages in peanuts, cotton, and a little tobacco supplemented primary crops
(corn, soybeans, and wheat), and half of Dodge County's farm income
came from hogs and cattle. Many farms moved toward irrigation to lower
the risk of drought. A comfortable middle-class lifestyle was now the norm
for those who had survived the transition from the low-productivity farming of the 1920s and 1930s.

In my final section, I argue that these historical and sociocultural conditions have led to (at least) three different notions of masculine personal
success in today's rural America: the agrarian, the industrial, and the
newly emerging "sustainable" models of agriculture. The contrasting sustainable perspective of masculinity has not emerged as fully in the South
as it has in the Midwest, although it has certainly begun, as farmers increasingly adopt no-till methods of agriculture. Thus, although researchers
can identify three different versions of rural masculine success, not all
farmers in all regions share the same tripartite view. In the following analysis of agrarian, industrial, and sustainable models of agriculture, I aim to
avoid the notion of a fixed "gender consciousness,"[40] and instead highlight
the more useful concept that ideas of gender shift along with cultural ideals according to time and place.[41]

## Agrarian Versus Industrial Views of Masculine Success Among Georgia Farmers

Farmers express *agrarian* values in their respect for farming as a way of
life, its connection with nature, and its autonomy and independence in

daily work. For men who embrace this definition of success, the ability to do the work they love is very important: "[It's] a special feeling in the spring when you get out and prepare the land and then plant, and when the trees begin to turn green and the crops begin to grow, you feel like you really accomplished something." Some farmers' voices even shift to a reverent tone when they share their deep connections to spirituality through their work: "You look at nature all day long—God is all around you." They speak of the engagement of their senses in their work: the smell of freshly plowed soil, the song of birds.

For those who hold an agrarian perspective, farming is valued as a family commitment, an integration of work, family, community, and land. Sustaining the family's livelihood is a complex enterprise, but one that is located in a particular place, with relatives and friends nearby. Usually, a rural church community provides a social and religious frame around farm life. Agrarian-oriented farmers express their values in conscious opposition to what they see as urban nuclear family isolation, secularization, and overemphasis on lifestyle consumerism ("greed"). Accumulating inheritable property is also a marker of success for some agrarian farmers. When such farmers contemplate new land, an irrigation system, or some other major expense, the decision is made in light of long-term plans for the farm, for their own lifetimes or from a multigenerational perspective. If no children wish to continue farming, the agrarian farmer is less likely to make a big investment. Agrarian men take pride in developing their farms and keeping up with new technology, but generally try to avoid risk and a heavy debt load. Cautious managers, most prefer to expand slowly and use savings or repair old equipment rather than go into debt.

The agrarian ideology is connected with views of marriage that see both husband and wife as partners in a shared enterprise that links production on the farm and in the home. Although women may have little involvement with farm work and may indeed be employed off the farm, they nevertheless identify with farm success and see their efforts as part of a family project. "Even while cooking, I'm helping us all out on the farm. . . . We're all fighting a common battle," said one woman. For farm men with an agrarian orientation, therefore, success may include continuing a farm tradition, sustaining an adequate standard of living for the family, and launching children into the career of their choice, while simultaneously maintaining obligations to support kin, church, and community.[42]

In contrast, farmers with an *industrial* approach see agriculture as a business, emphasizing financial success. For them, farming is an occupational choice, evaluated like other possible jobs. This group rarely mentions the spiritual and lifestyle satisfactions of farming. As one explained: "You can feel as close to God as a research scientist in a lab as being a farmer." Another highly entrepreneurial man said he chose farming because he hoped to become a millionaire "and retire by fifty." Farmers with an industrial orientation are proud of their stock portfolios and big investments on the farm, and may be less concerned with the "craft" of a weed-free field. If they can obtain higher profits by expanding farm scale, even with "slapdash" farming methods, they feel that it reflects well on their success. In contrast, one agrarian/cautious farmer refused to expand his farm because "You can't get it done like it should be."

As we saw with Richard at the beginning of this chapter, farmers with a more entrepreneurial approach are proud to take big, "courageous" risks. Even those with quite modest-sized farms are delighted to demonstrate their competence with the latest technology and new equipment. Their conversations use, for example, accounting calculations to assess the break-even point for a possible new investment. The entrepreneurial farmer takes account of social competition: "There's always a pecking order." This industrial vision of success is not as concerned with long-term stability in the farm operation; it is less likely to make decisions within a multigenerational time frame, focusing instead on individual financial success in one generation.

The farmer who embraces an industrial vision of success expects to be the primary family breadwinner. For these farmers, it is important to support their wives, who are ideally full-time homemakers: "I've always said, it's my job to make the living and her job to make the living worthwhile," said one farmer. This group of Dodge County farmers thus has obvious parallels with Kimmel's description of the 1950s vision of suburban masculinity: "the American male, by definition, must provide for his family. He is *responsible* for the support of his wife and children."[43] Even when farming conditions make fulfilling this goal difficult, some men cling to these ideals. One man forced out of farming while his wife continued in a job commented sadly, "I didn't ever want a lot of money—a big house or a big car. I just wanted to make a decent living, have my wife not to have to work . . . to *provide*."

Two men of similar age, one with an industrial perspective and one with more of an agrarian, have similar modest redbrick farm homes, and illustrate these divergent orientations to material possessions. "You always would like something nicer," admitted the industrial farmer, dissatisfied with his home, while the other asserted, "I'm not greedy; I'm happy with what I got." Another older farmer clarified these two value orientations, saying, "I never wanted much, never had much, neither. But I don't want no pots of money. Nowadays, some people farm to get rich!" By contrast, a large-scale farmer with a more industrial orientation toward financial success—a man who chose farming to "be as independent as a pig on ice"—illustrates a mixture of perspectives in his desire for the autonomy of agriculture: alongside his desire for independence, he also thought farming would give him more freedom to be outdoors and to "be respected as a good businessman as well as a good farmer."[44]

## Personal Failure Versus Marital Partnership: Emotional Consequences

My conversations with Dodge County farmers suggest that these divergent views of masculine success have different emotional consequences, particularly in periods of financial crisis. In the 1980s and early 1990s, high input costs, low product prices, and fluctuating land values threw many American farms into the red. In the same period, droughts and floods increased the risk of financial loss. Farm incomes declined in both the Southeast and the Midwest, forcing many families into stringent budgeting and deferring consumption goals. Many examples show that during financial hard times farm men struggle with a sense of loss and personal failure, often displaying symptoms such as depression, anger, and anxiety.[45] One important response to falling household income is to turn to off-farm work. Men, however, rarely seek such jobs, because diverting their effort from the farm requires a major restructuring of daily farming operations and usually fails to save the enterprise, anyway. More commonly, then, women either take jobs off the farm or seek to expand part-time work into full-time work.

Although all farmers naturally were upset by declining incomes and worried about possible bankruptcy and farm loss, those whose definitions of personal success emphasized family income, consumer goods, and farm entrepreneurship seemed to carry a different emotional burden. Their personal self-worth was more likely to be challenged by the farm's low income. In terms of wives' employment, especially, a man's definition of success made the difference between seeing his wife's income as a relief and blessing or as a personal failure.[46]

Bill, a young, energetic farmer, lives not far from Mack and shares Mack's agrarian ideals, although Mack is old enough to be his father. Bill struggles mightily with a huge debt for the farm he has bought, although so far he has been able to meet his mortgage payments. With the help of his wife's job, the couple finds the family's standard of living acceptable. Their current strategy, as Bill explains, means that his wife "makes the living" and her income allows him to focus on making the farm break even. He is calm about the need for his wife to have a job; his sense of success centers on the family partnership and on progress toward the shared goal of a viable farm operation. Notably, both younger and older agrarian farmers spoke of their wives' jobs as necessary, saying: "It takes two to make the living nowadays." These agrarian-oriented men seem to experience little discomfort in saying, "My wife makes the living," and, although they know that some people might consider such a situation undesirable, the arrangement is harmonious with their values.

In contrast, men with a different sense of masculine obligations to family are sometimes devastated by the necessity that their wives get a job off the farm—typically these are men with a more industrial approach to farming. One working wife said that her husband cried in humiliation when she got a job: "He didn't want to admit he couldn't support [me]." Another man agreed that if a wife buys the groceries, it makes the husband feel he "is falling down on the job." Still another expressed his desire to "provide the living" as a matter of pride, "and if I couldn't, I hope folks would say I really *tried*."

These very different emotional reactions occur on farms of similar sizes and states of financial solvency. Clearly, men of similar age, education, and farm background draw different meanings from their wives' employment based on whether they have previously embraced a breadwinner norm. Farmers rarely discuss such issues with each other, but when I described the industrial definition of masculine success to (agrarian) Bill, he agreed that industrial farmers "play from a different book." Sometimes, a man's sense of masculine inadequacy means that he "plays from a different book" from his own wife. One woman from a more agrarian background than her husband, who enjoyed her job in town, expressed helplessness as her husband struggled with insomnia and depression: "He's very defeated."

The Iowa Youth and Families Project (a study of economic hardship, family relationships, and psychological well-being) reveals some interesting parallels with the Georgia case.[47] Farmers who scored low on questions relating to materialistic values and the importance of financial success also earned somewhat less money than those who scored high. Nevertheless, these farmers seem to find themselves more empowered in their daily lives. Those with higher "materialistic" scores had a lower sense of mastery, perhaps because they base their sense of mastery not on the firmer ground of craft and farm skill but on the shifting sands of income and prosperity.[48] The group with high materialistic values also showed a statistically significant correlation between depressed mood and self-reported inadequacy in providing materially for the family, a much higher correlation than that observed for the low materialistic values group.

## An Emerging Third Masculine Ideal

As the majority of farmers in the Midwest and Southeast struggle with these two conflicting paradigms of success, a third option is emerging as part of a new paradigm of alternative agriculture. Farm management techniques in the Iowa sustainable agriculture movement, as Peter and his colleagues describe them,[49] challenge conventional farming values and constitute an alternative vision of masculine success. To create their alternative identity as sustainable farmers, these farmers collapse the agrarian and industrial variants described above and articulate their own emerging values of good farming in opposition to "the other guys"—that is, the conventional or traditional practitioners.

Peter and his colleagues found that Iowa farmers committed to sustainable agricultural practices are less likely to use the language and practices of toughness, independent individualism, hard work, machines, and a generally phallocentric approach to the "impregnation" of the earth.[50] "In place of toughness," they explain, "sustainably oriented farm men spoke openly of their mistakes, their failures, and their sense of having less than total control of their farming. In place of independent individualism, they often spoke of the need for community support. In place of hard work, they often spoke of a different conception of what constitutes 'work.'" These farmers also emphasized farm diversification and new economic strategies: "In place of machines, they often spoke of the pleasures of livestock, and in place of phallocentric imagery for the land . . . they often spoke of an ecological . . . vision of the landscape."[51]

Iowa sustainable farmers tend to have more diversified farm enterprises, with less emphasis on grain and increasing livestock and less reliance on machines. One such farmer characterized the psychology of conventional grain farming as "a power trip or image of authority: 'I can do this because I've got 400 horsepower under the tractor and I can make sixty feet black.'"[52] One sophisticated farmer in Georgia responded to hearing this statement by saying: "You can find yourself saying that: 'I've got a four-row cotton picker!' But I know I wouldn't be proud to say, 'I'm an earth farmer and I don't use chemicals and I pick up after the horses in Savannah. . . .' That has no allure for me." *What would people say if you did that?* "I'd think of myself as an absolute nut."

In contrast to midwestern conventional agriculture, in which "nobody ever wants to talk about their failures," according to Peter and his colleagues, the sustainable farming organizations provide a supportive community for discussing both successes and failures: "They like to share with people." Thus sustainable farmers articulate a "less individualistic, less competitive, more community-oriented vision of the masculine self."[53] In comparison, a conventional Georgia farmer emphasizes that "farmers today have so many toys and tools. We have so much more technology; we know so much more [than farmers of the past]. For me, I want to do my best and see *increase* . . . every day, I want to put on the right chemical." He celebrates pushing the envelope of production, developing the farm in a new way, and extending the "improvements" of the early pioneers who first cleared the land. Sustainable agriculture proponents, on the other hand, are focused less on "increase" than on discovering the incremental steps that will build a whole new paradigm of production.

Salamon's research in Illinois among farmers committed to sustainable agriculture also shows a shifting pattern in how they measure success.[54] For example, these men are satisfied to use older, smaller tractors, rejecting the view of conventional farmers that old equipment is proof of financial stress. Sustainable farmers are similarly less likely to celebrate their farm achievements: "they strive for a goal that is continually refined, so that full achievement is rarely acknowledged." One explained, "I'm not there yet, but I know what it takes to get there" (267). Sustainable farmers tend to be frugal and cautious in their use of all resources, not just chemicals. These Illinois farmers echo the "if you can't pay for it, don't buy it" ethos found among more agrarian Georgia farmers. They are also more likely to embrace a modest lifestyle (268). Sustainable farmers flout conventional norms of farm skill as expressed in weed-free fields, preferring to save fuel and avoid chemical use by mowing only when weeds become "serious." Sustainable farmers get support in this alternative approach to farming through peer mentors and organizations such as the Illinois Sustainable Agriculture Network.

Because alternative agriculture represents a break with several dimensions of farming success, men and women committed to sustainable farming must negotiate between the support of alternative agricultural organizations and like-minded peers, on the one hand, and the different norms of family, neighbors, and other members of the geographical community on the other. As Salamon reports, both husbands and wives are vulnerable to judgments that see these new farming techniques as examples of laziness, poor skills, or financial failure, particularly as midwestern sustainable farmers commonly experiment (most in the Illinois study have test plots underway) (269). Sustainable farm operations are, on average, smaller in size than conventional ones, one indication to the conventional farmer of less successful management. Similarly, sustainable farmers' delight in discussing their ways of "tweaking the system" is seen by their neighbors as evidence of poor management. One conventional farmer said, "I see them changing their practices every year. What that tells me is they're not sure what they are doing" (270).

The power of masculine competitive peer pressure also affects sustainable farmers as deeply as it does conventional farmers. Some Illinois sustainable farmers report, for example, that they feel reluctant to participate in one forum in which men commonly gather, the local coffee shop, where stories and farming commentary are a primary focus of conversation. As one sustainable farmer explained, "If I went to the coffee shop I wouldn't be using no-till [a technique to reduce erosion by leaving plant material covering the soil, unlike the cleared fields of conventional farmers]. Everyone would have shamed me into not using it" (269). While research in Georgia in 2002 found several Dodge County farmers taking steps toward sustainable agriculture by adopting no-till planting methods, many farmers still describe this system as leaving the fields "a damn mess." But criticism by fathers or neighbors can be offset by encouragement from regional meetings, as found in the Midwest. Therefore, although peer criticism remains "rough" for many, one older farmer admitted, "Years ago, people would have laughed at you, but now it's common."

Wives of sustainable farmers, however, can be caught in the middle, absorbing the negative judgments of their conventional parents, siblings, or neighbors ("He's crazy. He's going broke") without benefit of a supportive peer group. Salamon concludes that while the alternative agriculture community seems to be doing a more successful job in sustaining a different set of status symbols and measures of success for their male members, this is not necessarily so for the wives, who may not be members (269).

The words of one Illinois farmer sum up his view of these different forms of farming masculinity: "I think all farmers divide into two types. Either you have power-genes or soil-genes. A power-gene guy likes machines, buys new the latest and most powerful he can. A soil-gene guy uses less horsepower, has old or used equipment, and does anything not to use as much horsepower. A soil-gene guy looks under the soil while the power-gene guy only cares about what's going-on on top" (270). Sustainable approaches also work within an expanded time horizon in terms of decision making. Transcending even multigenerational agrarian farmers, alternative agriculturalists often think in terms of very long-term chemical consequences to the food chain, aquifer contamination, and ecosystem diversity. The alternative or sustainable farmer thus embraces a global "systems perspective"—a far broader perspective than that of either of the two types of conventional farmer.

## Conclusion: Urban Parallels

These examples of a new masculinity on the midwestern farm echo Kimmel's description of an emerging new masculinity in urban America. Kimmel describes an urban "third wave," in which "a globally aware, environmentally sensitive, freely flowing androgynous cultural identity" replaces the capitalistic self-made man "animated by hierarchy, marketplace, rationality, and order under marketplace-based individualism."[55] According to this argument, competition, domination, and power—the masculine touchstones of the self-made (industrial) man—are evolving into accountability, responsibility, compassion, and "a fierce egalitarianism."[56] In keeping with this evolution, Kimmel also argues that in the postmodern, globalizing economy, the workplace has "collapsed" as an arena in which to test and prove masculinity, and that post–Reagan-era attempts to redefine masculine ideals are characterized by greater concern with generativity, attention to fatherhood, and renewed spirituality. Although the workplace has not "collapsed" in agriculture—and indeed remains a central locus of contested meanings and practices—similar values are echoed in these studies of sustainable farmers of Illinois and Iowa. The emerging ideas of masculine success among these alternative farmers are less likely to be defined by "instrumental dominance and power dominance" than traditional models, thus reflecting wider postmodern trends to define masculinity in "more diffuse and flexible" ways.[57]

The third wave of rural masculine ideology emerging among alternative and sustainable farmers means that these men construct their identities not only through public, competitive, and homosocial practices, but also through private relations with nature, orientation to the divine, and stewardship of resources. As the evidence from Iowa, Illinois, and Georgia shows, it is vital to expand our awareness of masculinity beyond the public sphere to explore these forms of family interactions and intensely personal judgments and emotions in order to analyze both masculinity and personal success.

This study of multiple ideologies of good farming, personal success, and masculinity within one occupational group highlights several fruitful directions for future research. Overall, we need better documentation and research in many areas, among them the complex enactments and tensions of these multiple models within local communities; the relationship between masculinity and personal success; historical regional differences and the changing political economy of rural America; varying American visions of partnership and moral obligation in marriage; the negotiated transformations of youthful masculine ideals over the adult lifespan; and the psychological consequences of different masculine ideals at different moments in life. Just as an industrializing global culture brings new imperatives for ecological sustainability and altered relationships with nature, so too are the shifts we can see among some sustainable agriculture practitioners in the webs of meaning and action that link masculine ideologies, farm management styles, and expectations about marriage and family partnerships echoed in other walks of life. Indeed, our global survival may depend on the speed with which personal definitions of success can change.

NOTES

1. Mack and other named farmers have been given pseudonyms, and minor details have been changed to protect their identities. Unless otherwise noted, all quotations are statements from interviews or conversations with specific individuals in my research in Dodge County, Georgia.

2. Moore (1994); Ortner (1996).

3. Collins (1990); Rubin (1976); Mohanty, Russo, and Torres (1991).

4. Brod and Kaufman (1994); Gutmann (1996); Hearn and Morgan (1990); Kimmel (1996).

5. Brod (1987); Johnson (1997).

6. Campbell and Bell (2000); Liepins (2000); Peter et al. (2000).

7. Unfortunately, the distinctive experience of African American farmers, particularly in the South, cannot be explored properly with the limited data available. The Georgia research found that the values about success in farming expressed by more than a dozen African American farmers were similar to those expressed by Euro-American farmers, suggesting some common ground. But these cases are not sufficient in number for a clear and subtle understanding. Consequently, this analysis is restricted to the experience of Euro-Americans.

8. Peter et al. (1996, 13).

9. Kimmel (1996, 26).

10. Peter et al. (2000, 219).

11. Kimmel (1996, 7).

12. Gutmann (1997).

13. Collier (1986).

14. Osterud (1991).

15. Hochschild (1989).

16. Liepins (2000); Dudley (2000).

17. Barlett (1993).

18. Ibid.

19. Barlett (1993); Liepins (2000); Salamon et al. (1997).

20. Peter et al. (2000, 225).

21. But see Dudley (2000).

22. Ownby (1991).

23. Ownby (1991), cited in Kimmel (1996, 125).

24. Dimensions of femininity are also part of farming, note some men. "You have to mother that crop," said one. "There's a little of both in it." In drawing out the masculine dimensions of agriculture, I do not want to deny the existence of other dimensions.

25. Fink (1992); Adams (1994); Sedgwick (1985).

26. Kimmel (1996, 14–18).

27. I omit Kimmel's third category, the "gentleman farmer," because it is not a major part of the Dodge County story, although echoes are present in the lives of some individuals. It may be a dimension of masculinity in other parts of the country, but it seems to be even less so in the Midwest than in the Southeast. The stereotype of southern agriculture as dominated by the plantation economy and the aristocratic traditions of an agrarian elite is supported by the overemphasis in southern history on such counties. Counties that were not heavily influenced by the plantation system (the so-called Yeoman South) are in the vast majority; in Georgia they make up 90 percent of the state, but historians have studied them less thoroughly.

28. Netting (1993).

29. M. Ryan (1981), for example, documents the emerging gender ideology of "separate spheres" in northeastern towns in the early 1800s, alongside the increased emphasis on women's value as mother and homemaker rather than producer (Cott 1977; Degler 1980; Margolis 1984). In this model, men's role as breadwinners is complemented by women's responsibility for the family. As these ideological ideals migrated into the Southeast and Midwest, they mixed with some

regional variants (Adams 1988; Fink 1992; McMillen 1992).

30. Salamon (1992); Friedburger (1988, 1989); Walker (1997).

31. Salamon et al. (1986); Barlett (1993).

32. Danbom (1979); Kirby (1987); Mooney (1988).

33. McNall and McNall (1983, 264–65).

34. Bennett (1982, 22).

35. Walker (1997).

36. Barlett (1993); Wetherington (1994).

37. Wetherington (1994).

38. Barlett (1993).

39. Men and women were interviewed separately in the interviews on gender and farm management in 1987. Research spanned the years 1982 to 1989 and included three periods of residence in the county, for a total of almost two years. Interviews were supplemented by participant observation on farms, in churches, at agricultural meetings, and in social contexts. Although this article draws mainly from the fifty-eight full-time farmers studied, 156 full-time, part-time, and retired farmers were part of the total study. Insights into masculinity were drawn from the work with all three groups and were supplemented by follow-up interviews with twenty farmers in 2002.

40. Livingstone and Luxton (1989).

41. Campbell and Bell (2000); Davenport (2000); Dudley (1994); Gutmann (1996); Peter et al. (2000).

42. The popular image of the family farm includes an important labor contribution by children, but commercial row-crop and livestock farms today are much less likely to depend on family labor than in the past (Adams 1994; Fink 1992). Dairy, poultry, tobacco, and truck farms are more likely to rely on cooperative family labor. In the Georgia study, the majority of farm children did no regular farm chores, although a minority (mostly boys) chose to help out, and their labor was important to the family. After-school activities and part-time jobs hamper the farm contributions of many teenagers, and most parents want to offer their children a choice regarding farm labor. This choice in adolescence is a precursor to the free choice many parents hope to offer their children with regard to an adult occupation. The majority of parents in the Dodge County study who love farming do not encourage their children to farm, in recognition of the high costs and risks of this occupation today.

43. Kimmel (1996, 248).

44. Barlett (1991).

45. Conger and Elder (1994); Elder and Conger (2000); Rosenblatt (1990).

46. Lobao and Meyer (1995b).

47. Barlett and Conger (2004); Conger and Elder (1994); Elder and Conger (2000).

48. Barlett and Conger (2004).

49. Peter et al. (1996, 2000). See also Peter et al., Chapter 2 in this volume.

50. Peter et al. (1996); Peter et al. (2000).

51. Peter et al. (1996, 21).

52. Peter et al. (2000, 228).

53. Peter et al. (1996, 22–23); Peter et al. (2000, 230).

54. Salamon et al. (1997). The following five paragraphs draw heavily on this work; page citations are given parenthetically in the text.

55. Kimmel (1996, 266). Wilkie's (1993) survey of American men's attitudes also confirms this shift toward a "third-wave" masculinity.

56. Kimmel (1996, 334).

57. Livingstone and Luxton (1989, 242); Peter et al. (2000).

# 4 Masculinities in Rural Small Business Ownership: Between Community and Capitalism

*Sharon Bird*

Recent research on masculinities, work, and organizations often focuses on the gendered nature of management practices in large companies and how these practices evolved under industrial capitalism, corporate capitalism, and multinational corporate capitalism.[1] Few studies, however, focus specifically on the gendered management practices of men as small business owners or the constructions of masculinity potentially produced in small business contexts. Likewise, there are few studies of the influence of rural location on how gender organizes small businesses and management practices, and men as managers in those businesses.[2] We do know, however, that in the United States the ratio of female-to male-owned businesses tends to be higher in rural than urban settings. And recent studies suggest that the sex gap in small business success is smaller in rural places than in urban places.[3] These findings suggest a need for studies that examine constructions of masculinities within rural contexts, where gender norms and practices may differ considerably from those found in large corporations and urban areas.

This chapter examines how masculinities—as socially constructed ideals, meanings, and identities—shape and are shaped by small business operations in one small town (population approximately eight thousand) in the midwestern United States. Unlike many previous studies that examine dominant models of management, men, and masculinities in large corporations, this study focuses on how men view themselves as business owners, as community members, and as men.[4] As I discuss below, the male small business owners I interviewed positioned themselves carefully between the community and "big business" by carving out gendered business niches where they are embraced as good husbands, fathers, and community troopers. Within these niches, male owners reinforce stereotypes and practices of masculinity and femininity consistent with their own gender ideologies. Although the themes of masculinity and management such men embrace in their businesses and daily lives differ somewhat from one owner to the next, the management practices these men employ fit clearly within a paternalistic model of management.[5] In turn, in most of their businesses, paternalistic management practices enable favorable relations with workers and sustain customer satisfaction, and therefore help owners maintain both socially valued masculine identities *and* business profits.

## The Study

The data for the study are drawn from a larger project that compares small business success in rural and urban communities. In the present investigation, I focus on the qualitative data collected for this study,[6] especially in-depth interviews with male owners of small rural businesses in a single town.[7] The population of the town is predominantly white, as were most of the small business owners surveyed (more than 95 percent). The community guide distributed by the local Chamber of Commerce describes the town primarily as a "farming community" with one large manufacturing plant. The town was first "settled" by white Euro-Americans in the 1800s and became incorporated in the 1870s.

All data were collected in the fall of 2001 and spring of 2002. All interviews were tape-recorded and transcribed. In the in-depth interviews, I asked the same set of questions of each owner but allowed the owners to elaborate on issues they felt were important regarding the success of their businesses and the vitality of their communities. More specifically, the questions asked of business owners focused on their relations with customers and employees; the owners' personal views on business ownership, business success, and balancing work, family, and friends; and the owners' personal backgrounds.

## Small Business Ownership and Male Owners' Views of Themselves

In many ways, owning one's own business is consistent with ideals of manhood and masculinity that have been prominent for many years in the United States and other industrialized capitalist societies. Business ownership offers, for example, the opportunity to make decisions relatively autonomously and to harvest the fruits of one's own labor. For all of the male owners I interviewed in Madison Town, business ownership was a central organizing aspect of life. In fact, these men found operating a business so routine that they spent little time thinking consciously about it. Many were thus initially at a loss for words when asked to explain how running their own businesses had shaped their lives over the years. On reflection, however, each owner was able to reveal several ways in which his business was central to his daily routine and how he viewed himself.

### "I Couldn't Work for Anybody Else"

When asked what he found the most fulfilling aspect of business ownership, Ray Goodman, owner of Madison Town's only jewelry store, Goodman Jewelers, responded: "Well, obviously being your own boss isn't too bad." Terry Reed, owner of Shady Street Sports Bar and Pizza Parlor (a restaurant known for its wide selection of beers and sports bar atmosphere), initially suggested that business ownership had little to do with his personality or self-concept, but then added: "You know, I'm forty-nine years old. My wife says I couldn't work for anybody else . . . because, she says, 'You're too opinionated on how to run a business.' And I says, well I think if, to me I'd love to have somebody that, like myself, that you don't have to tell how to do things that's used to doing by themselves so . . . I probably at this point in life I wouldn't change but, you know, it always crosses your mind because, like I say, the hours are hard on people."

Similarly, Jim Rathke, owner of Main Street Manor, the restaurant widely recognized as Madison Town's finest dining establishment, said: "Well, I . . . I would suppose that if I was to sell this and go to work for somebody, that'd be awful hard to do for me. Because I've worked for myself for so long. When there's something that comes up I can make a decision right now and don't have to go to anybody. . . . And I think it's the, uh, the freedom of a small business that I arranged for myself."

Each owner explained that the primary reason he would continue to make his living in small business ownership, despite economic hard times and long inconvenient work hours, was that he could not accept taking orders from others.

Being one's own boss is consistent with pervasive and romanticized ideals of masculinity in the American capitalist economy. Business ownership, however, does not necessarily reflect or produce the same kind of idealized manhood for each male owner. According to my interviews, small business ownership enables men to construct a reality in which their own visions of appropriate gender "roles" are not only accepted but also continually affirmed.

## Ownership Is Consistent with Owners' Views of Desirable Manhood/ Masculinity

Small business is also central to these men's lives in that their businesses allow them to create an atmosphere consistent with their own personalities and primary interests. Although the owners' interests differed, they nevertheless shared a distinct gender theme. That is, each male owner emphasized aspects of his business that highlighted characteristics and practices he saw as more appropriate and common for men than women.

Dick Johnson, owner of Sports World, Madison Town's only sporting goods store, for example, explained that his business creates opportunities for him to work with local and regional sports teams at several age levels. Dick is an avid runner and golfer, enjoys attending sports events at the local junior high and high school, and likes to attend football games at one of the state's public universities.

When I asked if anyone in his family helps out with the business, Dick replied that his brother sometimes fills in for him, and then added: "My wife, she doesn't, she's not involved with this; very, very little. The main reason is because she doesn't relate to, she just doesn't . . . feel comfortable, especially with the hunting and fishing stuff. But she's had, she's in education and that's been her thing so she's never really taken an active part in the business, although she helps with the Christmas decorations and that kind of stuff."

Dick then explained that his daughters, two of whom are in college and one in high school, sometimes worked at the store. "The girls have helped me with trends . . . women come in and buy shoes and . . . well, you know, [they say,] 'I kinda like that one with the pink stripe.'" But male workers, he added, "even if they don't hunt or fish, can talk the lingo a bit better, can just converse with somebody," so for "the entire picture of the store, a male usually works better for all departments."

Like other men, Dick views himself as interested in and knowledgeable about sports. He views women, on the other hand, as interested in and knowledgeable about fashion. He explained that his store allows him to connect with "other people who are excited about the same things I'm excited about." These "other people," however, are not generic people; they are men who presumably are able to talk about sports even if they do not know much about them.

Interestingly, Dick uses levels of interest in sport to position himself (and other men) as opposite women, even though—as he revealed toward the end of our interview—his daughters were very interested in and good at sports. Dick's youngest daughter, for example, "is a very good athlete; they won the state softball championship this summer. She's in track, and right now she's in basketball. . . . I go to every one of those games." Thus Dick places himself and other men opposite women within the context of his own business, despite the obvious contradiction that his own daughters' accomplishments pose to his gender and sports ideology.

Terry Reed, the owner of Shady Street Sports Bar and Pizza Parlor, emphasized a similar theme as he discussed his wife's role in his business. He noted, for example, that his wife is the only female who ever tends the bar at the restaurant and that she only fills in when none of the "guys" (regular employees) are available. He elaborated that he would prefer that his wife not work behind the bar because she does not care much about sports. Interestingly, however, my observations of the owner, his wife, and customers during regular business hours indicated that the wife was indeed quite knowledgeable and seemed very enthusiastic about sports. She sat for more than fifteen minutes at a table in the restaurant next to mine talking with two middle-aged male customers about the upcoming basketball season at the local high school, the anticipated victory of her favorite National Football League team, and her latest golf club purchase—a putter.

Terry also described his Sports Bar–Pizza Parlor as a place where everyone can feel welcome, "a *Cheers* type of thing, not one of those places where you walk in and everybody turns around and looks at you." The physical and symbolic setting of the restaurant itself underlines what Terry means when he describes his restaurant as a place where everyone feels welcome. His comment about "a *Cheers* type of thing" refers to the neighborhood sports bar atmosphere featured in a U.S. television show that ran for several years in the 1980s and 1990s. Posters of sports teams line the walls of the building, along with multiple televisions of various sizes. A large basketball "shoot-out" game sits opposite the main entrance. A poster advertisement for a domestic beer featuring a woman in a skimpy swimsuit hangs prominently just inside the door. The televisions are either tuned to sports channels or turned off. During six hours of observations on two occasions—one weeknight and one weekend, once as part of a three-woman group and once alone—I overheard dozens of conversations initiated by men, very few of which had anything to do with topics other than sports, politics, or local gossip. Most customers were men, but women were also well represented (approximately 30 percent of all the customers I observed). Most female customers were accompanied by one or more men, although three small all-woman groups made brief visits to the restaurant during my observations. Women were, with very few exceptions, peripheral to men's conversations. The women sat with the men primarily as spectators, not participants. I noted only four brief exchanges in which the women sitting with men initiated conversation. In each instance, the women asked the men questions about their work or leisure activities.

The larger proportion of male customers, the décor, and the televised sports events, together with the all-male staff in the front of the restaurant/ bar (except for the owner's wife), indeed creates a *Cheers*-type atmosphere. But to suggest that everyone feels similarly comfortable in Terry's bar would be a stretch. The owner, as he clearly testifies, feels at home in his restaurant, as do others interested in men's sports activities, beer, and women in swimsuits. But this is not necessarily an environment in which all types of customers would feel at home. The restaurant affirms Terry, as an owner, a man, and a sports fan, and those who, like Terry, enjoy a masculinist sports' fan atmosphere.

When asked to describe the atmosphere in his restaurant, Don Becker, owner of Pine Forge Inn, a small steak house, also emphasized the friendliness of his place. He, like Terry Reed, stressed that he felt his restaurant was a place where regulars and occasional customers alike would feel welcome. He said he enjoyed creating an atmosphere where "everybody can talk to everybody," a "close atmosphere," not one with "little stalls where you sit and don't see who's there." Initially, the atmosphere Don described was very similar to the kind of atmosphere Terry aimed to nurture in the Shady Street Sports Bar. But Don specifically distinguished himself from other restaurant owners in town when he noted that he and his wife pay attention to everyone, unlike "a lot of other restaurant owners in town" who "keep their noses in the air." "We welcome everyone," Don explained, "regardless of social circles or high-class educations or whether they're into sport."

The atmosphere of Pine Forge Inn, like that of the Shady Street Sports

Bar and Pizza Parlor, provides a necessary context for interpreting Don Becker's comments on restaurant atmosphere, and how his business and gender ideologies coincide. The steak house is divided into three large dining areas, each partly partitioned from the others so that one can see through the columns separating these spaces. Movable chairs are positioned around approximately thirty round wooden tables, each of which is covered with a vinyl tablecloth. The décor consists primarily of antiques and framed prints of desert and mountain scenes. There are no televisions or beer advertisements hanging on the walls, though a few light fixtures over the bar located just inside the front entryway do feature domestic beer logos.

In the two and a half hours I spent at the restaurant early one weekend evening, I witnessed numerous interactions between the owner's wife, the waitresses, and the customers. These interactions were central to what the owner meant when he said his restaurant was a "friendly place." I noted, for example, that the owner's wife and the waitresses were attentive to both male and female customers. The waitresses doted on the male customers, who in return joked with the waitresses about such things as how they might steal them away from their husbands, how they should work harder for tips, and how local politicians were not doing their jobs very well. With female customers, the waitresses were more likely to share bits of information heard "over the grapevine." The male and female customers, unlike those observed at the sports bar, engaged together in conversations that focused on both the women's and the men's daily lives.

In his interview, Don explained that while both he and his wife contribute to the business, they have distinct roles. When I asked whether his wife contributes to the success of the business, Don replied: "Oh yeah, she trained the waitresses to be real friendly to the men. I mean, we get a lot of compliments on how we train our front employees. Our back employees are a little different 'cause they don't know how to act with customers." "Front" employees, I learned, was the term Don used to refer to waitresses, who were all women, while the "back" employees, all men, were cooks. Don explained that the front helpers were always more inclined to interact in a "happy and cheerful" way with customers, whereas the back employees "just aren't too good at it." He believes, that is, that women are better at expressing themselves emotionally and positively, while men are more suited to work that does not involve being "cheerful" or waiting on people. When this owner described the friendly atmosphere of his business, therefore, he meant an atmosphere in which women and men contribute to conversations and work but enact different gender scripts.

But while Don claimed that his wife did most of the talking with and befriending of customers, he also provided many stories about his own nurturing relationships with customers, stories that demonstrate disjuncture between ideology and action. "I had this one old lady, Jessie, she was eighty-four, and I used to walk her to her car and Jessie fell in love [with me] and up to the time she died, I went to see her. We really actually took care of her. Her lawyer called and asked us what to do and stuff like that. I mean that's how my *wife* gets involved with some of our customers. It's always been that way" (emphasis added).

In this story, Don frames his wife's role as instigating friendships with customers but at the same time highlights the affection that Jessie expressed for him, seeing himself as the gentleman taking care for a helpless woman but deemphasizing his own emotional work. Don also talked about using his business to help other community members (all customers) in need: "We, well, I, had an auction in my restaurant. In the first auction we raised $9,000 [for a male customer's heart transplant]. [A different male customer] is another one that got hurt over there so I had another auction for him and we raised $19,000. We had little pigs in there and everything, auctioning them off."

Thus we see again that when Don describes his restaurant as a friendly place where all feel welcome, he is envisioning an atmosphere where he feels comfortable and where women and men play different roles. Note that the specific roles Don envisions in the steak house differ clearly from the roles that Terry envisions. Owners' and customers' ages might help explain some of the differences in the kind of atmosphere created and enjoyed, and the intersection between gender and work roles, in each restaurant. My survey of local businesses, in conjunction with the interview data, indicates that Terry, like many—although certainly not all—of the customers who frequent the Shady Street Sports Bar, is in early middle age, while Don, like many of his customers, is in his early sixties.

Jim Rathke, owner of Main Street Manor, also explained that his restaurant "gave people a level of comfort." When I asked what his customers liked best about the restaurant, he replied, "I always like to say it's their place, you know. They come in and they feel comfortable." Like the other owners, Jim emphasized the distinct roles that he and his wife play in the business and in life, explaining that they had always agreed that his primary duty in life was to run the business while hers was to raise the children.

The atmosphere of Main Street Manor helps us understand how Jim's vision of customer comfort and appreciation coincide with his own gender ideology. Main Street Manor is a family-style restaurant with an American "Old West" theme. Swinging saloon-style doors hang in each doorway. Antique brass lamps with bell-shaped shades and gold fringe dangle over each of the booths located along the largest of the four separate dining rooms. The same lampshades adorn the tall lamps that stand like proud guardians beside the rustic wooden tables scattered throughout the restaurant. Some of the tables and booths seat as many as ten or twelve people. Although the restaurant serves alcohol, only the antique soda fountain is visible to customers. Toward the back of the main dining room Jim has a pinball machine and a few other arcade games "for the kiddies." More private rooms and booths are also available. Jim notes that the mix of private rooms and family dining makes his restaurant attractive to families as well as romantic couples, appropriate for women "out to lunch after a morning shopping trip," as well as "businessmen who need to discuss private matters over drinks."

As noted above, Jim views women's primary roles as being wives and mothers and men's primary role as being breadwinners. Jim holds this position despite the fact that his wife spends a great deal of time working in the restaurant. When asked about his wife's contributions to his business, for example, Jim responded: "She has her thing, I do my thing. We put it together and we, you know, Saturday night and Friday she's got the front end, and I got the kitchen."

His wife, according to Jim, has worked full time at the restaurant since it first opened. Even so, he was careful to position his wife as primarily a homemaker. Jim noted more than once, for example, that his "wife has always kept the, uh, mother's hours"; "for the most part, she's home a lot," and "she'd always make darn sure that the family sat down and ate together." Again, although his wife has characteristically worked full-time at the restaurant, her hours were nonetheless "mother's hours." He cast himself, by contrast, as the self-sacrificing breadwinner. "I am very self-disciplined. If I need to be here some morning at six o'clock, I'm here. And if I need to stay some night till midnight, I'm here. It could be the same day that I was having to be here at 6 A.M., you know. Whatever it takes, I do."

Like his assessment of his wife's "mother's hours," this assessment of himself is not entirely consistent with his description of his own typical workweek. He notes, for example, that he liked owning his own business not only because he could be his own boss but because it enabled him to take a few days off each week during golf season to "hit balls with his buddies at the country club."

When asked specifically whether his family expected him to work such long hours or to sacrifice time with family to business, Jim responded with a brief story about how he had once made a poor decision in an effort to increase business profits. "I made a big goof, I mean a six-figure [financial] goof a while back, and I was the one that was the most bothered by it. I sat the family down and poured myself out to them and they told me how silly I was. No big deal [they said]. Don't worry about it."

This was not exactly the story I was expecting to hear. Jim had described separate work and family roles for his wife. He framed these separate roles as though one were primary (family) and the other secondary (business) for his wife, but as if the two were largely unrelated, as if his wife's work at the business reflected little on her work at home, and vice versa. I had therefore anticipated that Jim would discuss the relation between business and family life for himself as well. But for Jim, there was apparently no division between his role as business owner and his roles as husband and father. Like the traditional "breadwinner," by making his business success-ful, he was fulfilling his duty as a good father and husband. If his business failed, he would also fail in his family roles.

Jim's approach to his employees, in addition, reflected an ideology of paternalism. He spoke of the waitresses as his "girls" and explained that he always made it clear to the "girls" that because "they may have little ones at home and little sick ones," he would not expect them to work full-time hours. In contrast, Jim explained how he tried to give the young men who worked for him opportunities to learn how to manage and possibly own a business of their own someday: "I worked for, uh [names three men] that, uh, really took me under their wing. And showed me a lot of things and I could ask questions and I'd always get an answer. And they shared their business with me. . . . So in turn I try to do that to young fellas that come . . . that work here."

Thus, from Jim's perspective, the workplace is primarily a man's place. "Businessmen" have business meetings; women, as "shoppers" and moth-ers "with little ones," take lunch breaks at his restaurant. While women may work a few "mother's hours," men are the primary breadwinners. Therefore, when Jim speaks of his restaurant being a place where customers "feel a level of comfort," he means a kind of comfort that is consistent with his views of himself and his vision of the primary roles in life that women and men are presumed to play.

As I said earlier, not all the men emphasized the same masculine role as they talked about the part their businesses played in their own lives. Each man, however, clearly positioned himself via his business role as opposite a woman's role—a role that variously defined women as less knowledgeable, as more dependent physically and financially on others, and as natural caretakers.

## Community Visibility: Building Loyal Customers and Giving Back to the Community

Male business owners in Madison Town stressed repeatedly that in a small town, unlike in cities, owners must be consistently visible to their customers and the community. Jim Rathke, owner of Main Street Manor, for example, had many stories about how his customers expected more of him personally than customers in larger communities expect.

> A friend of mine used to run the bowling center on the edge of town here. And he says, you know, he'd work sixty to seventy hours a week but once in a while take a night off. People would come in and say, "Yeah, well, where were you the other night? You never work?" That's a big deal in a small town. Now recently he got another bowling center in [large city about two hours away]. . . . So he moved down there to work that. He says, you know, the funny thing about [this large city] is those people don't care who owns the business. That's not a big deal to 'em. Uh, if they come in and get what they want and have a good time, that's all that's important to them.

Visibility, these men explained, gives customers a sense of trust in the business and a sense of belonging in the community. Visibility therefore creates customer loyalty and commitment to the business. The owners' belief that their contributions to the town via business ownership were one of the few barriers standing in the way of the "evils" of corporate capitalism was closely linked to this idea. The owners effectively positioned themselves as the exceptions in a world quickly being overrun by big business. As Terry Reed explained,

> It begins with corporate America and everything, where the owners are never in businesses anymore, you know, you can see that local people are a little bit that way. You know they want to come in and see you or something 'cause when you've been doing it for as many years as I have you know 99 percent of the customers. Like last week . . . we had a little bit of a help shortage and I put in a lot of hours. But if I'm not here for like one hour and somebody comes in [the customer says]: "Jeez, I was in here to see you. Weren't you working?" You know, I think I probably got in like seventy-five hours that week.

Ray Goodman, owner of the jewelry store, shared a similar thought:

> Being here . . . they like it when we're here. Yeah, they definitely do. When we've gone to market, people call it our vacations . . . but it's usually a working situation and you can always tell who's been in and knows you've been gone because they'll come back, and a lot of times if there's something they specifically want to know about, they'll wait until we come back to have it taken care of. . . . They seem to know they get caught up with your mall shopping and they realize, oh, well, I can't get this for two more weeks. Then they realize, I better take it to where they can do it faster. We end up with that.

Visibility as a storeowner helps build trust with customers and townspeople. In turn, the greater the level of trust between owners, their employees, and the community, the more successful the business and the more likely the owners are to support other small businesses in the community. When asked what makes his business successful, Jim Rathke explained that he actively cultivates an image of care with his customers and employees. Jim gave the following story as an example:

> Customers like to be noticed. They like to have you know that they came in and did business with you. . . . For instance, last Saturday

night there's a family. . . . They come in quite a bit and, you know what, I couldn't tell you their names, but I know 'em by sight and the two little kids with 'em. For the two kids with them, I grab two quarters out of the cash register and on the way out the back door I put 'em in the machine for 'em, you know. I mean, it's, I think it comes down to a lot of that personal touch that, uh, you develop over a period of time.

When I asked him to describe the kind of relationship he has with his employees, he explained:

They know all our family. I know all their families. Hey, we'll have a little get-together at a certain time of the year. In fact, we have a little sign-up sheet here, this reminds me. We have a sign-up sheet, we're gonna clean some things that we've, that get neglected here. We're gonna kinda spruce things up. . . . So here's a sign-up sheet. [Then he asks rhetorically:] What are we looking at? We [the employees] are signing up just to come in and work [for free]. Well, everybody signed up! And so, uh, I quickly saw that this, let's work with this, you know? So I said okay, listen, about five o'clock I want your husbands, your spouses, and kids to come down and we'll, uh, have pizza. . . . And the girls that work here, they're all close, you know.

Jim's examples of relations with customers and workers indicate that by emphasizing family and family loyalties he is also able to nurture an image of generosity and thus encourage a more productive workforce. In this atmosphere, Jim views himself as the symbolic father who cares for his loyal family members and the community.

Robert "Bob" Johnson, owner of Johnson's Pharmacy, the only locally owned pharmacy in town, shared a similar story about his relations with customers when I asked him how his business remained viable despite increased competition from corporate-owned pharmacies operated out of local supermarkets and discount stores: "Townspeople know who we are. They trust us. We've been here for sixty-one years. [Customers] go into some place else and go, 'Who are they?' [Corporate pharmacies] don't have the same connection that we've had with the local people."

Bob, like most of the other owners with whom I spoke—including his brother Dick, who owns Sports World—viewed their businesses as key players in the fight to save local communities from big business. He spoke passionately about his pharmacy's role in the community: "I don't want another business to go out so I feel some type of a, that I owe the town this." He also explained that his pharmacy had increased sales over the last decade despite two chain grocery stores' introducing in-store pharmacy services during that time. Bob said there was a simple reason why his pharmacy was still doing well: people looking for medical attention "aren't going to go to the corporate thieves who don't give a crap about human beings." His brother Dick shared similar thoughts: "I've watched for twenty-five years the decline of this downtown, my hometown. . . . It gets frustrating and you look at what's going on in the cities and that they just keep building, building, more malls, more larger [discount stores]. . . . But you know, the [discount store] can't come in, create a team logo for your little league team with a [team mascot] and a bat on it . . . they don't see the kids get excited about that; [the kids] just think that Lynx is the greatest thing in the world."

As the owners clearly pointed out, their businesses, and the location of those businesses in a small rural community, enable them to help preserve a way of life—a world where people know and take care of each other. Interestingly, while all the male owners I interviewed in Madison Town enthusiastically condemned big business from outside the town for eliminating small businesses, as well as for the lack of care they showed local residents and employees, all but one of them had bought out other small business owners in town to increase sales volume in their own stores and restaurants. Pharmacist Bob Johnson, for example, explained that when he first took over his father's store, "there were three drug stores . . . so I bought my competition out." He added that his brother, Dick, had "bought his competition out across the street, so that eliminated that." Similarly, Jim Rathke, owner of Main Street Manor, said that when he decided to expand his restaurant from fifty to 250 seats ten years earlier, he bought the restaurant located next door, determined to make his place the only place in town where someone would go for a "really nice, I mean as good as it gets" meal. He explained: "There's somebody else that's always wanting to start up these big nice places; but I have a chance here for the long term because now the competition is a little less likely to come in." Ray Goodman, the jewelry storeowner, told a similar story: "When we came into town there were three jewelry stores. We bought one . . . and then in five years the second one."

Thus, while these male owners positioned themselves as protectors of the town from the pitfalls of big business, at the same time they expanded their businesses—and thus their profits—by eliminating other small businesses in town. While these small business owners helped protect a trusting owner-client relationship in town, they also shared in common with outside big businesses a practice of eliminating the range of potential consumer options. Some local owners even had plans to expand their businesses by further eliminating competition.

## Male Small Business Owners in Rural Places: A Picture of Paternalism

Owning and managing small businesses in a small town provides these men with independence, enables them to construct environments consistent with their own vision of desirable masculinity, and makes them feel indispensable and positively visible within their communities. The gendered practices these men use, their ability to maintain positive relations with employees and townspeople, and the elimination of competitors has allowed them to maintain these businesses despite declining small town infrastructures and economies in the Midwest over the past few decades.

As I have outlined in this study, links between small business success, gender practices, and male owners have interesting (if problematic) theoretical and practical implications. The stability of these male-owned small businesses hinges, in part, on gendered practices that construct women and femininity as subordinate to men and masculinity. Gender inequality, therefore, helps keep these male-owned businesses up and running, thus sustaining the local economy. The owners are committed to their community, in part, because the community provides affordable labor and consistent patronage. Again, these exchanges of labor, wages, and patronage depend on gender practices and ideologies that render women, as wives, mothers, daughters, and workers, subordinate to men as husbands, fathers, and bosses. Gender relations, therefore, are intertwined with relations of expropriation, all of which are embedded in community social institutions. The male owners, as local citizens, business leaders, and family members fulfill roles that their community embraces and rewards—

indeed, the gender practices maintained by these male owners appear to be agreeable to both women and men in Madison Town. Cindy Goodman, Ray Goodman's partner in ownership and marriage, explained, that in business, as in the family, Ray is her "boss," and she would not encourage her two daughters to pursue business ownership because "this might go against what is best for their family." Cindy explained that the worries associated with operating a successful business in a small town should be a man's responsibility. Similarly, two women, both clerks at the local chamber of commerce, explained that one reason their town has remained so lively despite economic hardships such as the farm crisis of the 1980s is that their men are "real gentlemen," willing to stick around, even when things get really tough. When I asked what they meant by "real gentlemen," the women said that while most men would have gone to the cities in search of more profitable employment, in Madison Town the tradition of locally owned businesses has remained fairly strong. Notably, neither woman mentioned women's roles in maintaining community vitality.

Like most workers in small communities, the people of Madison Town have few job options that pay a living wage, but they also find commuting to a larger city undesirable because of the distances involved (at least forty miles).[8] Thus workers in small towns are often highly dependent on a few employers.[9] When this dependence endures over long periods, business owners gain the authority necessary to shape what workers view as their own "best interests." Likewise, the more the employer invests in community welfare, the more likely workers are to support the employer's interests. Furthermore, the greater visibility the owner has with the workers, the more personal the relationship between the two. In turn, this personal relationship encourages mutual trust and workers who are more likely to believe they share interests with owners.[10]

These conditions lend themselves to a model of management (and of social control) called paternalism.[11] Some research on contemporary work organizations and in society more generally suggests that paternalism as a means of control in business operations is an anachronism.[12] But in this case the model appears to fit. Under the paternalistic model, owners and managers sit at the head of the industrial "household" with the responsibility for providing for the workers' "moral welfare."[13] Workers accept the authority of the management and owners in return for some minimum level of welfare. Paternalism in management evolved with industrial capitalism out of an even older patriarchal model modeled on the preindustrial patriarchal family. With industrial capitalism, the family and the "public sphere" of business became more distinctly separate operations. The more centralized and specialized the organization of labor, the more removed owners were (and are) from the workers' activities.[14] The power once exercised by the patriarch is thus appropriated by capital and transformed into a system of relations between owners as *symbolic* patriarchs and workers as symbolic family members.

Under paternalism, the world of paid labor symbolizes masculinity and manhood and the world of domestic affairs symbolizes femininity and womanhood. The "abstract worker" is socially constructed as a man and the abstract homemaker as a woman.[15] The workplace thus becomes a male and "masculine" preserve, defined as opposite women and femininity. In turn, as symbolic fathers, male owners receive status, respect, and profits in exchange for their commitment to care for their workers and the community, even during economic hard times.

As noted by the male owners in Madison Town, however, retaining low-wage workers in a town where the consumer base is stagnant, regardless of how faithful those consumers are, is not enough. For these men, the success of their businesses over the years has also depended on their ability to buy out their competitors. This strategy, they explain, is the only way to remain viable when large corporations, like the large nationally and internationally franchised discount stores and fast food operations, increasingly draw their customers away. These male owners know their businesses will never be as financially successful as they may have been in a larger city, in part because of their location in the service and retail sectors, but also because of their location in a rural place. Those men who wish to pursue higher wages or, as business owners, higher profits, move out of small towns. Therefore, for male owners of small businesses in a rural community like Madison Town, the reasons for staying in the community extend beyond how much money they can make. Their incentives include cheap, loyal labor, a level of profit that enables them to maintain a decent standard of living, and the status and privileges they hold as men—men who are, furthermore, "gentlemen" and heroes.

Is gender inequality the price small towns must pay to remain viable? In what ways, if any, do female-owned businesses help offset the forces of paternalism in male-owned businesses? Previous research suggests that female-owned businesses are more likely than male-owned ones to employ women.[16] Thus female-owned businesses could help increase the status of women as owners, managers, and employees. If business ownership elevates the status of women as citizens and community leaders, what effects might this have on the vitality of male-owned businesses of small towns, given the reliance of male-owned businesses on gender inequality? These are among the many questions that remain for future research.

## NOTES

1. For example, Connell (2000); Hollway (1996); Kerfoot and Knights (1993, 1998); Roper (1994).

2. Campbell and Bell (2000); Collinson and Hearn (1994).

3. Bird and Sapp (2004); Clark and James (1992).

4. For example, Burris (1996); Hollway (1996); Morgan (1996).

5. For example, Hearn (1994); Kerfoot and Knights (1993); T. Lawson (1981).

6. Pseudonyms are used to refer to all places, businesses, and people in the study.

7. I conducted twelve in-depth interviews with owners of businesses in the food, retail, and service industries. I also conducted twenty-two hours of observations in sixteen businesses located in these same industries. My observations focused on interactions between owners, workers, and customers. I also made extensive notes and sketches of the physical structure of the businesses (for example, of the spaces within which owners interacted with workers and customers). Some additional information was drawn from a survey of small businesses on Main Street (n = 18) and from interviews conducted with female owners in the same town (n = 8). All the male owners interviewed were white, heterosexual, and ranged in age from forty-six to sixty. All the female owners interviewed were also white and heterosexual, and ranged in age from twenty-five to fifty-eight.

8. See Nelson and Smith (1999).

9. For example, Brueggemann (2000); Joyce (1980); T. Lawson (1981); Staples (1987).

10. Jackman (1994).

11. Ibid.

12. Brueggemann (2000); Jackman (1994).

13. Kerfoot and Knights (1993, 665); Jackman (1994).

14. Ferguson (1984).

15. Acker (1990).

16. For example, Carrington and Troske (1994).

# Real Men, Real Locals, and Real Workers: Realizing Masculinity in Small-Town New Zealand

*Hugh Campbell*

Within the broader study of rural masculinity, there is generally a significant lack of ethnographic research engaging with the practices and processes that construct masculinity both as rural and within rural space. In this chapter I return to my earlier ethnographic study of rural masculinity to examine how the practice of masculinity in pub drinking, notions of work, and the construction of both local history and ideas of "localness" have important consequences for gendered power within a rural community.[1] Ethnographic analysis generally tries to create insight by engaging in a comparison across similar ethnographic cases. In the absence of a secure body of "ethnography of rural masculinity," however, we need to search elsewhere for a relevant body of comparative ethnographic insights on which to base this analysis. Unusually, this chapter does not turn directly toward two obvious bodies of ethnographic work: the ethnography of rural society or the ethnography of gender. Rather, I want to engage here with a less obvious body of work best represented by Arjun Appadurai's meditation on the "ethnography of locality."[2] Appadurai argues that locality, and the day-to-day cultural labor required in the production of "reliably local subjects,"[3] form an important part of the production and reproduction of gender in rural communities. In this chapter I take Appadurai's production and reproduction of locality and incorporate it with notions of hegemonic masculinity, gender performance, and resonance to create an understanding of how, in this particular community, the reliably local subjects invariably turn out to be male. Further, when we add these theoretical ideas together, we can "decode" the key gender dynamic in this community: a residential pattern of male stability and female exodus (what Appadurai calls strategies of exit) or "replacement." In other words, this study asks where—or rather why—have all the women gone?

By building on prior work in this ethnographic locale, this chapter examines the relationship between hegemony and legitimacy in a way that explains why some forms of masculinity are so difficult to challenge.[4] Here

I also explore the relevance of competing histories, notions of localness, and representations of labor in understanding the power of particular constructions of masculinity. The relevance of these issues to masculinity is particularly important in recognizing how particular masculinities are embedded in local spaces and histories—in this case specifically rural spaces and histories—and how this embeddedness reinforces the claims of hegemonic masculinity and secures its ongoing legitimacy. Consequently, we move away here from rural masculinities that employ the rural locale only as circumstantial evidence when studying gender in rural space, toward a more dynamic understanding of the relationships between masculinity, locality, history, and rurality.

To analyze these issues, this study draws on ethnographic data from a small rural community in New Zealand. Within this community, working men gather in the local pubs each day after work and engage in the performance of what I term "pub(lic) masculinity."[5] Men are powerful in this community: they dominate the traditional labor market, hold most local political offices, write their own version of history, and successfully meet any challenges to the legitimacy of their activities. Most important, they seem to achieve such power with a high degree of consent from other members of the community—effectively, as my earlier study suggests,[6] their power is unchallenged. While my previous research investigated how masculinity operated *inside* the pub, this chapter goes an important step further. By looking *outside* the pub at patterns of residence and employment, and how these patterns are linked to constructions of history, locality, and labor, I aim to establish both why these men are so powerful and the ways in which potential resistance to men's power is constantly undermined in the wider community.

## The Research Site

My ethnographic research took place in a rural community (permanent population approximately one thousand) in the Canterbury region of New Zealand, and it involved participant observation in community life, facilitated by my living in the field locale. I targeted the first eighteen months of participatory research directly at the local pubs,[7] while my second, more extended, period of participatory fieldwork examined the changing social and economic nature of farming in the area.[8] The combination of these two periods of fieldwork (adding up to nearly five years' residence in the community) provided more than a hundred formal interviews, in excess of two hundred hours of participant observation in the pubs, and an even greater abundance of informal discussion and dialogue with members of the community.[9]

The village formed as a labor pool for sheep and wheat farming in the latter part of the nineteenth century. During the first half of the twentieth century, large sheep runs were subdivided into small farms and the need for hired labor declined. Nevertheless, a group of permanent laborers remained in the village and took jobs in farm service industries. In the 1970s, a ski field was developed near the town, which provided a range of new economic opportunities in tourism. Although apparently a positive development, many long-term residents—particularly men—took no part in the new, nontraditional economic activities.

Despite the changing nature of the village's economy, some evidence persists of its early, often disreputable, role as a pooling point for local labor. While the billiard halls and brothels have disappeared, the two historic pubs remain. These have attracted a faithful clientele since the nineteenth century and remained well patronized by local drinkers even as a proliferation of other, tourist-centered, drinking venues sprang up around the town. During the period of ethnographic research in this community, 150–200 local men drank at these pubs every day over the course of an average week, almost exclusively after finishing work in the town.[10] Overall, in any given week, some 300–350 men in the community participated in some way in public drinking at pubs or in local sports clubs. This group of drinkers is the most visible expression of "pub(lic) masculinity," which incorporates all those men in this community who separate their work life from their home life by spending several (or more) hours at the pub each day.[11] This term recognizes that pub behavior by men occurs in the public domain, so is constantly under scrutiny by other men. It also suggests[12] that those men who drink in *pubs* are the same men who dominate almost all other *public* leisure sites in this community, like sports clubs and voluntary associations.[13]

By contextualizing such behavior inside the pub with wider community perceptions about gender, an interesting paradox emerges. While pub(lic) masculinity is continually subjected to rigorous and intense scrutiny by other drinking men, there is seemingly little attempt by anyone in the broader community—that is, outside the pub—to engage in a similar scrutiny of men's activities. In fact, as I interviewed local women and newcomers to the community during the research process, numerous people expressed relief at being able to criticize the dominance of men's drinking culture in the town, finding that an interview with a researcher/outsider created an opportunity for critique that was absent in everyday life. People were not ignorant of male power, but my key argument in this chapter is that they could not find any stable place to stand in order to mobilize a critique—or, more specifically, a critique that seemed legitimate to community members. The primary focus of this chapter, therefore, is this tension between the slippery and unstable social terrain occupied by such women and "newcomers," and the stability and enduring legitimacy of pub(lic) masculinity.[14] The framework for this tension, and for the more complex aspects of pub(lic) masculinity that it implies, can be found in ethnographic data outlining local patterns of residence.

## Continuity of Male Residence: Who Stays, Who Goes

When examining patterns of residence, we can take two basic concepts for granted: first, that residence inevitably is closely linked to the availability of work and the arrangement of the local labor market; and second, that any such labor market will have certain gendered dimensions. In this particular locale, relationships between gender, work, locality, and tradition have specific and far-reaching implications for social legitimacy. The most concrete manifestation of these can be seen in the area's demographic dynamics, which indicate that while a majority of young men stay locally resident throughout their lives, far fewer young women either remain in the district or return to it after leaving.

Census data show there is an imbalance between young men and women who remain resident in the area after schooling.[15] While the numbers of young men and women in the local district are relatively similar for all age cohorts under age sixteen, in the cohort aged seventeen to twenty the number of young women resident in the community declined by 44 percent. In striking contrast, the number of young men declined by only 15 percent. As might be expected, some of this cohort (both male and female) leave the community to attend tertiary education institutions, travel, or seek work in the city, and certainly some women do return after finishing tertiary education. Crucially, however, while it is clear that a significant number of young men remain and are employed in the community, the number of young women who remain in the community is much smaller.

This demographic trend does not hold true for older age cohorts: census data also show that the balance between men and women returns in the cohort aged twenty-five to twenty-eight, and indeed remains so throughout the cohort aged twenty-five to forty.[16] Who are these women? We need to look beyond simple statistics to deconstruct this demographic trend, because while census data show the degree to which women either leave or live in the community, they cannot show the degree to which resident adult women may be "outsiders" entering the community. In fact, the increase in females aged twenty-five to forty typically does not represent "returning" female residents who left after school, but "replacement" women from other areas who marry men in the community. These data, therefore, disguise the continuity of men as permanent local residents as opposed to the relative "newcomer" status of many women. Given this study's parameters, it is vital to establish why men either leave and return, or remain in the community after school, while women leave and are often replaced by "outsiders."

Many of these reasons become clear when we expand the census data through interviews and ethnographic observation. The rest of this chapter, therefore, examines the key dynamics that seem to operate behind this difference in residential patterns. In brief, for the wider farming community, continued male residence was explicitly linked to the vast predominance of male-inherited farmland. For those who lived in the village, young men had the option to remain and become incorporated into both the social institutions of pub(lic) masculinity and local blue-collar workplaces, while young women characteristically perceived they had "no future" in the community (something that was reinforced in my interviews with their teachers). This chapter argues that both the male-dominated operation of the informal labor market and the overwhelming rejection of women and femininity by pub(lic) masculinity acted as a disincentive for young women to remain in the community.

Both census data and ethnographic interviewing, therefore, show that more local men remain in the community than local women. Likewise, these men tend to experience relatively stable work patterns, which results in a degree of intergenerational continuity of residence and work among local men. In contrast, women in the community are less likely to come from established families in the area, are often newcomers or outsiders, and work in the less stable casual job market. In turn, their daughters see little future in the community and are less likely to remain. The implications of this finding are highly significant for understanding the power of pub(lic) masculinity in this locale. By focusing on the operation of the local labor market, therefore, we can gain entry to a much wider understanding of how pub(lic) masculinity is legitimized, and how such legitimacy is profoundly linked to wider male power in this community. This chapter goes on to "unpack" the interlinking, interlocking labor/locality issues behind the ways in which pub(lic) masculinity engages with, and encourages, this dynamic. As we shall see, behind the material realities of locality lies the cultural work of producing masculinity, history, and localness.

## Masculinity, Proxies, and Resonance

Clearly, the ethnographic data from this locality show a general pattern of male residence and female exodus or "replacement." This section addresses how this demographic dynamic is indexed (or related) to local labor market conditions, which are themselves indexed to the power and legitimacy of pub(lic) masculinity in this community. We now need to bring some theoretical approaches to bear on this intersection of legitimacy, locality, labor, and gender in order to examine in more detail why young men of this district feel "legitimate"—and legitimated—within it, while young women do not. Here, therefore, we turn to the idea of resonance and "defense by proxy" to discover the key relationships and social categories that defend and empower masculinity. Resonance and "defense by proxy" also help us understand how men's behavior is linked strongly to more stable and enduring aspects of community life like "localness," labor, and history.

To understand legitimacy more fully, we need to include Raewyn Connell's idea of "defense by proxy," an argument that, in combination with Mike Bell's concept of multicategory social meanings,[17] introduces and underpins the concept of resonance.

Connell suggests that sometimes masculinity can be defended through "surrogates" such as the gun lobby, which operate as an arena in which men (and sometimes women) defend issues of masculinity "by proxy," or through a different medium—in this case through resistance to gun control.[18] Literature on masculinity has already begun to examine the degree to which other causes or projects—like the gun lobby—become a defense by proxy for masculinity. Rachel Woodward, for example, analyzes the way in which the British army deliberately links particular notions of rurality to issues of masculinity during training.[19] Similarly, Tony Horwitz documents how a particular southern U.S. masculinity reemerges through the rigors of detailed reenactment of civil war battles.[20] In these examples, defense of guns, the military, land/territory/the South, and rurality all can be argued to operate as proxies for masculinity. The next section looks at these proxies and articulates a theoretical idea—"resonant performance"—that deconstructs the way these proxies work in specific settings.

## The Resonant Performance of Pub(lic) Masculinity

Too much research into masculinity isolates a particular construction of masculinity into a resolute, independent monolith, dominating a particular social setting. The idea of defense by proxy, however, clearly shows that masculinity often operates in conjunction with other aspects of social life. We can identify and explain how this interlinking happens by using the concept of "resonant performance."

Bell uses the term "resonance" to describe the way in which the social meanings of "nature" and "society" engage with each other in different ways for people from different class groups.[21] Resonance, in this sense, recognizes that people actively derive meanings for certain ideas (such as "nature") that are similar across different social realms of experience. In fact, Bell argues, "It seems most reasonable to expect that people feel the most ideological comfort when they find their categories work across the realms of their experience—across realms of the natural other, the generalized (that is, social) other, machines, the body and more."[22] Instead of specifying a single, concrete social mechanism of resonance, Bell suggests that ethnographic research should try to unravel the multiple, subtle, and often unintentional ways that the social meanings of things such as nature and class resonate with each other in social practice, and to explore the implications this has for social power and legitimacy.

Like nature and class, the legitimacy of pub(lic) masculinity is based crucially on a degree of resonance, in this case between the notion of masculinity and other realms of meaning in the community. David Savran's argument about the "performance" of gender is particularly useful here. While working along lines similar to those of the more popularly cited Judith Butler, Savran suggests that gender performativity has specific and central material aspects, and is thus a form of behavior closely embedded in the everyday "concrete" world.[23] Savran's theory, with its emphasis on the physical manifestations and ramifications of gender, enables us to integrate resonance directly into what happens both inside the pub and between pub(lic) masculinity and the wider community.[24] The idea of resonant performance thus enables us to move beyond a sole focus on the masculine practice of pub(lic) masculinity and see the ways in which a particular version of masculinity is legitimized through its resonant relationships with several other categories of meaning. Put another way, we need to understand how pub(lic) masculinity achieves a *resonant* performance in order to understand how pub(lic) masculinity also achieves a *legitimate* performance. For participants in this ethnographic locale, pub(lic) masculinity resonates specifically with two crucial realms of meaning: localness and labor.[25]

## Resonance and Localness: Pub History, Biography, and the Local

Appadurai suggests that locality and localness cannot be taken for granted.[26] Rather, "locality is ephemeral unless hard and regular work is undertaken to produce and maintain its materiality. . . . Much that has been considered local knowledge is actually knowledge about how to produce, and reproduce locality under conditions of anxiety and entropy, social wear and flux."[27] He would have recognized immediately the pubs in this community as sites where this kind of cultural work constantly takes place. This section outlines how the business of producing and reproducing Appadurai's "reliably local subjects" simultaneously helps produce locality *and* gender.

For example, the following conversation—echoed many times during fieldwork—took place between me and a couple of men in the pub. As research was my "work" (and a somewhat poor attempt at working, by masculine reckoning), men would question me about it:

> Geoff: So, what do you actually do?
> Hugh: Basically talk to as many people as I can, try to find out all sorts of things about the place.

Geoff (heavily ironic): Hard work!

Rich: But *who* are you talking to?

Hugh: Well, I can't actually say that, it's not part of how we do things . . .

Rich: Just make sure you talk to the right people, people who know what's going on.

Geoff: Yeah, talk to the *real* locals like [X] and [Y] over there.

Rich: They won't talk to him!

Rich was right: a researcher needs to talk to the "real locals," and the real locals often did not want to talk to me. For men in the pub, X and Y (and other nominated "real locals") were, not coincidentally, also the men of the highest status in the pub—paragons of pub(lic) masculinity. There was a clear and constant association by drinking men between "real locals" and those men I observed to be the dominant performers of pub(lic) masculinity. Here was my first clear performance of masculinity by proxy through the performance of localness, because in this location the "real men" were also the reliably local subjects in Appadurai's sense. The degree to which a man could also be considered a local was generally arbitrated through his ability to be connected to local histories. This clear connection between pub(lic) masculinity and "localness"—a connection that was repeatedly enacted in pub performances by drinking men—became heightened around what I term "pub history."[28]

In this community local history takes two different forms: one—"pub history"—directly connected to pub(lic) masculinity, and the other—"official history"—starkly opposed to it. "Official" history concentrates on the rise of "respectable" pastoral family farming in the twentieth century.[29] Such "respectable" history was also evident in ethnographic data from a nearby village.[30] This history is constructed and promulgated in written histories of the area and also discussed in the context of the local historical society and museum. In contrast to this, pub(lic) masculinity deploys its own "pub history" of the village—a somewhat different narrative of the past. Here, the pub, and public leisure space in general, act as the sites in which people (that is, men) contest knowledge about the past, competing interpretations, and generally accepted events before incorporating them into the narrative of pub history. Pub history rejects respectable history as illegitimate—coming as it does from (male) farmers who spent their lives

in "ignorant" isolation on farms, while "real" knowledge was being generated by "reliably local" men at the pub.

In pub history, the town is described as always having been a "drinker's
town." This narrative celebrates the wild, unrestrained character of the
early colonial history of the town, and laments the rise of forces of respectability (an opposition that Jock Phillips found to be commonplace within
masculine discourse in New Zealand).[31] Unsurprisingly, pub history sees
the "victory" over prohibition—when the village voted to stay "wet" in contrast to the surrounding district—as a high point, a definitive moment in
the town's character. Through subsequent years of economic development, "local" men were at the forefront of new economic initiatives—
typified by one local man's heroic efforts in driving a bulldozer up the side
of a nearby mountain to show that a ski field could be established and
accessed by road. This ski field subsequently became the subject of a perceived betrayal of "the local," as farmer-shareholders and "outsiders" sold
the ski field to a large nonlocal company.

While these key events plot the broad chronology of pub history, pub(-
lic) performance weaves a rich body of detail into this narrative. Men passionately articulate the role of their own families and forebears in pub
history, dictating various jobs, schemes, adventures, parties, and other
events (including the occasional spectacular death) witnessed or experienced by them or their (male) predecessors. It is this ability to integrate
oneself biographically into pub history via the performance of pub(lic)
masculinity that marks a man as "local."

As I outlined in my previous study,[32] this appeal *to* pub history, or the
ability to integrate one's biography *with* pub history, carries a great deal of
legitimacy in the performance of masculinity. This dynamic can be understood as a *resonance* between the idea of being a "local" and the idea of
masculinity. Both the "local" and the "masculine" are embedded in a sense
of history that provides the legitimizing power of tradition, thus stability,
and therefore normalcy. Likewise, establishing continuity between contemporary and past practice connects these locals to an earlier way of life
that was closer to nature or represented a simpler, better, and what was
perceived to be a less gender-confused form of social relations. Significantly, such ideas of localness are not limited to the participants in pub(lic)
masculinity but are shared by many community members. This link
means that masculinity can be defended by proxy through resonance with
a body of ideas about localness that has legitimacy for a wider group in the

community. But this resonance between localness (and local history) and masculinity is not mere serendipity—rather, it is underlined and reinforced by the resonance between labor and masculinity.

## Resonance and Labor: Men's Work, Women's Work

In terms of pub(lic) masculinity, the engagement between masculinity and labor creates an even more compelling relationship between masculinity, localness, and history. Predictably, like ideas of localness, this engagement is forged in the pub. For pub(lic) masculinity the links between the workplace and the pub are highly significant and highly resonant. For these local men, moreover, both work and pub(lic) masculinity are defined by negating femininity and the domestic sphere.

This resonance between masculinity and labor is important, as masculinity is constantly enacted, by proxy, through the social categories of work and labor. Activities within the various worksites around the community provide a constant arena of discussion, while workplace performance is often inseparable from drinking performance as men are scrutinized during pub drinking. Men's ability to work, their enthusiasm for hard physical tasks, the embodied performance of skill, stamina, and strength in the workplace, and their particular relationships with machines[33] are constantly discussed—and thus open to scrutiny from other men—in the pub.

I was particularly interested in the question of which workplaces constituted appropriate sites for men's work, as the boundaries of acceptability were clearly demarcated in the eyes of pub(lic) masculinity. Generally, acceptable worksites included the gamut of farm service industries, including farm supply firms, seed-dressing plants, grain storage, transport, farm machinery sales and repair, garage workshops, and various movable vegetable-processing facilities (mainly for grading potatoes).[34] Also acceptable were other light industries such as an aluminum window factory (which was acceptable only on the margins as it had no history in the town), and the many workers who were owner-operators of contract machinery, or farm laborers, or who generally traveled around the area each day, such as stock buyers and seed buyers. I also noted that various unacceptable businesses were mentioned in passing during pub conversation and humor. Extracts from my field notes included these statements about unacceptable forms of work:

General retail: "women's work."

White-collar professionals (accountants and lawyers): "money for nothing," "pen-pushers," "button boys" (the last referring to the use of calculators).

Ski-industry workers: "tragic," "a pack of losers," "futile," "dress-ups" (a reference to ski workers' clothing), "gutless," "uncommitted," "brain-dead," and many others.

As these comments indicate, the area of men's work that attracted the most ridicule from pub(lic) masculinity was work on or around the ski field. Such opprobrium was mild, however, in comparison with the humor and ridicule attracted by women's work, which was often associated with "new" or nontraditional areas. Apart from some long-term jobs in the retail sector, teaching, nursing, and local government, women in the community tended to work in short-term or casual jobs. In particular, women from blue-collar households (and with husbands who drank at the pub) often worked in the burgeoning hotel and food service sectors in the tourist industry. Women cleaned motel and hotel rooms, worked in hotel kitchens and laundries, and prepared food in the many cafés and restaurants catering to skiers. The gender division of labor between women in the new, casual sector and men in traditional (albeit often casual) jobs was so strong that in a 1996 study we identified this as a major factor influencing the strategic responses of families during New Zealand's rural crisis in the 1980s.[35] Women had no hesitation in accepting work in the new industry, while men trenchantly stayed within established masculine work areas.[36]

In this locale, however, each occupation was judged as legitimate or illegitimate not only in terms of masculinity but according to its historical depth—was it part of the "reliably local" world? Given these parameters, despite the apparent social and economic benefits of women's taking up employment in "new" areas, "women's work" provided a persistent focus of derision in the pub. In practice, the valued blue-collar occupations were ones that were embedded in pub history and had been the sites of work for high-status men (and their fathers, brothers, and uncles) over a long period. Clearly, there is a distinct body of work that is considered appropriate by pub(lic) masculinity, and the men who are most successful in the pub also tend to be those who are centrally located in this world of work (or have retired from these jobs). Furthermore, as I suggested earlier, those qualities central to pub(lic) masculinity are the same qualities celebrated in the workplace. In other words, for both the participants in pub(-lic) masculinity and for many other members of the community, the social category of masculinity resonates powerfully with the social category of labor. At the same time, both these categories also resonate with the ideas of localness that are legitimized by pub history.

## Pub(lic) Masculinity and the Informal Labor Market: Jobs for the Boys

The critical resonance between pub(lic) masculinity and workplace masculinity is clearly revealed in the role of pub(lic) masculinity as a gatekeeper to the local labor market. In turn, this gatekeeping role has critical implications in terms of residence and ideas of localness. In brief, the cultural work of pub(lic) masculinity simultaneously involves the production of reliably local subjects and reliably masculine workers.

I was alerted to the relationship between pub(lic) masculinity and the local labor market by a specific fieldwork incident. During an evening at the pub, one of the men I knew to be an owner-operator of a potato-digger was moving through the pub with a local farmer, approaching many groups of men. When I asked what was going on, I was simply told "potatoes"—that is, the potato harvest had begun and contractors were looking for men to work in the grading sheds. In the course of the year, as different crops came into harvest, men were similarly approached in the pubs and sports clubs to participate in work. On a more sporadic basis, some men seemed to move from job to job throughout the year, although each new job was still situated safely within the canon of acceptable occupations in the pub. This kind of activity suggested the role of pub(lic) masculinity as a port of entry into local blue-collar work. In contrast to the typically competitive performance of pub(lic) masculinity, a high degree of cooperation existed in ensuring that local men (with sound biographies and reputable work histories) were never unemployed. An interview with the local high school careers advisory officer confirmed my suspicions. "Local boys don't bother to darken my doorstep," he explained. "They've got their own careers office down the road" (meaning the two pubs). Likewise, two years later, while interviewing farm families in the area, I asked two large potato producers where they obtained their casual staff. Unhesitating, they answered, "at the pub." When I asked one to explain this recruiting strategy, he was explicit: "[Z] down the road took some kids on from the Employment Office. They were worse than useless, certificate or no certificate, they just didn't know what hard work was."

This statement illustrates several characteristics of pub(lic) masculinity's wider understandings of work. First, as far as this construction of masculinity goes, government training schemes, and for that matter any form of formal education, do not indicate whether a worker is skilled or suited for a job, because these schemes and courses do not resonate with the key relationship between labor and masculinity. Second, most unemployed people are "suspect" and prone to laziness. The pub, however, offers the possibility of hiring skilled workers, disciplined both socially and physically and accountable for their workplace performance to their peers. This logic was repeated to me in an interview with the manager of the local government employment service. He argued that despite many hundreds of casual and seasonal jobs in the area, and a large pool of unemployed people, he had managed to place only twelve male workers in what he termed "traditional agricultural work" over the previous year. As he put it, "local employers don't trust our workers, they never have." It is specifically men (and a particular kind of man acceptable to pub[lic] masculinity) who are absorbed into the informal labor market: in contrast, many women in the area readily obtain work through the employment service.

While this may be overplaying the significance of the pub itself as an alternative "careers office" relative to the wider network of pub(lic) masculinity, throughout my five years of ethnographic participation in the community I continually observed both the sons of long-term local residents and men who had become unemployed gain jobs in workplaces that were populated by (or owned and operated by) the participants in pub(lic) masculinity. Thus, although both men and women worked in areas of casual employment, the forms of this casual employment were strictly demarcated by gender. Women worked in new jobs associated with the ski industry (which necessarily shut down for seven months of each year). In contrast, men not only worked in jobs with a long history in the area but also moved within a powerful informal labor market that ensured that even those relying on casual work were, in effect, constantly employed.

This dynamic is not uncommon and has been noted in other studies. Ray Pahl's study of the Isle of Sheppey documents an informal labor market and black economy that incorporated nearly every long-term resident on that island—with the pub as one site where such informal activities

were often arranged.[37] Similarly, Lydia Morris's ethnography of unemployed men in south Wales shows the same trend, noting moreover that
men reached a new level of poverty when they could no longer afford to
drink at the pub and therefore maintain access to casual work.[38] What
these studies have not observed, however, is the way that control over the
informal labor market has, in the case of pub(lic) masculinity, given men
far more power than simply the ability to keep themselves in what they
consider appropriate work. The contours of such power lie in the way that
this form of labor market capture has long-term historical effects on the
hegemonic power of some men in these communities.

## Discussion: The Embedded Legitimacy of Pub(lic) Masculinity

In summary, the performance of pub(lic) masculinity draws on strongly
marked categories of meaning that have a shared significance for many
members of this community. At the heart of legitimate pub(lic) masculinity lies a series of relationships that define masculinity by association and
resonance with the idea of localness and work. First, the high-status men
within the performance of pub(lic) masculinity are those who can link
themselves biographically to pub history and therefore make solid claims
about their status as "local" men. Second, masculine legitimacy is intimately tied to labor and work performance. The same masculine disciplines that broadly characterize drinking performance (embodied control,
skill, and accumulated knowledge) also characterize workplace performance. It is the resonance between these three categories of social meaning—masculinity, work, and localness—and the fact that many individuals
outside pub(lic) masculinity share these ideas about localness and labor,
that accords pub(lic) masculinity a high degree of legitimacy.

This, however, tells only part of the story. Clearly, the *stability* of these
resonances over time is highly significant in creating a sense of legitimacy.
Certain features of local history and local work mutually constitute each
other in a way that embeds pub(lic) masculinity as a powerful and enduring feature of community life. In other words, it is stability over time that
eventually normalizes pub(lic) masculinity to the degree that it becomes
difficult to challenge.

The process of becoming "reliably local" is central in explaining this
stability and embeddedness, because localness has a powerful legitimacy

within pub(lic) masculinity. Furthermore, as men position themselves biographically within pub history, their performances of pub(lic) masculinity
constantly revalidate and reinforce these resonant links between masculinity and localness. But this is not simply a case of men pursuing a particular
strategy to defend themselves. Men *have* been literally embedded in local
history because men have experienced a greater continuity of local residence than local women or participants in the ski industry. By effectively
controlling the local labor market, pub(lic) masculinity has, over a long
period, ensured that men who participate in pub(lic) masculinity retain
jobs, are employed in the same industries that employed their male kin,
and have a greater tendency to remain in the community when they leave
school, so they will be present as participants in the ongoing formulation
of pub history. Men, therefore, have a stability of presence in the community and this stability gives them the opportunity to undertake the cultural
work that legitimizes them as local.

What this dynamic does not make clear, however, is that this localness
is also distinctly masculine. As we have seen, the associations between
masculinity, work/labor, and localness/history have become resonant
owing to their enduring and stable association over a long period. Similarly, because this resonance has existed for so long, the association between these realms of social activity and meaning is unreflexive, assumed,
and therefore highly legitimate. As the pub is the site where men generate
understandings of pub history (and therefore arbitrate the notion of localness), evaluate everyday events, and maintain ongoing control over the
informal labor market, the resonant power and legitimacy of pub(lic) masculinity thus overwhelmingly remains within the control of pub(lic) masculinity itself.

To conclude, the self-reinforcing triangle of labor, localness, and masculinity is powerfully apparent in this particular rural community. By stepping back, we can argue that such dynamics might be common in many
small rural communities, where blue-collar men's work has retained a
continuity over generations. Given this context, the only way for young
rural women who grow up in such communities to escape the male gender
order is to leave. While men in these kinds of communities reside securely
in the rural virtues of their gender (reliably masculine, reliably local, reliably employed), it is little wonder that for so many young women growing
up (unreliably local) in such communities, escape to the city represents a

calculated political act. The true opposition to the resonant performance of rural masculinity is the performance of absence by young rural women.

## NOTES

1. Campbell (2000).
2. Appadurai (1996). I am indebted to Carolyn Morris for uncovering this far from obvious, but very productive, engagement (see Morris 2003).
3. Appadurai (1996, 181).
4. Fairweather and Campbell (1990); Campbell (2000).
5. Campbell (2000).
6. Ibid.
7. Fairweather and Campbell (1990). I would like to acknowledge the contribution of John Fairweather, who directed the first stage of this project.
8. Campbell (1994).
9. Fairweather and Campbell (1990) discuss these research methods in detail.
10. Fairweather and Campbell (1990); Campbell (2000).
11. Campbell (2000).
12. As do Campbell and Phillips (1995).
13. While the power of male control of public space is clearly widespread, future reference to pub(lic) masculinity will mean specifically this particular group of men engaged in pub drinking.
14. While this situation appears quite extreme, a similar dynamic is revealed in the ethnographic work of C. Morris (2003), who studied a nearby community of sheep farmers and identified a very high degree of legitimacy within the male-dominated rural gender order.
15. Department of Statistics (1986).
16. Ibid.
17. M. Bell (1994).
18. Connell (1995a).
19. Woodward (1998).
20. Horwitz (1998).

21. M. Bell (1994).
22. Ibid., 238–39.
23. Savran (1998).
24. Ibid.
25. These two are instructive but by no means exhaustive. Sport provides another interesting area of resonance for masculinity in the context of this ethnography, while Lovelock (1999) provides ethnographic evidence from a similar locale in New Zealand that unravels the relationship between masculinity and machines, including both workplace machinery and the intriguing bonds between men and cars.
26. Appadurai (1996, 180).
27. Ibid., 180–81.
28. Campbell (2000).
29. For example, Ackland (1930); McCausland (1979).
30. Hatch (1992).
31. Phillips (1987).
32. Campbell (2000).
33. See also Lovelock (1999).
34. The employees of these worksites were not the only ones who drank at the pub. Several business owners also tended to drink there, but they were often those owners who participated in worksite operations alongside their employees. Owners who took a purely managerial role were highly unlikely to patronize the pub, except during Christmas and New Year's celebrations.
35. Coombes and Campbell (1996).
36. This was true even when new jobs available on the ski field—like grading the roads—were very similar to many "traditional" jobs.
37. Pahl (1984).
38. L. Morris (1985).

# Rooted and Routed Masculinities Among the Rural Youth of North Cork and Upper Swaledale

*Caitríona Ní Laoire and Shaun Fielding*

Research on gender relations has played a pivotal role in contributing to the resurgence of rural studies. Growing recognition that mainstream rural studies have marginalized women's experiences and voices has contributed to a wealth of research about rural women's lives.[1] At the same time, our understanding of "the rural" itself has been deconstructed, highlighting its dynamism and instability. This "cultural turn" has resulted in researchers' embracing issues of otherness, difference, and fluidity, and destabilizing essentialist constructions of rural people and places.[2] Consequently, gender and rurality are no longer seen as fixed and unchanging but as "unstable and interactive reference points."[3] More important in terms of this study, the focus of research has expanded from an emphasis on the experiences of rural women to include studies addressing the gendered nature of representations of the rural and the agricultural. It is here that studies of rural masculinity—influenced by wider sociological research addressing the construction and performance of masculine identities and experiences—have received increasing attention.[4]

Masculinities research encompasses a range of theoretical perspectives, from the feminist to the antifeminist. However, most share a concern with the relations between gender and power.[5] These perspectives involve moving beyond conventional, homogeneous, and unproblematic associations of privilege and power with maleness, and moving toward recognizing *multiple* masculinities in different social and spatial contexts. Furthermore, as Raewyn Connell argues, some "hegemonic" masculinities occupy more dominant, authoritative positions than others.[6] These hegemonic masculinities are reproduced through the association of signs and symbols of masculinity with power and authority. Masculinities researcher Berit Brandth, for example, highlights the role of the tractor as a sign of male farm identity, a sign that symbolizes work, technology, and control over nature. Via this research, Brandth deconstructs the imperatives of masculinity and rurality in order to understand the socially constructed nature of gendered identities and practices.[7]

This chapter uses Brandth's type of discourse analysis to explore competing narratives of masculinity among young men in north Cork, Ireland, and upper Swaledale, England, to highlight the similarly complex relationship between masculinities and power relations in two different rural contexts. By examining these gendered power relations, we unpack the confusions and contradictions involved in contemporary discourses of masculinity in these places through a conceptual framework based on the tension between "rootedness" and "routedness."

## A Comparative Approach

Not only do multiple and competing masculinities exist in different contexts, but some of these masculinities are hegemonic in nature—that is, they are the most powerful, or most "honored" within a particular social context, and thus are influential in the marginalization of women and less powerful (or "subordinate") masculinities.[8] These two ideas indicate that we need to understand the social, geographical, and historical contexts of particular constructions of (rural) masculinity.[9] In their collection of ethnographies of masculinity, Andrea Cornwall and Nancy Lindisfarne display the value of a comparative ethnographic approach in teasing out the contextual and specific nature of relations between gender, power, and masculine identities: "The shifting and contingent relation between 'masculinity' and 'men' and power becomes clear when we examine the *enactment* of hegemonic and subordinate masculinities in a single setting."[10] In other words, while an ethnographic approach illuminates the richness of local detail, a comparative ethnographic approach takes this even further. Moreover, a comparative approach also illuminates the contingent nature of relations between gender and power.

This chapter is located within the comparative ethnographic tradition. Like other contributors to this volume, we use ethnographic methods to examine concrete practices in particular types of rural places.[11] The chapter draws on our own research: two distinct yet comparable studies of local geographies of power and identity among young people living in two marginal rural regions.[12] One study focuses on the gendered nature of experiences of growing up in, leaving, or staying in rural Ireland.[13] This study draws on research in one locality in north Cork involving focus-group interviews with local secondary school students, and in-depth interviews with young migrants and young male farmers. The other study explores the marginal cultural identities in upper Swaledale, in rural North Yorkshire.[14] This project involved participant observation and interviews with local people in key sites such as a local pub and the local festival.

Although the study areas are characterized by different institutional and cultural contexts, both are sites undergoing considerable economic restructuring and social recomposition. Increased agricultural commercialization and consolidation threaten "traditional" primary industries (dairy, cattle, and hill farming). Conventional agricultural systems are being rationalized and are gradually being replaced by a more diversified economic base. Upper Swaledale, in particular, is experiencing a continuing rise of the service-sector industry characterized by tourism and leisure (although the 2001 outbreak of foot-and-mouth disease has curtailed this somewhat). North Cork is characterized more by a shift toward limited manufacturing industry such as food processing and construction. These economic changes have significant social and cultural implications, especially through continued youth out-migration (in both areas) and service class and retirement in-migration (mainly in upper Swaledale).

## Young People in North Cork and Upper Swaledale

The ways in which the two groups of young people exist in and view their environments are highly significant. Discussions with young people growing up in rural north Cork revealed life-worlds characterized by considerable conflict and contradiction. They perceived their environment as combining elements of a stereotypical rural idyll (with characteristics of safety, freedom, and a sense of community), but also complained about a lack of "things to do" and the restrictiveness of local society. Many of the young men talked about the role of sport, including their involvement in local football (Gaelic football) teams, as an important focus in their lives, while many saw farming as central to their lives. In comparison, for the young women, a lack of sporting activities was an issue, as was the restrictiveness of local social and cultural structures. Local society was clearly highly gendered, a gendering most obviously reflected in the male dominance of local labor markets and social networks. As the young people left school and made their transition to adulthood, local gender relations affected their career and migration decisions in powerful and complex ways.

In upper Swaledale, one of the most notable observations was the relative invisibility of young people. This invisibility is partly explained by most young people's social/gender relations' tending to be located outside their immediate locality and toward the lower dale around Richmond, where they went to school or had their friendship groups. Culturally, this area boasts a strong musical tradition, and many young people played in the two local music groups (at Reeth and Muker), while others were involved in folk groups. There were also a few youth church groups, although these tended to be frequented by the dale's younger children.

In both study areas, it was evident that the ways in which young people used space was highly gendered. Young men were more likely to appropriate (or be admitted to) public spaces, in particular the pub and the playing field. This accessibility reflects the association of masculinity with the dominant local institutions of sport and leisure. In turn, this social dynamic is reinforced by the male dominance of local labor markets, with young men more likely than young women to view farming as an important source of belonging and identity in both areas.

As this demographic indicates, these local worlds were highly gendered in general terms. These were also worlds in tension with wider global networks of consumption, migration, and information. As in other small rural communities, many young people looked outside the local area for their leisure activities, either toward Richmond or Darlington (in Swaledale) or Cork city (in Cork). In many cases, young people also left the locality as soon as they left school. Given the gendered nature of these local worlds, we can link such movements and social relations to the construction of masculinities. These connections are most clearly seen if we analyze them through the dual critical concept of "rootedness and routedness."

## Rootedness and Routedness

Rootedness and routedness are concepts that help us examine the complex social and political processes that historically form identities. Identities and, more generally, cultures have "roots" or origins that are typically seen as timeless, traditional, authentic, and natural, associated with a sense of place and often with "the land" itself. Similarly, identities and cultures also have "routes," or the constantly shifting economic, social, cultural, and political patterns that make them subject to restructuring, alteration, reframing, or "re-outlining." While they may seem mutually exclusive, roots and routes coexist and operate in dialogue with each other in complex ways. Our definitions of roots and routes draw primarily on Paul Gilroy's work, which in turn coheres with theories outlined by Gillian Rose and Catherine Nash.[15]

In his examination of the cultural exchange between Africans and Europeans, Gilroy criticizes the conventional opposition between tradition and modernity, a dualism that attributes history, progress, reason, and rationality to the West and consigns the non-West to perpetual otherness.[16] Gilroy uses the concepts of the "Black Atlantic" (his term for the cultural connections between Europeans and Africans so far neglected in theories of modernity) and "double consciousness" to criticize the "cultural insiderism" of modern forms of belonging.[17] His study emphasizes the complex social and political processes that historically form identities and places most emphasis on identifying the "routes" that map the outline of the "Black Atlantic," rather than discovering the "roots" that allegedly represent its origins. Gilroy's perspective highlights the compound and dynamic nature of identities, which, he argues, are being shaped by modernity without being fully part of it. This in turn creates a state of "double consciousness." Here people experience simultaneous attraction and repulsion as they recognize the doubleness of their own identity. Gilroy suggests that this "double consciousness" can provide lessons and understandings that are not just restricted to black people in the West.[18]

Rose argues that a similar dualistic distinction between nature and culture lies behind many aspects of (geographical) knowledge. She points out that culture is constructed in masculine, modern terms while nature is associated with femininity, tradition, and rurality.[19] Rurality, in this context, can be seen to represent tradition and the natural environment. In terms of a specific location, Rose's approach coheres with Nash's study of identity, gender, and landscape in Ireland, in which she argues that the Irish "rural" is associated with femininity, nurturing, and home and has connotations of pastoralism and ecology. Such symbolism is part of a wider tendency to see peripheral rural communities as the repositories, or *roots,* of national cultural symbols.[20]

The concept of "roots" is driven by a tendency to invest new ways of belonging with these timeless forces of nature and tradition. "Roots" are expressed through such symbols as the soil and the landscape, and identities are constructed through a natural association between people and place. Hence there is great comfort and popularity in a sense of shared common memory and shared roots that generate essentialist and absolutist forms of identity. Gilroy uses this concept to focus on "the nation," but such frameworks can also apply to discourses of rurality and masculinity. For example, rootedness is evident in the construction of a particular kind of rural masculinity involving a natural/biological connection with the land, often legitimized by reference to "localness" and "local history."[21]

The difficulty with legitimizing such a "rooted" rural masculinity is that it does not exist in isolation; as we have argued, it coexists in a constantly shifting set of economic, social, cultural, and political circumstances—its *routes.* For example, restructuring within the rural economy is shifting the ideological focus of farmers to a more businesslike and "high-tech" masculinity.[22] Modern phenomena such as migration and globalization make a bounded/traditional sense of belonging less relevant. For some men, this means coping with significant changes to "the way things are done," while for others it leads to migration and a disruption of the connections to place.

Tradition itself is neither outside nor opposed to modernity but is reconstituted continually through interaction and conflict with it. "The traditional" cannot store fixed identities of time and place—of "what it once was like"—because "the traditional" exists as a series of breaks and interruptions where identities are viewed as unstable and shifting outcomes of historical, social, cultural, and political processes.[23] In this approach, identities are always unpacking and reworking themselves as people encounter each other's overlapping territories and intertwined histories—their *routes.* Through such encounters, identities struggle for meaning and control. This struggle produces identities (in our case, rural masculinity) that can be seen as the products of interconnected histories and cultures.[24] In the next two sections, we explore the use of rooted and routed identities among young people in two marginal rural areas to provide an insight into the concept of rural masculinity.

## Rooted Masculinities

Tradition, or "rootedness," is a hegemonic discourse in constructions of rurality and masculinity in both north Cork and upper Swaledale. In both locations, values of purity, authenticity, and stability are associated with a sense of belonging to "the rural" and are constructed in opposition to "the urban," which symbolizes modernity, progress, and change. Many young people in north Cork and upper Swaledale subscribe to a series of "cultural repertoires" that look to the roots of local culture and society in a search for authenticity, coherence, and stability. In other words, they are drawing on and contributing to a rooted masculinity.

These "cultural repertoires" are highly gendered, reflecting a masculinist view of place. Traditional discourses of rurality in both Ireland and England draw on a myth of a romantic agrarian past. Selective elements of a way of life that existed in the late nineteenth and early twentieth centuries are idealized in this myth.[25] Unsurprisingly, this way of life that involved a highly gendered social structure based on patriarchal systems of land ownership and control. Femininity was associated with domesticity, while the public spheres of work and visible leisure activities were constructed as masculine domains. Rooted constructions of rurality draw on these gendered identities, reproducing gendered uses of space. As we have already mentioned, gendered space is highly evident in both north Cork and upper Swaledale, where public spaces of leisure tend to be male dominated: the pub, the football (soccer) field (in north Cork), and the village green (in upper Swaledale).[26]

The ways in which a rooted rural masculinity develops in north Cork or in upper Swaledale is contingent on a particular constellation of ideologies and social structures in each place. In both areas, a rooted masculinity is intimately bound up with the reassertion of an agriculture-based, male-dominated value system, with a fixed local identity rooted in "how it once was"—a golden-age construction of the past:

> There is a real sense of bereavement for a way of life that has changed out of all recognition and will never be retrieved. . . . People love to look at the past like that was the real dale. [Interview, local man, upper Swaledale.]

> Before, like, they'd go out and milk the cow, put it into the jug and put it up on the table, it never killed 'em like. Now they're all [talking about] "bacteria" and "tests," and . . . in the old days, they'd be a lot harder than us, like, they'd stand up to a lot more, like. [Focus group interview, fifteen-year-old male, north Cork.]

As these statements indicate, in both areas masculinity is symbolized by powerful "rooted" themes such as land, locality, and history. In upper Swaledale, many people expressed an intense cultural, almost spiritual, attachment to the land, even though it represented the site of their socio-economic marginalization. This sense of attachment is particularly significant among the young men as a way of maintaining their own identity and informing their life decisions: "I am really touched by the way that the young men sit up in the hills; as if they see the countryside as their life, and even though they have never moved out of the dale they still do not take it for granted" (interview, local woman, upper Swaledale). Similar expressions of and connections with the land were identified in north Cork: "'Tis a farmer I am, 'tis a farmer I'll be. A conscious decision [to become a farmer]?—no. 'Tis in the blood. I can't explain it. . . . I suppose I love what I do. . . . I stick with it . . . the land and cattle: that's my way of life" (interview, young male farmer, north Cork).

In both areas, alongside such associations with the land, a strong sense of local or regional culture and history reflects a preoccupation with an "authentic" rooted form of belonging to the place. A rooted sense of masculinity is thus asserted through events and activities routinely taken as symbolic of traditional culture—for example, through farming, music, song, and religion in upper Swaledale, and through farming, Gaelic football, and Catholicism in north Cork. In north Cork particularly, a local identity is affirmed and essentialized through sport. A fifteen-year-old male from the north Cork village of Kiskeam emphasizes the role of sport in providing a focus of identity when he refers to the image of Kiskeam as a small, run-down, depopulated place in comparison to the nearby small town of Newmarket, which also houses a popular nightspot for the surrounding area, the "Highland": "They say Newmarket [has] the 'Highland,' Kiskeam [has] nothing. They'd be boasting what they have. We gets 'em back when we beats 'em in football" (focus group interview, fifteen-year-old male, north Cork).

For young men, the decision to leave or stay in the rural area is tied to the extent to which they do or do not, can or cannot, locate themselves within this rooted masculinity. In this respect, staying behind is often seen as an expression of such an attachment to place. In examining similar demographic dynamics in Norway, Mariann Villa argues that the modernization of rural society has involved changes in farmers' life modes and life courses. For example, the decision to enter or stay in farming is no longer taken for granted among the young men; it is much more a matter of choice for the individual young person.[27] As a result, attachment to the land or rural place becomes a charged issue for many young rural men, when for previous generations it may have constituted an unquestioned part of everyday life. In this respect, the roots of traditional everyday life and culture are in tension with contemporary rural economic and social relations, or *routes,* which we examine in more depth in our next section.

One outcome of rural restructuring processes is the out-migration of young people for education and employment. In other words, many young people may find that the place that is at the very core of their identities can no longer support them economically. One strategy used by young people to cope with the physical separation from place is to maintain some attachment to the area—for example, by continuing to participate in traditional activities in their new location (such as music and sport), by staying in touch and frequently visiting the area, or by surrounding themselves with artifacts and memories of their life there. In these cases, although the life paths of these young people are now *routed* to other places, they are still *rooted* in north Cork or upper Swaledale. "Although many of the young people have left, for many of them there is always a large bit of Swaledale that is with them all the time" (interview, local woman, Swaledale). This is also reflected in the commitment to "returning home" at some point in their life:

> I s'pose a lot of the time I felt for my parents; there was only one of us at home. And, I s'pose that . . . was part of the decision as well [to return to Ireland]. Whether at the time I would have admitted it or not is another thing, 'cause I s'pose a young fellow at that age doesn't want to admit to too many family ties. [Interview, twenty-five-year-old male return migrant, north Cork.]

> It's some place I want to go back to, definitely. [Interview, twenty-seven-year-old female migrant, north Cork.]

In these cases, although young people may be outside north Cork and upper Swaledale physically, they are still part of these places culturally.

The current economic shift in rural areas also challenges traditional patriarchal household structures and therefore, it can be argued, challenges traditional gender roles and identities. One way of coping with the contradiction between a rooted masculinity and the changing structures of rural life is constantly to adapt the discourses of rootedness to changing demands. For some rural men, therefore, while their identity is still *rooted* in the place, it is constantly shifting and adapting as it is *routed* through the changes brought by economic restructuring and social recomposition. For example, Brandth contends that for rural men, the rooted masculinity of the rugged, strong, dirty, manual mechanic is now being routed and negotiated through the necessities of diversification and a more business-like type of masculinity.[28]

Villa traces a similar negotiation over three generations of farm house-holds and outlines how farmers' lives and expectations have changed. She argues that economic diversification has reduced the status of the farmer in the rural community and also the support networks available to farm-ers.[29] In this respect, it can be argued that a rooted masculinity is under threat.[30] In relation to rural masculinities, however, most theorists agree that although the discourses of masculinity are reworked and adapted to changing circumstances in rural areas, masculine hegemony is main-tained in key spheres of rural life.[31] What concerns us here is that very process of negotiation and/or adaptation.

Young men in and of north Cork and upper Swaledale, then, can use discourses of rootedness to express their masculine identities. However, a rooted masculinity is difficult to maintain in the context of contemporary rural restructuring processes that threaten traditional social structures and value systems and that can result in a movement away from farming, or in out-migration, for local men. These tensions and contradictions are po-sitioned within local power relations, as the more powerful local groups are those that can adapt unproblematically to changing circumstances, while others may find their livelihoods and identities under threat.

## Routed Masculinities

We have demonstrated that young men in north Cork and upper Swaledale can "invest" in a masculinity that is *rooted* in particular ways of interpret-ing local social and cultural traditions. Those rooted values of authenticity and purity are idealized, and are expressed through potentially exclusion-ary practices such as farm work, sport, and drinking in pubs. Because of such exclusionary performances of rootedness, those young people—

especially young women and particular groups of young men—who do not or cannot participate in such activities, or whose belonging is not rooted in such activities, may experience alienation and marginalization. In this sense, rooted masculinities operate as hegemonic masculinities, because although a rooted masculinity may be under threat in these cases, it still has the power to marginalize the "voices" of many young people.

In contrast, routed masculinities can challenge the hegemony of rooted masculinities. Young people also look beyond their localities for a sense of belonging and connection, away from their social and cultural roots and toward their social and cultural *routes*. Although physically located in the local, they can construct identities that are routed through institutions such as the media and the education system. A desire to find cultural connections beyond the rooted can also be expressed through physical movement away from the locality, either through migration from the area or through involvement in leisure activities in more urbanized areas nearby (in these cases, the lower dale, the town, or the city):

> There is much more for us to do in places like Newcastle or Leeds, there is the cinema, the pubs, the shops, I can't get any decent clothes here, and then there are the jobs and if you want those sorts of things, you have to move. [Interview, local woman, upper Swaledale.]

> I don't know, I'm afraid I'd go mad here or something! It's very boring, all right. I think you'd have more to do in the city. [Focus group interview, fifteen-year-old female, north Cork.]

As well as identifying with more urbanized localities, people in upper Swaledale and north Cork expressed resistance to the hegemonic masculinist views of local identity. For example, several people in north Cork were aware of the power of sport and its association with a particular form of masculinity: "Friends of mine from school invariably talk about football matches, local matters, or something like that. Fair enough, I mean, it's because one becomes accustomed to that. . . . One is kind of forced by local society to conform to norms" (interview, twenty-six-year-old male migrant from north Cork). Young women in particular were aware of their exclusion from this powerfully masculine local institution: "The boys have handball, soccer, volleyball, and football during the summer. . . . The boys get handed [everything] and the girls have to do it themselves. . . . They think we're weak like 'cause we're girls but . . . I don't think it's the boys' fault. . . . It's a man's world!" (focus group interview, fifteen-year-old female, north Cork). On a more profound level, both men and women believed that to belong locally, it was necessary to conform to an essentialist construction of what it meant to be "a local": "One tends to stand out like a sore thumb basically if you do something differently . . . rewards are linked up with the conformity . . . you get rewarded in the sense that you get accepted" (interview, twenty-seven-year-old male migrant, north Cork).

Another way of resisting rooted masculinity is to leave, to break all connections to community, and to embrace routedness. Here, the rural is seen as a place to escape from rather than return to, and migrants can tap into the popular discourse of migration as escape from the constraints of rural life, a discourse that opposes tradition and rurality to modernity and urbanism. This is still a highly masculinist discourse, whereby the migrant is constructed as a "hero" who exerts "his" independence by leaving home, or as someone who is a "hero" because of the hardships experienced during migration. This is a paradoxical situation for two reasons. First, outmigration from both north Cork and upper Swaledale continues to be female dominated. Second, this routed discourse of resistance and escape is actually *rooted* in the historical traditions of migration in rural areas—a fact reflecting the interconnectedness of rootedness and routedness.

Furthermore, the histories, cultures, and traditions that are thought of as "authentically" rooted—and against which there is some resistance among young people—are, for the most part, routed through other places, people, and cultures: "We found dances that came down from places as far away as Poland and Norway . . . and also the old lead mining song *Four Pence a Day*, that was not from here, but was brought down by the miners from Teesdale . . . and there was also a song that came from London to the music halls of the northeast and then down here" (interview, festival worker, upper Swaledale). In other words, a rooted masculinity was being inscribed through cultural symbols that were routed, and a routed masculinity was inscribed with cultural symbols that were rooted. Thus both north Cork and upper Swaledale had histories and identities that were fractured, broken up, and reconstituted by different people from different places. As a result, there was no single coherent rural masculinity to invest in or to resist.

To borrow from human geographer Doreen Massey, young people living in both north Cork and upper Swaledale had "extroverted senses of place." They could become vessels of intersecting social relations that lay within and beyond their boundaries.[32] Doreen Massey exemplifies this idea with the place she calls "home"—Kilburn, North London: "Kilburn may have a character of its own, [but] it is absolutely not a seamless, coherent identity, a single sense of place that everyone shares. It could hardly be less so. People's routes through the place, their favourite haunts within it, the connection they make (physically, or by phone, or post, or in memory or imagination) between here and the rest of the world vary enormously. If it is recognised that people have multiple identities, then the same point can be made in relation to places."[33]

Likewise, within north Cork and upper Swaledale, people have multiple identities based on their experiences routed through multiple places and a whole range of historical, social, and cultural encounters. Hence the various social groups within north Cork and upper Swaledale will be "differently located" according to these complex social relations. In turn, their own reading and interpretation of those social relations will be distinct: "The geography of social relations forces us to recognise that our interconnectedness underscores the fact that both personal identity and the identity of those envelopes of space-time in which and between which we live and move (and have our 'Being') are constructed precisely through that interconnectedness."[34]

But how does this perspective help to illuminate the concept of rural masculinity? The answer, we feel, lies in understanding that rural masculinities are being pulled in different directions all at the same time. A rooted masculinity with an emphasis on tradition is under threat from the routes of economic and social restructuring. Yet the roots on which this masculinity is based are in fact routed through other people, places, and cultures. At the same time, routed masculinities are invoked to resist the dominant view of tradition expressed in rural masculinities. This rootedness, however, is often expressed through the practice of migration, a practice that is rooted in the traditions of rural life. In other words, roots are routed and routes are rooted.

We have demonstrated that the concepts of rootedness and routedness enable the unpacking and reworking of rural masculinities in north Cork and upper Swaledale. The rooted rural masculinity of the more powerful (that is, the male) elements in these communities is associated with a search for authenticity, coherence, and stability, and is presented as the

"true" local identity. However, we have also demonstrated that rural masculinities in north Cork and upper Swaledale are highly fractured and interconnected with other people, places, and spaces, thus emphasizing their
routedness as opposed to their rootedness. In both north Cork and upper
Swaledale, a rooted masculinity nevertheless prevails through the traditional patriarchal and masculinist structures of the local societies.

In this chapter we have been concerned with the interconnecting discourses that compete for the "hearts and minds" of young rural people and
specifically young men. The competition of these discourses has created a
double bind, in which a rooted masculinity also has elements of routedness, and a routed masculinity has elements of rootedness. But what are
the implications of this interconnectedness? If, as we suggest, a routed
masculinity is marginalized by the more powerful rooted discourses
within rural society, this suggests a need to move away from a rooted perspective in order to understand the dilemmas being faced by many young
rural people (and equally by "other," less powerful rural people). Having
said that, to neglect the traditions, histories, and roots of people and places
is to disregard the bedrock on which any new social relations can be based,
and thus any such new understandings cannot necessarily come from a
total immersion in a routed perspective. What is required, then, is to understand the routedness of the rooted and the rootedness of the routed.
This mutual recognition implies opening up the space between the two
discourses, thereby providing a new conceptual tool for understanding the
construction of rural masculinities.

NOTES

1. For examples of important texts in
the United Kingdom, see Little (1987);
Whatmore, Marsden, and Lowe (1994).

2. For a useful introduction to "the
cultural turn" in rural geography, see the
debates between Philo (1992, 1993) and
Murdoch and Pratt (1993, 1994). For a
good overview of the development of this
way of thinking, see Cloke and Little
(1997).

3. Whatmore, Marsden, and Lowe
(1994, 4).

4. Saugeres (2002a); Villa (1999);
Woodward (1998).

5. Connell (1995a); Cornwall and
Lindisfarne (1994); Mac an Ghaill (1996);
Segal (1990).

6. Connell (1995a).

7. Brandth (1995).

8. Connell (2000).

9. Connell (1995a, 2000); Mac an
Ghaill (1996).

10. Cornwall and Lindisfarne (1994,
10).

11. See Chapters 4 and 5 in this volume, by Bird and Campbell, respectively.

12. Fielding (1998a, 1998b, 2000); Ní
Laoire (1997, 1999, 2002).

13. Ní Laoire (1997, 1999, 2002).

14. Fielding (1998a, 1998b, 2000).

15. Rose (1993); Nash (1993).

16. Gilroy (1993).

17. Ibid.

18. See Gilroy (1993). For a more in-depth investigation and critique of this work, see Kale (1996); King (1995); B. Williams (1995).

19. Rose (1993).

20. Nash (1993).

21. Campbell (2000); Saugeres (2002a).

22. For example, see Brandth (1995); Ní Laoire (2002).

23. Gilroy (1993).

24. For a wider discussion of the role of "promiscuous geographies," see Jacobs (1996).

25. For a discussion of these myths, see Brown (1995); Short (1991).

26. Gilroy (1993) recognizes the similar highly gendered nature of rooted concepts when applied to cultural or national identity, whereby the development of nations is seen as dependent on the establishment of a particular kind of gender hierarchy.

27. Villa (1999).

28. Brandth (1995); Campbell (2000).

29. Villa (1999).

30. Connell (1987) argues that the current gender order in Western society generally is characterized by a series of crisis tendencies related to contemporary processes of social and economic restructuring.

31. Brandth (1995).

32. Massey (1994).

33. Massey (1995, 153).

34. Massey (1994, 122).

# "White Men Are This Nation": Right-Wing Militias and the Restoration of Rural American Masculinity

*Michael Kimmel and Abby L. Ferber*

In a 1987 illustration in *W.A.R.*, the magazine of the White Aryan Resistance, a working-class white man, in hard hat and flak jacket, stands proudly before a suspension bridge while a jet plane soars overhead. "White Men *Built* This Nation!!" reads the text. "White Men *Are* This Nation!!!"

Most observers see the statement's racist intent immediately, but rarely do we see its deeply gendered meaning. Here is a moment when racial and gendered discourses fuse, when both race and gender are made visible. "This nation," we now understand, "is" neither white women nor nonwhite people of either gender.

The White Aryan Resistance that produced this illustration is situated on a continuum of the far right that runs from older organizations, such as the John Birch Society, the Ku Klux Klan, and the American Nazi Party, to Holocaust deniers, neo-Nazi or racist skinheads; white power groups like Posse Comitatus and White Aryan Resistance; and radical rural militias like the Wisconsin Militia and the Militia of Montana. This last set of organizations, the rural militias, appeared in the 1990s in the farm belt (and Rust Belt) and became especially visible after the standoffs in Ruby Ridge, Idaho, and the bombing of the federal building in Oklahoma City.

In this chapter we examine the ideology and organization of the rural militia movement, which reached its peak in the mid-1990s. First, we locate the emergence of this movement in the farm crisis of the 1980s. Second, we describe the movement's social composition. Finally, we explore its ideology. We argue that the militias, like many far-right groups, are both fiercely patriotic and simultaneously against capitalism and democratic government—or, more accurately, against corporate capitalism and federal government. To resolve that apparent contradiction, the militias, like other groups, employ a gendered discourse about masculinity both to explain the baffling set of structural forces arrayed against them and to provide a set of "others" against which they can project a unifying ideology.

"White Men *Built* This Nation," from *W.A.R.* By permission.

## The Rural Context

The economic restructuring of the global economy has had a dramatic effect on rural areas throughout the industrial world.[1] The Reagan Revolution in general meant corporate downsizing, declining real wages, changing technology, an increasing gap between the wealthy and everyone else, uncertainty in the stock market, new waves of Latino and Asian immigrants to the United States, and a steady decline in manufacturing jobs (typically replaced by lower-paying jobs in the service sector). Increased capital mobility and the elimination of tariff barriers have also weakened the bargaining power of labor and left the average American worker feeling vulnerable and betrayed.[2] Between 1980 and 1985 alone, 11 million American workers lost their jobs through plant closures and layoffs. Of those who found new jobs, more than half experienced downward mobility.[3] Rural Americans in particular have found their economic insecurity compounded by threats to traditional Western industries like logging, mining, ranching, and farming, where consolidation has also proceeded rapidly and markedly.[4] Squeezed between corporate capital (agribusiness) and federal government (regulations, environmentalism, and the like), many farmers feel themselves to be the "victim[s] of the global restructuring of the rural world."[5]

Since 1980, America has lost nearly 750,000 of its small and medium-size family farms. During the farm crisis of the 1980s, Linda Lobao and Katherine Meyer point out, "farmers faced the worst financial stress since the Great Depression."[6] For affected farmers, this economic disaster dashed the American Dream of upward mobility and replaced it with the stark reality of downward mobility. As Osha Davidson notes, "Many of the new rural poor had not only shared American cultural goals—they had achieved them for a time. They had been in the middle class, of the middle class. They had tasted the good life and then had fallen from it." Davidson also notes the irony—crucial to our analysis—that "the victims of this blight, the inhabitants of the new rural ghettos, have always been the most blindly patriotic of Americans, the keepers of the American dream."[7] This state of rural crisis continues today as "family farms, which use little hired labor and whose households are sustained through farming alone, are being edged out."[8] While many may speak of a "new farm crisis," it is more accurate to say that the crisis of the 1980s never truly ended.[9]

For many, the continuing farm crisis is also a gender crisis, a crisis of masculinity. Many white, rural American men feel under siege and vulnerable, unsure of their manhood. They are furious and are looking for someone to blame. Some direct their rage inward, even to the point of suicidal thoughts and actions; others direct it outward. "Many debt ridden farm families will become more suspicious of government, as their self-worth, their sense of belonging, their hope for the future deteriorates," predicted Oklahoma psychologist Glen Wallace in 1989. "The farms are gone," writes Joel Dyer, "yet the farmers remain. They've been transformed into a wildfire of rage, fuelled by the grief of their loss and blown by the winds of conspiracy and hate-filled rhetoric."[10] Rural men are not alone in facing wrenching economic transformations, however. Many urban men, too, have tasted the good life and fallen from it. "It is hardly surprising, then, that American men—lacking confidence in the government and the economy, troubled by the changing relations between the sexes, uncertain of their identity or their future—began to *dream*, to fantasize about the powers and features of another kind of man who could retake and reorder the world. And the hero of all these dreams was the paramilitary warrior."[11] The militia movement is one embodiment of this dream, one that is strikingly rural both in the population from which it draws and in the location of most of its activities.

## The Militia Movement

The militia movement is not easy to define. There is no central organization or leadership; rather, the movement is composed of loosely connected paramilitary organizations that "perceive a global conspiracy in which key political and economic events are manipulated by a small group of elite insiders."[12] These numerous unrelated groups form private armies, mistrust the government, and have armed themselves to fight back. According to the Militia Watchdog, an internet organization that tracks the movement, the militias grew out of the Posse Comitatus and the Patriot movement, which were strong in the 1970s and 1980s. (The Southern Poverty Law Center, which tracks right-wing extremist groups, lists the militias as a subset of the Patriot movement.)

Like their predecessors, militia members believe that the U.S. government has become totalitarian and seeks to disarm its citizenry and create a "one-world government." Militia members believe that traditional political reform is useless and that they must resist U.S. laws and attack the government. They believe that armed confrontation is inevitable. While not unified in any traditional sense, the movement nonetheless is tied together through the internet, where groups and individuals share stories and advice. At survivalist expositions and gun shows, they sell literature, recruit new members, and purchase arms and survivalist gear.[13] Some groups sell their wares via mail-order catalogs, and many meet on the weekends to train in guerrilla warfare tactics. Militia organizations subscribe to the magazine *Soldier of Fortune*, frequent *Soldier of Fortune* conventions, and draw members from *Soldier of Fortune* enthusiasts. The Militia of Montana has had booths at *Soldier of Fortune* expositions, where it peddles T-shirts reading "Angry White Guy" and bumper stickers proclaiming, "I Love my Country, but I Hate my Government."[14]

The Militia of Montana (with the deliciously unironically gendered acronym MOM) provides us with a "prototype" of the American militia. Founded by former Aryan Nations member John Trochman, his brother, and his nephew in the aftermath of Ruby Ridge, MOM was the first significant militia organization and the largest national distributor of militia propaganda.[15] At MOM meetings and through mail-order distribution it sells its own manuals, as well as a variety of books and videos, including *A Call to Arms, Battle Preparations Now, The Pestilence* (AIDS), *America in Crisis, The Illuminati Today, Booby Traps,* and *Big Sister Is Watching You* (discussed below). Their numerous manuals encourage and train readers in kidnapping, murder, and explosives, urging acts of terrorism.[16]

Estimates about the size and appeal of such militias vary. Since the first modern-day militias began appearing in the early 1990s, their numbers have expanded to include between 50,000 and 100,000 members in at least forty states.[17] In 1996 the number of militias and similar Patriot groups hit an all-time high of 858, with militia units or organizers in every state.[18] That number declined to 435 in 1998, of which 171 were classified as militias, and in 2001 only 158 Patriot groups remained active, with 73 classified as militias. We attribute this decline to a variety of factors. According to Mark Potok of the Southern Poverty Law Center, "They have gone home, disillusioned and tired of waiting for the revolution that never seems to come. They have been scared off, frightened by the arrests of thousands of comrades for engaging in illegal 'common-law' court tactics, weapons violations and even terrorist plots. And they have, in great numbers, left the relatively nonracist Patriot world for the harder-line groups that now make up most of the radical right."[19]

Few sharp divisions separate the various subgroups of the radical right. People flow between groups and have overlapping memberships and allegiances.[20] At the peak of the militia movement, one observer wrote, "It is the convergence of various streams of fanatical right wing beliefs that seems to be sweeping the militia movement along. Overlapping right wing social movements with militant factions appear to be coalescing within the militias."[21] This demonstrates the important point that far-right groups are intricately interconnected and share a basic antigovernment, anti-Semitic, racist, and sexist/patriarchal ideology. Equally, the extent of involvement in the movement varies; some men simply correspond over the internet and read militia literature; others attend training sessions, stockpile food supplies and weapons, and resist paying taxes. In its most dangerous form, small, secret cells of two to ten people plan sabotage and terrorism. These cells have been linked to several terrorist acts, including the Oklahoma City bombing, the derailment of an Amtrak train in Arizona, and multiple bomb plots targeting "the Southern Poverty Law Center, offices of the Anti-Defamation League, federal buildings, abortion clinics and sites in the gay community."[22]

As these activities suggest, militias provide training in, among other things, weapons use, target practice, intelligence gathering, encryption and decryption, field radio operation, navigation, unarmed defense, the manufacture of explosives, and demolition.[23] Vietnam War veterans, Gulf War veterans, and active military and law enforcement officers provide much of the instruction.

## Social Composition of the Militias

Who are militia members? While no one has undertaken a formal survey of the militias (for obvious reasons), we can nonetheless discern several demographic characteristics. First and most obviously, militia members are overwhelmingly white and male. These white men, moreover, are commonly rural men. Numerous researchers have documented the rural nature of the militia movement; its roots are strongest, for instance, in the intermountain Montana and Idaho panhandle.[24] Potok similarly notes that the militia movement is "almost entirely rurally based."[25] Historian Carol

McNichol Stock situates the militia movement within the historical tradition of rural radicalism on both the left and the right, a tradition rooted in the values of producerism and vigilantism. Stock explores what she labels the "ideology of rural producer radicalism." "The desire to own small property, to produce crops and foodstuffs, to control local affairs, to be served but never coerced by a representative government, and to have traditional ways of life and labor respected," she writes, "is the stuff of one of the oldest dreams in the United States."[26]

Many militia members are also military veterans. Several leaders served in Vietnam and were shocked by the national disgust that greeted them as they returned home after the debacle.[27] Some veterans believed the government sold them out, caving in to effeminate, cowardly protesters; they no longer trust the government to fight for what is right. Louis Beam, for example, served eighteen months in Vietnam before returning to start his own paramilitary organization, which was broken up in the 1980s by lawsuits. He now advocates "leaderless resistance," the formation of underground terrorist cells.

Another militia member, Bo Gritz, a former Green Beret in Vietnam, returned to Southeast Asia several times on clandestine missions to search for prisoners of war and provided the real-life basis for the film *Rambo*. He used his military heroism to increase his credibility among potential recruits—one brochure describes him as "this country's most decorated Vietnam veteran," a man who "killed some 400 Communists in his illustrious military career."[28] In 1993 Gritz began a traveling SPIKE (Specially Prepared Individuals for Key Events) training program, a rigorous survival course in paramilitary techniques. Gritz and colleague Jack McLamb, a retired police officer, created their own community, "Almost Heaven," in Idaho. Gritz embodies the military element of the militias; he represents men who believe they are entitled to be hailed as heroes, like earlier generations of American veterans, not scorned as outcasts. He symbolizes "true" warrior-style masculinity, the reward for men who join the militia.

The militias are also Christian, and thus the movement is strongest in states with high concentrations of fundamentalist Christians. Many have embraced Christian Identity theology, which gained a foothold on the far right in the early 1980s. About half of the militia members in South Carolina, for example, are also followers of Christian Identity.[29] Christian Identity's focus on racism and anti-Semitism provides the theological underpinnings for the shift from a more "traditional agrarian protest" to the paramilitarism of the militias.

According to several researchers, actual militia members tend to range in age from the late thirties to fifties, while the active terrorists tend to be somewhat younger—in their twenties.[30] Many teenagers who commit hate crimes "graduate" to militias and other far-right organizations when they reach their twenties.[31] Like other groups of ethnic nationalists, the militias and their followers consist of two generations of dispossessed and displaced lower-middle-class men—small farmers, shopkeepers, craftsmen, and skilled workers. Some are men who have worked all their adult lives, hoping to pass their family farm to their sons and retire comfortably. Tom Metzger, head of the White Aryan Resistance, for instance, estimates that while 10 percent of his followers are skinheads, most are "businessmen and artisans."[32] These men believed that if they worked hard, their legacy would be assured, but they are able to leave their sons little but foreclosures, economic insecurity, and debt. As Timothy McVeigh, from Lockport, New York, wrote in a letter to the editor in his hometown paper a few years before he blew up the federal building in Oklahoma City, "the American dream of the middle class has all but disappeared, substituted with people struggling just to buy next week's groceries."[33] The sons of these farmers and shopkeepers expected to—and felt entitled to—inherit their fathers' legacy.[34] And when they realized the extent of their dispossession, some became murderously angry—at a system that not only emasculated their fathers but also threatened their own manhood.

Of course, the militias are not composed entirely of "sons." Lori Linzer, a militia researcher at the Anti-Defamation League, found that there are a few women involved in the movement. These women, however, are most likely to become involved with internet discussions and websites and less likely to be active in paramilitary training and other militia activities. Although some women are actively involved in the movement, their presence does not change the fact that most militias are "vastly, mainly, white Christian men."[35]

This demographic certainly coincides with the dominant gender ideology in rural areas. U.S. farming communities are characterized by a prevalent "domestic ideology" that depicts men as farmers and women as their helpmates.[36] This ideology erases the significant labor of women on farms from view and reinforces a sexual division of labor that defines different areas of work for men and women.[37]

While many members of the militia movement were not born or raised in rural areas, many have moved to such areas because they seek companionship with like-minded fellows. Moreover, in relatively remote areas, far from large numbers of nonwhites and Jews, they can organize, train, and build protective fortresses. Many groups thus seek to establish a refuge in rural communities where they can practice military tactics, stockpile food and weapons, hone their survivalist skills, and become self-sufficient in preparation for Armageddon, the final race war, or whatever cataclysm they envision. For example, while preparing for Y2K, some groups set up "covenant communities," self-sufficient and heavily armed rural settlements of white people who feared that "when the computers crash, government checks to minorities in the inner cities will stop. Then starving Hispanics and blacks will flood into the rural parts of America, armed to the teeth and willing to stop at nothing in order to wrench food from the tables of white Christians."[38]

In addition, far-right extremist leaders see rural areas as strong potential recruitment bases. Accurately reading the signs of rural decline and downward mobility, these leaders "see an opportunity to increase their political base by recruiting economically troubled farmers into their ranks."[39] While Davidson explains that "the spread of far-right groups over the last decade has not been limited to rural areas alone," we can certainly see that "the social and economic unraveling of rural communities—especially in the Midwest—has provided far-right groups with new audiences for their messages of hate."[40] Many farmers facing foreclosure have responded to promises from the far right to help them save their land; extremist groups offer them various schemes and legal maneuvers to help prevent foreclosure, blaming the farmers' troubles on Jewish bankers and "one world government." In stark contrast to the governmental indifference many rural Americans encounter, a range of right-wing groups, most recently the militias, seem to provide support, community, and answers.

In this sense, the militias simply follow in the footsteps of the Ku Klux Klan, the Posse Comitatus, and other far-right groups that recruited members in rural America throughout the 1980s. In fact, rural America has an entrenched history of racism and an equally long tradition of collective local action and vigilante justice. There remains a widespread notion that "Jews, African-Americans, and other minority-group members 'do not entirely belong,'" which may, in part, "be responsible for rural people's easy acceptance of the far right's agenda of hate."[41] "The far right didn't create bigotry in the Midwest; it didn't need to," Davidson concludes. "It merely had to tap into the existing undercurrent of prejudice once this had been inflamed by widespread economic failure and social discontent."[42]

What characterizes these descendants of small-town rural America—both the fathers and the sons—is not only their ideological vision of pro-ducerism, threatened by economic transformation, or their sense of small-town democratic community, an inclusive community based on the exclusion of broad segments of the population (blacks, Jews, homosexuals, and so on), but their sense of entitlement to economic, social, political—and even military—power. To cast the straight, white, middle-class man as the hegemonic holder of power in America entirely misses the daily experience of these straight white men. They believe themselves *entitled* to power—by a combination of historical legacy, religious proclamation, biological destiny, and moral legitimacy; but they feel powerless. Power, in their view, has not only been surrendered by white men—their fathers—but stolen from them by a federal government controlled and staffed by legions of newly enfranchised minorities, women, and immigrants. Furthermore, they believe these minorities all serve the "omnipotent" Jews, who control international economic and political life. "Heaven help the God-fearing, law-abiding Caucasian middle class," said actor and NRA spokesman Charlton Heston to a Christian Coalition convention, especially the "Protestant or even worse evangelical Christian, Midwest or Southern or even worse rural, apparently straight or even worse admittedly [straight], gun-owning or even worse [National Rifle Association] card-carrying average working stiff, or even worst of all, male working stiff. Because not only don't you count, you're a downright obstacle to social progress."[43]

Downwardly mobile rural white men—those who lost the family farms and those who expected to inherit them—are squeezed between the omnivorous jaws of capital concentration and a federal bureaucracy that at best is indifferent to their plight and at worst gives them a solid push down the slippery slope.


## Militia Ideology

Militia ideology reflects this squeeze yet cannot fully confront its causes. Rooted in heartland conservatism, the militias have no difficulty blaming the federal government for their ills, but they are less willing to blame capitalism. After all, in terms of capitalist economics, they are strong defenders of the self-made man,[44] and many have served in the armed forces defending the capitalist system that they believe ensures individual freedom. As a result, they must displace their potential criticism of capitalism onto another force that distorts and disfigures the pure capitalist impulse. Thus they combine racism, sexism, homophobia, and anti-Semitism into a rhetoric of emasculating "others" against whom the militias' fantasies of the restoration of American masculinity are played out.

The antigovernment position is central to the militia ideology. It is big government, not big capital, that is eroding Americans' constitutional rights. International economic arrangements, such as NAFTA (the North American Free Trade Agreement) and GATT (the General Agreement on Tariffs and Trade) are understood as politically disenfranchising white American workers. Recent governmental initiatives, such as the Brady Bill and the Crime Bill, which require a waiting period before handguns may be purchased and ban certain assault rifles, are seen as compromising the constitutional right to bear arms and are perceived as a threat to white men's ability to protect and defend their families. Gun control is seen as a further attempt by the government to emasculate white men. The 1993 FBI/ATF (Alcohol, Tobacco, and Firearms) shootout at the Branch Davidian compound in Waco, Texas, and the 1992 standoff and shootout with white separatist Randy Weaver at Ruby Ridge, Idaho (which resulted in the death of Weaver's wife and son), have further exacerbated distrust in the federal government.[45] Restrictions on the right to bear arms are perceived as just further steps in the government's attempt to disarm and eventually control all citizens, leading inevitably to a United Nations invasion and establishment of a totalitarian new world order.

Militia publications are replete with stories of government conspiracies, and many militia members believe that the U.S. government is working with international forces to control U.S. citizens. For example, some argue that black helicopters are spying on citizens, that monitoring devices are being implanted in newborns, that Hong Kong police forces are being trained in Montana to disarm U.S. citizens, and that markings on the back of road signs are secret codes to direct invading UN forces.[46] In response, militias have established "common-law courts"—self-appointed groups that usurp the authority of the law, stage their own trials, and issue their own legal documents.

In many respects, the militias' ideology reflects the ideologies of other fringe groups on the far right, from which they typically recruit and with which they overlap. While the militias may not be as overtly racist and anti-Semitic as some other white supremacist groups, many researchers have documented extensive links between the two.[47] For example, militias embrace white supremacist theories of the international Jewish conspiracy for world control. They likewise take their idiosyncratic reading of the Bible from Christian Identity groups, which hold that Jews are descendants of Satan (through Cain), that people of color are "pre-Adamic mud people," and that Aryans are the true people of God. Militia member Rodney Skurdal, for instance, uses Christian Identity theology to justify his refusal to pay taxes, arguing that if "we the white race are God's chosen people . . . and our Lord God stated that 'the earth is mine,' why are we paying taxes on 'His land'?"[48] And from all sides the militias take racism, homophobia, nativism, sexism, and anti-Semitism. Like antigovernment ideology, these discourses provide an explanation for militia members' feelings of thwarted entitlement and fix the blame squarely on "others" whom the state must now serve at the expense of white men.

Central to our analysis here is that the unifying theme of all these discourses, which have traditionally formed the rhetorical package Richard Hofstadter labeled "paranoid politics," is *gender*. Specifically, it is by framing state policies as emasculating and problematizing the masculinity of these various "others" that rural white militia members seek to restore their own masculinity. In this, militias can claim a long historical lineage. Since the early nineteenth century American manhood has pivoted around the status of breadwinner—the self-made man who supports his family by his own labor. The breadwinner is economically independent, king in his own castle, embedded in a political community of like-minded and equally free men. When this self-made masculinity has been threatened, one response from American men has been to exclude others from staking their own claim to manhood. Like the Sons of Liberty who threw off the British yoke of tyranny in 1776, these contemporary "patriots" see "R-2" (the second American Revolution) as restorative. Their goal is to reestablish traditional masculinity on the exclusion of others.

That such ardent patriots as militia members are so passionately antigovernment might strike the observer as contradictory. After all, are these not the same men who served their country in Vietnam or the Gulf War? Are these not the same men who believe so passionately in the American

Dream? Are they not the backbone of the Reagan Revolution? Indeed they are. As we have shown, militia members face the difficult theoretical task of maintaining their faith in America *and* in capitalism. Simultaneously they must aim to rationalize what seems at best an indifferent state, or at worst an actively interventionist one, coupled with contemporary versions of corporate capitalist logic that leave them, often literally, out in the cold.

It is through a decidedly gendered and sexualized rhetoric of masculinity that this contradiction between loving America and hating its government, loving capitalism and hating its corporate iterations, is resolved. First, like others on the far right, militia members believe the state has been captured by evil—even Satanic—forces; the original virtue of the American political regime has been deeply and irretrievably corrupted. In their view, environmental regulations, state policies dictated by urban and northern interests, and the Internal Revenue Service are the outcomes of a state now utterly controlled by feminists, environmentalists, blacks, and Jews.[49]

According to this logic, feminists have captured the welfare state, so that now, like all feminists and feminist institutions, it serves to emasculate white manhood. Several call for the repeal of the Thirteenth and Fourteenth Amendments, which eliminated slavery and provided equal protection for all.[50] One leader, John Trochman, argues that women must relinquish the right to vote and to own property.[51] Likewise, one book sold by the Militia of Montana, *Big Sister Is Watching You: Hillary Clinton and the White House Feminists Who Now Control America and Tell the President What to Do,* argues that during the Clinton era Hillary Clinton and her feminist co-conspirators were controlling the country and threatening Americans' rights and national sovereignty. The author, Texe Marrs, claims that "Big Sister" intends nothing short of a new world order, to be accomplished through a "10 Part Plan" that includes:

> the replacement of Christianity with feminist, new-age spirituality. . . . History will be rewritten, discarding our True heroes. . . . Homosexuality will be made noble, and the male-female relationship undesirable. . . . Patriotism will be smashed, while multiculturalism shall be exalted, and the masses will come to despise white, male dominated society as a throwback to the failed age of militarism and conflict. The masses shall be taught to revile nationalism, patriotism, and family . . . abortion and in-

fanticide . . . encouraged. . . . Women will dominate in all walks
of life—in law, medicine, literature, religion, economics, enter-
tainment, education, and especially in politics.[52]

In this vision, feminism, multiculturalism, homosexuality, and Chris-
tian-bashing are all tied together, part and parcel of the new world order.
On the other hand, Christianity, traditional history, heterosexuality, male
domination, white racial superiority and power, individualism, meritoc-
racy, and the value of individual hard work all describe the true America
that is at risk and must be protected. Because these facets are so closely
intertwined, multicultural textbooks, women in government, and legalized
abortion can all be taken as individual signs of the impending new world
order.

This text suggests several themes of interest to us here. The notion that
the state has been taken over means that it no longer acts in the interests
of "true" American men. The state is an engine of gender inversion, mas-
culinizing women through feminism and simultaneously feminizing
men. Feminist women, it turns out, are more masculine than men are.
Not only does this call the masculinity of white men into question, it uses
gender as the rhetorical vehicle for criticizing "other" men.

The militia movement is also strongly anti-Semitic. According to militia
logic, it is not capitalist corporations that have turned the government
against them but the international cartel of Jewish bankers and financiers,
media moguls, and intellectuals who have already taken over the United
States and turned it into a ZOG (Zionist-Occupied Government). The Wisconsin Militia's pamphlet *American Farmer: 20th Century Slave* explains
how banks have been foreclosing on farms because Jews, incapable of
farming themselves, had to control the world's monetary system to control
the global food supply.[53] "Is this what you work your fingers to the bone
for—to pay usury to a private group of bankers who make up the Fed?"
asks a militia publication, *Why a Bankrupt America?* Eustace Mullins, a
popular speaker on the militia circuit and author of the anti-Semitic *Secrets
of the Federal Reserve*, argues that militias are "the only organized threat to
the Zionists' absolute control of the [United States]."[54]

Since Jews are incapable of acting like real men—strong, hardy, virtuous manual workers and farmers—a central axiom of the international
Jewish conspiracy for world domination is their plan to "feminize White
men and to masculinize White women."[55] *The Turner Diaries* similarly de-

"The Aryan That Made a Man Out of 'Mac,'" from *W.A.R.* By permission.

scribes the "Jewish-liberal-democratic-equalitarian" perspective as "an essentially feminine, submissive worldview."[56] Embedded in this anti-Semitic libel is a critique of white American manhood as having already become soft, feminized, and weak—indeed, emasculated. According to *The Turner Diaries,* American men have lost the right to be free; slavery "is the just and proper state for a people who have grown soft."[57]

## Militias and Manhood

For the men involved in the militia movement, the militias offer a way to restore and revive American manhood—a manhood in which individual

white men control the fruits of their own labor and are not subject to the emasculation of Jewish-owned finance capital or a black- and feminist-controlled welfare state. This is the militarized manhood of the heroic John Rambo—a manhood that celebrates a God-sanctioned right to band together in armed militias if anyone (or any governmental agency) tries to take it away from them. If the state and capital emasculate them, and if the masculinity of "others" is problematic, then only "real White men" can rescue this American Eden from a feminized, multicultural, androgynous melting pot. The militias seek to reclaim their manhood gloriously, violently.

We conclude this article as we began it, with a cartoon from *W.A.R.* This deliberate parody of countless Charles Atlas advertisements shows the timid white ninety-seven-pound weakling finding his strength as a man through racial hatred. In the ideology of the white supremacist movement and its organized militia allies, racism enables white men to reclaim their manhood once again. The amorphous groups of white supremacists, skinheads, and neo-Nazis may be the symbolic shock troops of this movement, but the rural militias are their well-organized and highly regimented infantry. These men of the militia are the displaced sons of rural America, the Jeffersonian yeomen of the nineteenth century, disfigured by global restructuring and economic downturns. These are Reagan's rural children.

NOTES

1. Bonanno et al. (1994); Jobes (1997, 331).
2. Gouveia and Rousseau (1995).
3. Weis (1993).
4. Jobes (1997).
5. Dyer (1997, 61).
6. Lobao and Meyer (1995b, 6).
7. Davidson (1996, 118–19).
8. Lobao and Meyer (1995, 61). See also Hanson (1996).
9. M. Bell (1999).
10. Dyer (1997).
11. Gibson (1994, 11).
12. Junas (1995, 227).
13. Rand (1996).
14. Lamy (1996, 26).
15. The 1992 confrontation in rural Idaho between white separatist Randy Weaver and U.S. marshals and FBI agents resulted in the deaths of Weaver's wife and son. Department of Justice reports have since exposed government misconduct in the siege on Weaver's home.
16. Stern (1996, 78).
17. Coalition for Human Dignity (1995); Potok (1999).
18. Militia Watchdog website; Southern Poverty Law Center (1999).
19. Potok (2002).
20. Berlet and Lyons (1999).
21. Berlet and Lyons (1995, 24).
22. Southern Poverty Law Center (1999, 23).
23. Ibid., 20.
24. Corcoran (1997); Dyer (1997); Stern (1996); Stock (1996).

25. Potok (1999).

26. Stock (1996, 16).

27. Gibson (1994, 10).

28. Mazzochi and Rhinegaard (1991, 4).

29. Potok (1999).

30. Aho (1990); Linzer (1999).

31. O'Matz (1996).

32. Serrano (1990).

33. Dyer (1997, 63).

34. Junas (1995).

35. Potok (1999).

36. Walter and Wilson (1996); Jellison (1993).

37. Lobao and Meyer (1995b); Walter and Wilson (1996).

38. Southern Poverty Law Center (1999, 13).

39. Young (1990, 15).

40. Davidson (1996, 109).

41. Snipp (1996, 127, 122).

42. Davidson (1996, 120).

43. Citizens Project (1998/1999, 3).

44. Kimmel (1996).

45. Dees (1996); Southern Poverty Law Center (1997); Stern (1996).

46. Southern Poverty Law Center (1997).

47. Crawford and Burghart (1997, 190).

48. Stern (1996, 89).

49. Dyer (1997).

50. Stern (1996, 82).

51. Crawford and Burghart (1997); Stern (1996, 69).

52. Marrs (1993, 22–23).

53. Stern (1996, 120).

54. Mullins (n.d., 28).

55. *Racial Loyalty* (1991, 3).

56. Pierce (1978, 42).

57. Ibid., 33.

# 8

## Rural Men's Health: Situating Risk in the Negotiation of Masculinity

*Will H. Courtenay*

Early feminist scholars were among the first to explore the topics of gender and health. They identified, for example, the absence of female subjects in health research and the use of males as the standard measure in health matters.[1] These efforts have had a wide-ranging, positive influence on health outcomes and on the health sciences. But they have also resulted in an exclusive emphasis on women. "Gender and health" has now become synonymous with "women's health."[2] Health concerns associated with men's gender have remained largely unrecognized.

Although male bodies have provided the means for carrying out much of the past century's health science research, male patients are rarely studied *as men*. Aside from some theorists of the mid-1970s,[3] only a few contemporary researchers have examined the influence of men's gender—or masculinity—on men's health,[4] or on the health of specific populations, such as college men[5] or men in prison.[6] Still fewer researchers have examined the influence of masculinity on rural men's health.[7] Even in rural studies that address risks more common to men than to women, the discussion of men's greater risks and of the influence of men's gender on these risks is often conspicuously absent. Instead, the "gender" that is associated with greater risk remains unnamed.[8] The consistent, underlying presumption in medical literature—and rural health literature—is that masculinity and what it means to be a man in America have no bearing on how men work, drink, drive, fight, or take risks. Left unquestioned, men's shorter life span is often presumed to be "natural" and inevitable.

In this chapter I use a social-constructionist framework to examine the previously unexplored territory of rural men's health and to achieve two primary aims. First, I review available research regarding the health behaviors and risks of rural men and women and of various specific populations of men. Examining gender differences in social activities and experiences (as well as differences among men[9]) can be a valuable social-constructionist strategy. It illuminates the process by which biological sex is transformed into gender and demonstrates how power is negotiated and structured through everyday social actions.[10] Second, I discuss rural men's health beliefs and behavior as a form of gendered practice. I provide a conceptual and theoretical framework that shows how the social practices that undermine men's health are often signifiers of masculinity and the instruments men use in negotiating social power—not only in relation to women but also within hierarchies of men.

## Men's Health

In the United States[11] men die six years younger than women and are more likely to die from all ten leading causes of death.[12] Men are twice as likely as women to die of heart disease, and one and a half times more likely to die of cancer.[13] Men are also more likely than women to suffer from chronic conditions such as heart disease and hypertension,[14] and they start suffering from them at younger ages. Nearly three out of four people under age sixty-five who die of heart attacks are men.[15] Men's health, furthermore, shows few signs of improving. The cancer death rate[16] for men went up more than 20 percent during the second half of the 1900s, while cancer death rates for women remained unchanged.[17]

People who live in rural communities are generally at less risk of death than people who live in cities,[18] but there are some notable exceptions. Heart disease, the leading killer,[19] mostly kills people who live in rural or nonmetropolitan areas.[20] People who live in rural communities are generally less likely than nonrural people to develop most forms of cancer, the second-leading killer,[21] but farmers are among those at greatest risk for developing certain types of cancer, such as leukemia, non-Hodgkin's lymphoma, melanoma, and cancer of the brain.[22] Overall, even though rural men have lower death rates than nonrural men, they have more health problems than urban men.[23] Most significantly, rural men have higher death rates than rural women for all leading causes of death.[24] But why?

The health and longevity of rural populations are both strongly influenced by social factors such as access to care, economic status, and ethnicity. But neither these factors nor genetic and biologic circumstances can explain gender differences in longevity.[25] We can, however, explain some of the gender difference in mortality among rural populations in terms of health practices. Many large and prospective studies indicate that individual health practices are the most important factors influencing longevity;[26] an evaluation of thousands of research studies suggests that approximately half of all deaths could be prevented through changes in personal preventive health practices.[27] These and similar studies also reveal consistent gender differences. Men and boys are more likely than women and girls to engage in thirty controllable behaviors conclusively linked to a greater risk of disease, injury, and death[28]—a gender difference that remains true across a variety of ethnic groups.[29] Despite these findings, however, men's poor health practices are rarely addressed by health scientists. Consequently, we know little about *why* men adopt these unhealthy attitudes and behaviors.

## Rural Men's Behaviors and Health Beliefs, and the Associated Risks

Here I use both empirical and epidemiological studies from the health sciences to investigate rural men's health and health behavior as a form of gendered practice. This section reviews these studies, focusing on evidence of rural men's behaviors and health beliefs related to tobacco use, diet and physical activity, unintentional injuries, alcohol use, using health care and seeking help, social support, perceived susceptibility, and beliefs about manhood as well as the health risks associated with these behaviors and beliefs. Because research examining gender and the health behavior of rural populations is limited, this review incorporates data on a wide range of often diverse rural populations—such as nonmetropolitan and farm populations. Whenever possible, I make comparisons both with rural women and with men nationally, because constructionist theorists are as concerned with differences among men (and among women) as they are with differences between women and men.

### Tobacco Use

Men are more likely than women to smoke and to smoke heavily, which are leading causes of heart disease and cancer.[30] The greatest proportion of smokers lives in nonmetropolitan areas.[31] Among youth, rural Euro-American males smoke more often than any other group.[32] Smokeless tobacco use has nearly tripled since the 1970s.[33] Smokeless tobacco is used almost exclusively by men, most heavily by young, nonmetropolitan, and rural men; in one rural Oregon high school, one in three young men uses it.[34] Although most cancers occur late in life, oral cancers are increasingly diagnosed in younger persons,[35] and they kill nearly twice as many men as women.[36]

## Diet

Research consistently shows that men have less healthy diets than women and that this increases their risk for heart disease, cancer, and many chronic diseases.[37] Men eat less fiber and fewer fruits and vegetables than women, and more cholesterol and saturated fat. Among rural African Americans in North Carolina, being a woman is one of the two strongest predictors of fruit and vegetable consumption.[38] One large study of both rural and urban older adults in six New England states showed that dietary cholesterol intake was considerably higher than recommended levels, particularly among men.[39] Among rural African Americans in Virginia, low levels of high-density lipoproteins—"good" cholesterol—were found in one in four men, compared with only one in twenty women.[40] In the New England study, the men were also less likely than women to have diets that provided adequate levels of vitamins.

## Physical Activity

Physical inactivity also increases the risk of the leading killers (heart disease and cancer) as well as other chronic diseases.[41] Among rural men in Iowa, it has been found to be a risk factor for prostate cancer.[42] Although equal numbers of women and men nationally engage in little or no physical activity, among those aged thirty-five to fifty-four, the number is significantly higher for men.[43] Among rural Kansas couples, although men are more physically active overall than women, they are two and a half times more likely to be sedentary between the ages of forty-five and sixty-four.[44] As noted above, this is the age bracket in which men are at much greater risk than women for experiencing a deadly heart attack. Physical activity may differ between various ethnic groups. Among African Americans in rural Virginia, for instance, far more women than men are sedentary—although both women and men are less sedentary than African Americans nationally.[45]

The type and intensity of physical activity also influence health. Contrary to popular belief, women have made the most beneficial changes in their levels of physical activity in recent years.[46] One large study of residents in rural counties in New York found that although women and men did not differ in their level of physical activity, the women—like women nationally—were more likely than men to engage in light to moderate and aerobic exercise.[47] These are the types of exercise that health scientists now agree are the best for maintaining good health.[48]

## Unintentional Injuries

Unintentional injuries claim the lives of two and a half times more men than women and are the leading cause of death for men under forty-five.[49] Among fifteen- to twenty-four-year-olds, young men account for three out of every four deaths—75 percent of which are caused by unintentional injuries.[50] Among farm residents, men suffer the most injuries. About 2,400 of these injuries result in death each year, while another 400,000 are disabling.[51] Among rural adolescents, boys are far more likely than girls to suffer unintentional injuries,[52] primarily from their work or their reckless driving.

## Occupational Injuries and Deaths

In terms of occupation, the industries of agriculture, mining, construction, timber cutting, and fishing have the highest injury death rates, while transportation, farming, forestry, and fishing account for the largest number of total deaths from injury.[53] These jobs are often performed by rural men. In one study, 83 percent of Wisconsin residents who suffered agricultural injuries were men.[54] In New Mexico, the occupational injury death rate for farm workers is four times higher than that for nonfarm workers, and, among farm workers, the death rate is four times higher for men than for women.[55] Most occupational injury deaths are motor vehicle–related.[56]

## Motor Vehicle Injuries and Deaths

Motor vehicle–related fatalities account for more than half of all unintentional injury deaths,[57] and the death rate for motor vehicle crashes is twice as high for men as for women.[58] Most of these deaths occur in rural areas.[59] Rural drivers in Michigan have a 96 percent higher risk of dying in a motor vehicle crash than nonrural drivers.[60] Among adults over sixty-four in rural Iowa, the risk of a motor vehicle crash is 60 percent higher for men than for women.[61] In Colorado, unintentional injury death rates are higher among rural than urban youth, and significantly higher for motor vehicle–related deaths. Among rural youth aged five to fourteen, motor vehicle death rates are from one and a half to two times higher for boys than for girls, while death rates for other unintentional injuries are thirteen to twenty-eight times higher for boys.[62]

Gender differences in the number of miles driven do not explain gender differences in motor vehicle–related deaths, but poor driving habits do.[63] For example, men are less likely than women to wear safety belts, while 96 percent of all those charged with drunk driving are men.[64] Compared with drivers in all other rural crashes, operators of farm vehicles—who are mostly men—have a greater proportion of convictions for driving while intoxicated.[65] Similarly, compared with urban teenagers, rural Iowan teenagers are less likely to use front safety belts or helmets, and young men are less likely than women to wear back safety belts or moped helmets.[66] In Mississippi, rural adolescent males are less likely than females to use safety belts.[67] One rural trauma center in West Virginia reported that 80 percent of the patients who required hospitalization from motor vehicle accidents had not used safety belts.[68] Consequently, the severity of injuries was 34 percent higher for unbelted than for belted drivers, and their need for extended care after leaving the center was 97 percent higher.

*Alcohol Use*

Both the quantity and the frequency of alcohol consumption are higher among men than among women.[69] Although alcohol use is generally less common among nonmetropolitan adults than it is among adults nationally, this is not true for those under age twenty-six.[70] Additionally, heavy drinking—five and a half times more common among men than women—is equally prevalent among metropolitan and nonmetropolitan adults.[71] Among rural Kansas couples, women are more likely than men to drink moderately or not at all.[72] Among rural adolescents, findings are equally consistent: boys are far more likely than girls to drink alcohol, to drink more often, to experience problems related to drinking, and to start drinking at a young age.[73] Researchers of one large Mississippi study found that gender differences in problem drinking among rural adolescents were particularly pronounced in ethnic minority groups. Compared with girls, problem drinking was one and a half times higher for Euro-American boys, nearly three times higher for African American boys, and five times higher for boys of "other" ethnicities.[74]

Men's alcohol use contributes significantly to their risk of disease, injury, and death. Findings from one rural trauma center revealed that nearly twice as many male as female trauma patients had been drinking (52 percent compared with 29 percent).[75] Most injuries suffered by eighth-grade students in another rural Maryland study were associated with both risky behavior and alcohol use, and most of the injured students were boys.[76] Furthermore, one Illinois study found that among rural adolescents who drank (predominantly young men), those who drank while driving also drank more often.[77]

## Using Health Care and Seeking Help

Men use fewer health care services than women,[78] a gender difference not explained by health status, access to care, income, or health insurance coverage. We can explain this discrepancy, however, by looking at men's attitudes toward seeking help. Men are less willing and have less intention than women to seek help when they need it.[79] Among rural people, men and boys are less likely than women and girls to be receptive to help, to seek support, or to visit a physician.[80] In any given year, farm and nonfarm women are equally likely to have had a medical checkup, while farm men are less likely than nonfarm men to have had one.[81] Farmers may be even less inclined than other rural men to seek help. In one study of Wisconsin residents who had suffered agricultural injuries—most of whom were men—farm residents were the most likely to delay seeking health care. Half of them waited for more than two hours. One in four of these farm residents waited more than twenty-four hours—twice the number of nonfarm residents who did so.[82] In Tennessee, more than half of farmers (compared with one-third of nonfarmers) reported waiting for emotional problems to go away rather than seeking support.[83] But often these problems do not simply disappear. Suicide among rural men is extraordinarily high, ranging from three to five times higher than national averages.[84]

## Social Support

Research consistently shows that men have smaller social networks than women, and that lacking social relationships is a risk factor for death—especially for men.[85] These findings remain true among rural residents. A twenty-year longitudinal study of rural older adults in Missouri showed that levels of social support predicted longevity and simultaneously revealed that men had less extensive networks and less frequent contact with friends than women.[86] Rural men who have never married have a 50 percent greater risk of death than married rural men.[87] Researchers have also found that depression is more common among farmers who have small families[88] and few friends nearby.[89]

## Perceived Susceptibility to Risk

While men are more susceptible than women to a variety of health problems, they are also more likely than women to believe they are not at risk for these problems.[90] With rare exceptions, people who think they are invulnerable take fewer precautions with their health—and thus have greater health risks—than people who recognize their vulnerability.[91] Young rural men and boys have been found to express significantly fewer concerns or fears than young rural women and girls about a variety of health problems.[92] Rural men are also less likely than women to report fearing crime,[93] even though rural men are most likely to experience all forms of crime (except rape).[94] One study that examined perceived risk of skin cancer among male farmers and their spouses found that 53 percent of men, compared with 45 percent of women, thought it was likely they would develop skin cancer in the future.[95] While this suggests that many farmers are aware of their increased risk of skin cancer, these percentages do not reflect that men are twice as likely as women to develop this disease.[96]

## Beliefs About Manhood

Empirical research increasingly provides compelling evidence that men who endorse dominant norms of masculinity—such as the belief that "a man should be physically tough even if he's not big"—adopt fewer health-promoting behaviors and have greater health risks than men who do not hold such beliefs.[97] Unfortunately, there is only one similar type of study of rural men: among male Canadian farmers, several dominant norms of masculinity have been found to have strong, if indirect, effects on farming-related accidents. Farmers who endorsed these norms, moreover, were more likely to minimize the likelihood of a farming accident resulting in injuries.[98] However, a study of national data examining gender indicated that southerners—particularly men and rural dwellers—held the most traditional views about gender.[99] We can extrapolate from these findings that rural men—at least those in southern states—have greater health risks because they endorse these beliefs. In fact, the leading killer, heart disease, is indeed most common among people in the nonmetropolitan South.[100] Among middle-aged white Americans, men in the nonmetropolitan South are nearly twice as likely to suffer from heart disease as men in the metropolitan Northeast.[101]

*Summary*

This review provides us with a preliminary profile of rural men's health behavior. Although limited, these data suggest that, like men in general, rural men have less healthy lifestyles than rural women. In some cases, rural men are also at greater risk than nonrural men. Overall, we can identify three behavioral risk factors more common in rural men than in either rural women or nonrural men: tobacco use; behaviors that lead to unintentional injuries (such as reckless driving); and reluctance to seek help or use health care. These three factors alone have an enormous influence on the health and well-being of rural men. Smoking is the single most preventable cause of illness and death, and car crashes—which kill twice as many men as women each day—are the leading cause of death from unintentional injury.[102] Similarly, underuse of health services and delays in obtaining timely health care can have profoundly negative consequences for men's health.[103] In terms of their health-related beliefs, compared with either rural women or nonrural men, rural men hold the most traditional attitudes about gender and masculinity—attitudes that have been linked with increased health risks. Four additional behavioral risk factors are more common among rural men than rural women: poor diet, heavy drinking, limited social support, and perceived insusceptibility to risk.

## Masculinity and Rural Men's Health

Clearly, rural men are at increased risk relative to rural women and some nonrural men because of their unhealthy practices. What remains unclear is why rural men adopt beliefs and behaviors that undermine their health. To explore this question, this section examines four critical topics: health practices as gendered social action; the association between masculinity and the individual health practices of rural men; the cultural dictates and everyday interactions that shape gendered health practices used in the structuring of social power; and the interaction between masculinity and other social structures influencing men's health.

### Health Practices as Gendered Social Action

From a social-constructionist perspective, gender is not something that individuals possess. Although it is often experienced as something deeply personal, masculinity is a social system or structure—or more specifically, multiple structures. Masculinity organizes daily life and social relations and shapes institutions such as rural governance,[104] agricultural industries,[105] and rural health care systems. Gendered social structures facilitate some men's access to positions of power and dominance (for example, physicians and farm managers) and frequently relegate women to subordinate roles (for example, nurses and housewives). Masculinity is also a way of structuring social practices—both the practices of individual men and the practices of groups of men. Many of these social practices significantly influence the health and well-being of men and boys, whether these are health care practices or the practices of sport, farming, and other forms of labor.

Previous explanations of the damaging health effects of masculinity have focused primarily on the hazardous influences of "*the* male sex role."[106] But men and boys are not passive victims of a singular, socially prescribed gender role, nor are they simply conditioned by their cultures. Rather, they are actors—active agents—in their own socialization, generating a *variety* of male "roles" that variously influence their health. Similarly, masculinity traditionally has been seen as originating in each man's individual psychology. For social constructionists, however, gender does not reside in the person, but rather in social transactions defined as gendered:

it is a dynamic "set of socially constructed relationships, which are produced and reproduced through people's actions."[107]

The activities in which men and women engage, and their gendered
ideas and beliefs, operate as "currency" in the continual transactions that
construct and demonstrate gender. Gender is "something that one does,
and does recurrently, in interaction with others."[108] It is achieved through
"sustained social performances."[109] Health practices—like language,[110]
work,[111] sports,[112] sex,[113] and crime[114]—become resources in negotiating
and reconstructing gender.[115] The ways in which women and men think
about health, and the social practices in which they engage that affect their
physical well-being, are signifiers of gender that simultaneously reinforce
and reproduce gender differences. By either rejecting or embracing
healthy practices, women and men are constructing gender.

The use of health practices to define oneself as a woman or a man—
unlike the presumably innocent effects of wearing lipstick or a tie—has a
profound effect on one's health and longevity. Many men and boys define
masculinity *against* positive health behaviors and beliefs. When a man
brags, "I haven't been to a doctor in years," or "I can drink and drive!" he
is simultaneously describing a health practice and situating himself in a
masculine arena. In this way, men's health risks are both a function of,
and a means of securing, socially dominant forms of masculinity.

## Health Practices and Rural Masculinities

Growing up on a farm, many rural boys learn that to demonstrate masculinity successfully they must adopt risky or unhealthy behaviors such as
operating heavy equipment before they are old enough to do so safely. As
one rural man said, "If you're over 10, you'd better be out doing men's
work, driving a tractor and that kind of thing";[116] while another said, "My
brother Tony and I started driving the pickup on the farm at age six, as
soon as we could reach the pedals. We also learned how to drive a tractor."[117] These gendered practices help to explain the extraordinarily high
rate of motor vehicle injuries and deaths among rural adolescent boys.
Other gendered practices of rural men are closely associated with risk.
According to one rural man: "If you were a guy . . . you were born to be a
total, typical, straight male—to play sports, to hunt, to do everything a guy
was supposed to do."[118] In performing these particular gendered social
practices, men sustain most of the estimated 3 million to 5 million annual

sports injuries and the 1,132 nonfatal and 139 fatal hunting injuries that occur each year.[119]

Social norms of rural masculinity—or "the rural masculine"[120]—dictate how rural men should perform gender. Imagery of the rural masculine, for example, "has implications for the concrete practices of the masculine rural, by providing widely recognized cultural categories of appropriate masculinity."[121] Much of this imagery also has implications for rural men's health, such as the influence of the Marlboro cowboy on the high rates of smoking among rural men. The rural media consistently portray farmers as rugged, strong, and tough.[122] Not surprisingly, the vast majority of Pennsylvania residents believe that farmers *"embody the virtues of inde-pendence and self-sufficiency"* (emphasis added).[123] As we have seen, many male farmers construct this idealized masculinity and consequently undermine their health by not seeking the social support or health care they need. Unquestioned social norms—such as notions about men's in-vulnerability—can have powerful indirect influences on men's health. For example, although rural young men have a higher risk of injury and death due to heavy drinking than nonrural men and young rural women, parents are more likely to disapprove of their adolescent daughters' drinking than that of their sons.[124]

Performing gendered health practices inextricably involves men's bod-ies, which are used as vehicles in negotiating the landscape of rural mascu-linities. Social norms—such as the rural masculine depicted in the media—dictate how the body should be used. Typically, the rugged, tough bodies of male farmers are portrayed with tensed muscles, accentuated veins, clenched fists, and flexed biceps.[125] Gender is signified through em-bodied enactments of these muscular portrayals and through the ways in which gender is inscribed on the body. Kathleen Long provides a vivid example of this gendered marking in describing a farmer who caught his finger in farming equipment while harvesting his wheat field. He pulled his finger out—severing it—then wrapped his hand in a handkerchief and finished his work before seeking medical care.[126]

Rural men construct a variety of masculinities—ethnic, professional, and farm masculinities, to name a few—that variously influence their health. The specific ways in which the body is used and the specific health practices employed by rural men in constructing masculinity are patterned by a variety of social structures and available resources. For a rural college baseball player, smokeless tobacco is a readily accessible and socially normative signifier of athletic masculinity. Likewise, for many hunters, alcohol is a ubiquitous prop in performing rural masculinity. Alternatively, a rural businessman may eat mostly high-fat restaurant food and engage in excessive drinking and smoking, while a rural farmer may drive recklessly and fail to "pamper" his body by getting sufficient sleep. However, because neither masculinity nor a man's demonstration of manhood are static, the same man may enact gender differently in different contexts—prohibiting himself from displaying pain at work or in front of drinking buddies, perhaps, but permitting himself to do so at home or with his wife.

In defining and operationalizing the health of "rural men," we run the risk of normalizing rural men's experiences and universalizing their risks. With increasing diversity in rural settings, however, it is apparent that rural men do not represent a homogeneous group.[127] There are often enormous health disparities among populations of men, which vary depending on their ethnic identity, marital status, social class, education, income, age, participation in the labor force, sexual orientation, and religious affiliation.[128] The health and health practices of rural men who are economically, socially, and politically disadvantaged can differ greatly from those of other rural men. To understand the basis for these disparities and the broader contexts in which men's health practices are displayed, we need to examine power and social inequality.

## Gender, Power, and Health Practices

Gender is negotiated through relationships of power. Microlevel power practices[129] contribute to structuring the social transactions of everyday life—transactions that help to sustain and reproduce broader social structures of power and inequality. Among other social practices, power relationships are located and constituted in the demonstration of health practices. Gendered health practices are used in patterning these social relationships and are used by men in negotiating their status and establishing their ranking in the hierarchy of men.

Among rural men, dominant masculinities subordinate lower-status, marginalized masculinities, such as those of gay men and "hillbillies." The male body is central to this structuring of gender and power. Rather than allow themselves to be relegated to a lower-status position, for instance, rural gay men may negotiate their status by engaging their bodies in physically dominant or aggressive behaviors; as one rural gay man put it, "I really hated football, but I tried to play because it would make me more of a man."[130] Researchers examining injuries among rural adolescent youth found that physically underdeveloped boys were among those at greater risk, and concluded that these boys may take unnecessary risks or pick fights to prove their manhood because they feel defensive about their size.[131] Playing fields, local bars, country roads, farms, hunting and recreational areas, and rodeo stadiums are all sites where the male body is enlisted to legitimize dominant forms of masculinity.

Disadvantages resulting from such factors as ethnicity, class, geography, educational level, and sexual orientation marginalize certain men. These men may attempt to compensate for their subordinated status by adopting hypermasculine beliefs and behaviors, or oppositional[132] or compensatory[133] forms of masculinity. Risk taking, physical dominance, minimization of risk, and rejection of health-protective behaviors are readily accessible resources and forms of social action for men who may otherwise have limited ways in which to construct masculinity. Dominant beliefs about masculinity are another readily accessible resource. In fact, men's endorsement of these beliefs is associated with lower educational levels, nonprofessional occupational status, lower income, African American ethnicity, and sexual orientation that is not exclusively heterosexual.[134]

Men also use other health beliefs, such as the minimization of and perceived insusceptibility to risk, as means of successfully performing and securing hegemonic masculinity. In a study of rural men's pub drinking in New Zealand, Hugh Campbell found that the successful performance of masculinity required men to retain fine motor coordination after drinking a lot, and that "highly disciplined and controlled men derided inept drinkers for 'drinking like girls.'"[135] Like the Canadian farmers in the study discussed above, it is likely that these "controlled" rural drinkers misperceive their actual risk.[136] In a unique study of drinking and diving, researchers found progressive and significant impairment of diving performance when divers' blood alcohol level reached just .04 percent—the level that the average man would have after drinking only two cans of beer in one hour.[137] The male divers themselves, however, were not aware of either their progressive impairment in diving performance or their increased risk of injury.[138] "Controlled drinkers" dismiss the high risks associated with their heavy drinking and ridicule "inept" drinkers as a means of situating themselves in positions of dominance in the hierarchy of men. This kind of gender performance not only reifies normative masculinity but simultaneously fosters the continuous reproduction of the marginal-ized or lower-status masculinities necessary to support the dominant norm.

Adopting healthy practices requires that men cross gendered bound-aries. The demonstration of even one healthy behavior—such as using sunscreen—can contradict, and require a man to dismiss, multiple con-structions of masculinity that would relegate him to the status of femi-nized masculinities. Farmers, who are heavily exposed to the sun, are at increased risk for skin cancers of all kinds,[139] which represent the most rapidly increasing form of cancer.[140] Men's lack of sun protection is a major contributor to their high risk of melanoma, which kills twice as many men as women.[141] Despite their risk, most Wisconsin dairy farmers do not use sun protection.[142] Among rural Michigan farmers, only 40 per-cent of men, compared with 65 percent of women, protect themselves from the sun.[143] The application of sunscreen as one form of sun protec-tion requires farmers to reject a variety of social constructions of gender: men are unconcerned about health matters; men are invulnerable to dis-ease; the application of lotions to the body is feminine; men do not "pam-per" or "fuss" over their bodies; and "rugged good looks" are achieved by getting a tan. In fact, one and a half times more men than women nation-ally believe that people look better with tans.[144] By not using sunscreen, a farmer is using a poor health practice to demonstrate endorsement of numerous social constructions of gender.

As several of these examples illustrate, it is not only the endorsement of masculine ideals but also the rejection, or negation,[145] of feminine signi-fiers of gender that contributes to the construction of masculinities and to the structuring of power. Rural men and boys who attempt to engage in social practices demonstrating feminine norms of gender risk being rele-gated to the subordinated masculinity of "wimp" or "sissy." A gay man who grew up on Indiana farms said he would have been ridiculed as a "sissy" had he done the tasks of cooking, baking, and sewing that he pre-ferred: "My uncle would have started it and it would have spread out from there. Even my grandfather would say, 'Oh, you don't want to do that. That's girl stuff.'"[146] I have demonstrated elsewhere that positive health practices are signifiers of idealized femininity.[147] They are, therefore, po-tentially subordinating influences that men must oppose with varying de-grees of force, depending on which other resources are accessible—or are already being used—in the construction of their masculinity. Disregarding risk and dismissing health care needs are means of rejecting "girl stuff." A man's visit to a bar instead of a rural health clinic, therefore, becomes a mode of signification through which gender is enacted.

Denial of physical or emotional discomfort is another means of demonstrating difference from women and from "weaker" men, who are believed to embody this "feminine" characteristic. Emotional stoicism is a performative signifier of masculinity. In the words of one rural man, "Geared toward being strong, silent and tough, I accumulated lots of layers as I went along. I didn't *feel* tough at all, but I certainly created a veneer for myself."[148] This and other public displays of robust masculine health and vitality serve to conceal—in the sense that Judith Butler uses this term— the contradiction that men are at greater risk than women for chronic disease, injury, and death.[149] Such performances render invisible the fact— based on most health indices—that men are the more vulnerable, if not the weaker, sex. These sleights of hand reinforce the social constructions that men are more powerful and less vulnerable than women; that men's bodies are structurally more efficient than and superior to women's bodies; that asking for help and caring for one's health are feminine; and that the most powerful men are those to whom health and safety are irrelevant.

## Interaction Between Masculinity and Other Social Structures

The social structures that women and men encounter elicit different demonstrations of health practices and provide different opportunities to conduct this particular form of gendered practice. Rural men and boys are constantly participating in dynamic relationships with social systems such as families, schools, churches, bars, and agricultural agencies, where their lives are structured by a broad range of material, political, religious, institutional, ideological, and cultural factors. These systems and social structures either foster or restrict the adoption of particular beliefs and behaviors that influence health.

By and large, social and institutional structures foster poor health practices among men and undermine men's attempts to adopt healthier habits[150]—a rural health care system that largely ignores men's gendered health care needs is but one example. Men and boys in the few countries where state or national rural men's health policies have been adopted, such as Australia,[151] may develop different health perceptions, beliefs, and practices than rural men in countries (such as the United States) that lack such policies.

Economic structures also profoundly influence health and shape rural men's health and health practices. Economically disadvantaged men have the worst health of any population.[152] Class systems and the structure of economic markets expose those working-class men involved in manual labor to a range of occupational health and safety hazards—one explanation for why men constitute 56 percent of the workforce yet account for 94 percent of fatal injuries on the job.[153] Rural working-class men labor in jobs that require the use of dangerous equipment, such as heavy machinery, and jobs that expose them to hazardous chemicals—construction, agriculture, oil and gas extraction, water transportation, and forestry.[154]

Relationships among various institutionalized social structures—such as governments, the military, corporations, the media, judicial systems, and health care systems—further mediate the health of men. The dynamic interplay of these institutional structures and other social structures (such as those related to ethnicity, economics, and gender) results in different opportunities for, and constraints on, realizing optimal health. The risks of rural working-class men, for example, are compounded by the interaction of various structural factors, such as limited or poorly implemented occupational health and safety policies, lack of health insurance coverage, limited financial resources for health care, substandard living conditions, and limited geographic access to health services.

In closing, it is important to note that these social and institutional structures are not simply imposed on men, any more than a prescribed male sex role is imposed on men: "Social structures do not exist autonomously from humans; rather . . . as we engage in social action, we simultaneously help create the social structures that facilitate/limit social practice."[155] Definitions of gender influence social structures, which guide human interactions and social practices, which in turn reinforce gendered social structures and the notion of gender as difference. Men and masculinity are complicit in shaping rural health care systems, and reinscribing rural health policy, in ways that ignore men's gendered health concerns. Indeed, men are often the very researchers and scientists who have ignored the subject of rural men's health. Such masculine-gendered patterning of social structures is what Hugh Campbell and Michael Bell term "the masculine rural."[156]

Men sustain and reproduce social structures—and the masculine rural—in part for the privileges they derive from preserving them. Similarly, rural men who work tirelessly, deny their stress, and dismiss their physical needs for health care also do so, in part, because they expect to be rewarded with money, power, respect in their communities, and reassurance that they are rugged, self-sufficient, "self-made" men. Men who achieve hegemonic ideals by engaging in poor health practices are often compensated with social acceptance, with diminished anxiety about their manhood, and with the rewards that such normative demonstrations of masculinity provide in their rural communities. In constructing these exemplary rural masculinities, however, men simultaneously recreate the social structures that limit the forms of social action necessary for good health.

NOTES

1. Courtenay (2000b).

2. Bayne-Smith (1996).

3. Goldberg (1976); Harrison (1978).

4. Courtenay (1998a, 2001a); Courtenay and Keeling (2000); Eisler (1995); Sabo and Gordon (1995).

5. Courtenay (1998b).

6. Courtenay and Sabo (2001).

7. Harrell (1986).

8. Donnermeyer and Park (1995).

9. Courtenay (2000b).

10. Crawford (1995).

11. Unless otherwise noted, all studies and statistics refer to people in the United States.

12. Department of Health and Human Services (2000).

13. Ibid.

14. Verbrugge and Wingard (1987).

15. American Heart Association (1994).

16. Women outlive men, so the female population as a whole is older than the male population as a whole. To account for this difference when comparing female and male deaths, health scientists use data that have been age adjusted.

These age-adjusted figures are referred to as "death rates."

17. American Cancer Society (1994).

18. Hayward, Pienta, and McLaughlin (1997).

19. Department of Health and Human Services (2000).

20. Gillum (1994); Pearson and Lewis (1998).

21. Monroe, Ricketts, and Savitz (1992).

22. Blair and Zahm (1991).

23. Hayward, Pienta, and McLaughlin (1997).

24. Hessler et al. (1995); Smith et al. (1995).

25. Courtenay (2000a).

26. Woolf, Jonas, and Lawrence (1996).

27. United States Preventive Services Task Force (1996).

28. Courtenay (2000a).

29. Courtenay, McCreary, and Merighi (2002).

30. Department of Health and Human Services (1997); United States Preventive Services Task Force (1996).

31. Department of Health and Human Services (1997).

32. Sarvela, Cronk, and Isberner (1997).

33. Centers for Disease Control (1993b).

34. Department of Health and Human Services (1997); McKnight, Koetke, and Mays (1995); Nelson et al. (1996); Salehi and Elder (1995).

35. National Cancer Institute (1991).

36. American Cancer Society (1994).

37. Courtenay (2000a); United States Preventive Services Task Force (1996).

38. McClelland et al. (1998).

39. Posner et al. (1994).

40. Willems et al. (1997).

41. United States Preventive Services Task Force (1996).

42. Cerhan et al. (1997).

43. Centers for Disease Control (1993a).

44. Holcomb (1992).

45. Willems et al. (1997).

46. Caspersen and Merritt (1995).

47. Courtenay (2000a); Eaton et al. (1994).

48. Courtenay (2000a).

49. Department of Health and Human Services (2000).

50. Ibid.

51. National Safety Council (1994).

52. Alexander et al. (1995).

53. Courtenay (2000a); National Safety Council (1994).

54. Stueland et al. (1995).

55. Crandall et al. (1997).

56. National Safety Council (1994).

57. Ibid.

58. Department of Health and Human Services (2000).

59. National Safety Council (1994).

60. Maio et al. (1992).

61. Foley, Wallace, and Eberhard (1995).

62. Hwang, Stallones, and Keefe (1997).

63. Courtenay (2000a).

64. Ibid.

65. Gerberich et al. (1996).

66. Schootman et al. (1993).

67. Pope et al. (1994).

68. Sokolosky et al. (1993).

69. Courtenay (2000a).

70. Department of Health and Human Services (1997).

71. Ibid.

72. Holcomb (1992).

73. Department of Health and Human Services (1997); Donnermeyer and Park (1995); Felton et al. (1996); Gibbons et al. (1986); Pope et al. (1994); Sarvela and McClendon (1988).

74. Pope et al. (1994).

75. Ankney et al. (1998).

76. Alexander et al. (1995).

77. Donnermeyer and Park (1995).

78. Courtenay (2000a, 2003).

79. Ibid.

80. Cook and Tyler (1989); Dansky et al. (1998); Hoyt et al. (1997); Sorensen (1994).

81. Muldoon, Schootman, and Morton (1996).

82. Stueland et al. (1995).

83. Linn and Husaini (1987).

84. Stamm (2003).

85. Courtenay (2000a).

86. Hessler et al. (1995).

87. Smith et al. (1995).

88. Belyea and Lobao (1990).

89. Linn and Hasaini (1987).

90. Courtenay (2000a).

91. Ibid.

92. Davidson et al. (1989); Weiler (1997).

93. Krannich, Berry, and Greider (1989).

94. Bachman (1992).

95. Rosenman et al. (1995).

96. Courtenay (2000a).

97. Courtenay (2000c, 2002, 2003).

98. Harrell (1986).

99. Rice and Coates (1995).

100. Gillum (1994).

101. Ibid.

102. Courtenay (2000a).

103. Courtenay (2000a, 2003).

104. Little and Jones (2000).

105. Liepins (2000).

106. Goldberg (1976); Harrison (1978).

107. Gerson and Peiss (1985, 327).

108. West and Zimmerman (1987, 140).

109. Butler (1990, 180).

110. Crawford (1995); Perry, Turner, and Sterk (1992).

111. Connell (1995a).

112. Messner and Sabo (1994).

113. Vance (1995).

114. Messerschmidt (1993).

115. Courtenay (2000b, 2002).

116. Fellows (1996, 173).

117. Ibid., 305.

118. Ibid., 307.

119. Courtenay (2000a); National Safety Council (1994).

120. Campbell and Bell (2000).

121. Ibid., 540–41.

122. Liepins (2000).

123. Willits, Bealer, and Timbers (1990).

124. Pope et al. (1994).

125. Liepins (2000).

126. Long (1993).

127. Hoyt et al. (1997).

128. Courtenay (2001b, 2002, 2003).

129. Pyke (1996).

130. Fellows (1996, 40).

131. Alexander et al. (1995).

132. Messerschmidt (1993).

133. Pyke (1996).

134. Courtenay (1998a).

135. Campbell (2000).

136. Harrell (1986).

137. Perrine, Mundt, and Weiner (1994).

138. Ibid.

139. Blair and Zahm (1991).

140. Courtenay (2000a).

141. Ibid.

142. Marlenga (1995).

143. Rosenman et al. (1995).

144. American Academy of Dermatology (1997).

145. Campbell (2000).

146. Fellows (1996, 12).

147. Courtenay (2000a, 2000c).

148. Fellows (1996, 13).

149. Butler (1993).

150. Courtenay (2000b).

151. Blackwell (2001).

152. Courtenay (2003).

153. Courtenay (2000a).

154. Ibid.

155. Messerschmidt (1993, 62).

156. Campbell and Bell (2000).

# PART 2
## Representations

If we accept conventional ideas about masculinity, we accept that real men don't eat quiche. They eat red meat, preferably meat they caught and killed themselves. Real men don't wear sandals. They wear boots, and they're not afraid of getting dirty or acquiring a few bumps and bruises, as they ride broncos and work the land. Real men don't ask for directions. Like the tracker or scout, they are always self-sufficient in choosing a path through the wilderness of life. These common images of a stereotypical masculinity may tell us little about any actual man, but they point to a sociologically significant feature of the imagined real man: in many important and resonant instances, he is a *rural* man.

In order to examine the interconnections between the rural and the masculine that create the power and persistence of such images, it is helpful to contrast the *masculine in the rural* and the *rural in the masculine*—or what we could more efficiently call the *masculine rural* and the *rural masculine*. To study the masculine rural is to explore, as the chapters in the first section of this book do, how masculine practice takes place in specifically rural sites. To study the rural masculine, however, is to explore how rural images, ideas, and representations influence *all* masculinities—both rural and urban. In this next section of the book, the authors focus on this second task.

But we need to introduce a note of analytic caution here. While the distinction between the masculine rural and the rural masculine is useful in conceptualizing the study of rural masculinities, it is, like most dualisms, something that we must quickly move past when we encounter the messy realities of our gendered lives. After all, as soon as we recognize that symbolic rurality influences *all* masculinities, some examples of the rural in the masculine turn out to be exactly the same as examples of the masculine in the rural. When Kevin Costner portrays a particular kind of rural masculinity in films like *Open Country*, for example, the viewers of that film are *both* urban and rural. Thus the practices of masculinity among rural people are no less informed by the rural tone of much masculine imagery than the practices of masculinity among urban people: both are open to the ideological power of rural concepts, ideas, and representations. Thus the masculine practices of the farmer on the tractor (whether that farmer is male or female) are imagined as much as they are enacted. Both Costner's audience and the tractor-driving farmer simultaneously demonstrate the masculine rural and the rural masculine.

Recognizing this point does not invalidate the dualism of the rural masculine and the masculine rural. Rather, it highlights the kinds of explanatory and theoretical readjustment we have to make to move beyond simply associating the way we "do" gender with the way we behave in particular social sites. While both gender and the rural unarguably have concrete dimensions linked to space and place, they also both have symbolic qualities that float free of particular social settings and can be consumed and reproduced in a variety of ways and at a variety of sites.

If this sounds like a recipe for analytical chaos and confusion, let us assure you that the following chapters demonstrate the exact opposite!

The first chapter, by David Bell, provides an intense and vibrant portrayal of the ways in which gay masculinity and rurality can be co-constructed. Bell not only spans the wide emotional distance between the charms of urban faerie movement rituals and the brutality of Matt Shepard's murder, he also does what all good analysts should: opens up social sites that were previously invisible or ignored by the average reader. As he shows, behind the heterosexual hegemonies of rural representation operate multiple and varied worlds of gay and rural masculinities. After reading this chapter, you won't be surprised to visit the International Gay Rodeo Association website and discover that—as of 2005—it had twenty-four regional chapters across the United States and Canada.

The following chapter, by Jo Little, provides the perfect complement, exploring the comfortable, unthreatening side of heterosexual hegemony in rural regions. Little explores the "work" of making heterosexuality and the ways in which rural people construct family life. Through three vignettes of country initiatives aimed at creating "unscary" heterosexuality in the countryside, she examines the need to civilize rural men into domestic, heterosexual, and stable family lives, and how far such projects can go in achieving this aim.

Unarguably, one of the key sites at which masculinities are represented and reproduced is the media, and two of our chapters directly target the ways in which the media reinforces some versions of rural masculinity while rendering others invisible. Robin Law analyzes the "Southern Man" beer advertising campaign in New Zealand. In this study she outlines a clear method for examining the specific "slants" of media activity and carries through an analysis of the multiple processes that eventually end up privileging one particular version of masculinity. Berit Brandth and Marit Haugen employ the same approach in their chapter on Norwegian forestry. They examine transitions over time within representations of forestry men in a Norwegian industry magazine to show that while the content of forestry's hegemonic version of masculinity subtly shifts, the underlying power of the men does not.

So this section introduces the reader to urban faeries, heterosexual vigilantes, naked elderly women in rural England, a love train coming to rescue lonely bachelors (perhaps all aspiring Southern Men) in rural New Zealand, and the triumph of the organizational man in the Norwegian forestry industry (a subtle balance of wielding a chainsaw and fighting battles in the boardroom). One compelling set of images remains: Rachel Woodward's examination of the discourse of the "warrior hero" in British army training. This military "he-man" conquers nature, survives ordeals in the wilderness, and rises from his *swamp de passage* in order to protect and save idyllic rural England. Then he gets posted to patrol a city in Iraq.

All these representations of the rural and the masculine exhibit the power of gender and the power of how we define the rural. Each author foregrounds the politics of sexuality, gender, and place in his or her analysis, and thus makes the case that studying rural masculinities is far from irrelevant to our day-to-day lives. On the contrary, rural masculinities are integral to how we all are shaped by, understand, and respond to the gendered world around us.

## Cowboy Love

*David Bell*

For some time now, there's been a developing interest in rural studies in issues of otherness, marginalization, and exclusion—a focus on questions like who belongs in the countryside, and who is made to feel like an outsider there? This has been paralleled by a growing interest in the discursive construction of the rural—how the countryside is made up in images and ideas as well as fields and farmers.[1] These agendas have pushed rural studies in all sorts of interesting and productive directions, one of which has been toward a consideration of sexuality's place in the country. Principally focused on homosexuality, but with some consideration of topics such as bestiality and naturism, this work explores both the lives of "sexual outsiders" in the countryside and the discursive construction of distinct kinds of "rural erotics."[2] This has been followed by work focused on the body in the countryside, itself part of a wider "rediscovery" of issues of embodiment in the social sciences. The embodied experience of the rural here reintroduces a material, experiential dimension to match (and sometimes counter) the emphasis on representation found in some work on rural others.[3]

It is to these bodies of work that my chapter endeavors to contribute. Its focus is on male homosexuality, expanding on my earlier work on men's bodies, male same-sex sexual activity, and rural cultures. Most of the work I shall be referring to in this chapter discusses the rural United States. I am mindful of the different meanings and forms of "countryside" that exist in different contexts, so the arguments I make here should not be taken as universally applicable. Even within the United States, of course, the rural is far from homogenous—the West being a very different

Special thanks to Jon Binnie for his very helpful comments on the chapter, and to Meredith Raimondo for her comments and for sending me her (as yet unpublished) essay and allowing me to quote from it here. Some first thoughts for this work came into my head at the Rural Economy and Society Study Group conference in Exeter, September 2000; thanks to Jo Little for asking me to that conference.

country from the South, for example; so we need to be careful not to ho-
mogenize country people and places. While I think there are some general
things to say here, particularly about constructions of the rural and the
urban, I would also want to stress the importance of location. I am equally
anxious about my somewhat uncomfortable use in this chapter of the term
"homosexual"—a term loaded with historical and geographical specificity,
an identity rather than a practice. Other writers have similarly worried
about this loaded terminology. For example, John Howard prefers the term
"homosex" when discussing same-sex sexual activity in his Mississippi
study, but also chooses the term "queer" as a label for his respondents.[4] I
feel that queer is equally contested, despite its often touted (but less often
operationalized) inclusiveness, so I go back to a strategy I have used before: to use words like "homosexual," "homosexuality," and "gay" quite
loosely, even at times to describe people who might not identify themselves in that way. This may seem like an act of antirural symbolic violence, but I do not intend it to be; it is really only an act of simplification
on my part. Apologies at the outset for its inadequacies—I hope they will
not detract from my arguments.

Those preliminaries dealt with, I begin the chapter by describing four
vignettes (or scenes), four sites where particular embodiments of male
homosexuality (remember: read the term broadly) meet distinct constructions of the rural. These four sites form the basis for my analysis, which
centers on the discursive and material constructions of "homosexual" and
"rural," constructions that then come together in complex and sometimes
contrary ways. To borrow from this volume's editors' discussion of rural
masculinities (but repurposing it to suit my needs), I want to draw a fuzzy
distinction between the *rural homosexual* and the *homosexual rural,* where
the former refers to the life experiences of gay men living in the countryside, and the latter refers to the countryside that lives in what Byrne Fone
calls "the homosexual imagination."[5] I agree with Campbell and Bell that it
is useful to keep these two terms in dialogue, acknowledging the interplay
between the symbolic and the experiential; as they say, "We can never
separate the two entirely: even rural folk have seen *Deliverance,* Marlboro
ads, and army training manuals."[6]

Recognizing the inadequacy of the terms homosexual rural and rural
homosexual, and mindful of any exclusions they might suggest, I nevertheless want to use them here as catchalls for a cluster of same-sex practices and/or identities and/or politics that are located and/or imagined in

places that are nonurban—in the country. Building on my previous writing in this area, I want to think some more about what these things have to tell us about how we see the countryside, how we see homosexuality, and how we see homosexuality in the countryside. First I will introduce my four scenes, and then trace some of the connections they make to the discourses and lives in which I am interested.

*Scene one:* Two well-built and well-hung men are locked in sexual embrace, clearly fucking, astride a large motorcycle in an open woodland setting. One man is naked, the other dressed in leathers. Their moustaches and styled haircuts, their hard bodies and hard cocks, symbolize a particular version of male homosexuality associated with urban gay culture, with pre-AIDS metropolitan gay life, with the "clone." Relocated in this woodland setting, the men appear like day-trippers, enjoying the countryside as a (sexual) recreational resource, fucking in the open air, basking in its tranquility. We can suppose from the image and from what we know about gay culture that they have ridden there on their motorbike to enjoy some outdoor sex like many (urban) men who favor the erotic setting of (rural) woodlands and open spaces. Wooded landscapes are complex symbols of nature; as Phil Macnaghten and John Urry write, there is a lot to be learned from looking at "how specific social groups . . . *engage with and perform their bodies in wooded environments.*"[7] Here, the woods evoke nature as an erotic topography, but an erotic topography quite unlike those most commonly associated with modern gay life—the bars, discos, and bathhouses of the urban clone scene. The scenario described here is depicted in a 1972 drawing by the artist Tom of Finland, well known for his illustrations of gay men.[8]

*Scene two:* A group of men stands in a circle, their naked bodies caked with mud, arms around each other, faces looking inward, their expressions intense. These men are improvising a "fairie" ritual, and the setting is the Arizona desert, summer 1979. One participant describes it as follows: "Buckets of water had been brought to a dry riverbed, and soon a great puddle of mud was produced. Cries for 'more mud' rang across the cactus fields as each man anointed the other. Twigs and blades of dry grass were woven through hair, hands were linked, and a large circle formed. Coming together, the group lifted one man above it, arms above shoulders, silently swaying in the morning sun."[9]

A second similar scene, this time from 1981 and referred to as "a dance of the fairies," is also described:

> We build a fire near the sweatlodge, in a field above the bubbling
> springs, and form a circle around it the night of the winter sol-
> stice. We evoke the elements, the four directions and then stand
> awkward for a while. Slowly, some men begin to sing or to join
> with others in a low rumbling chant. We draw instinctively closer
> as the sounds grow in intensity and men, young and old together,
> begin to move. Some break from the circle and dance to shaking
> rattles and the voice of automatic tongues.[10]

The scenes mirror those associated with the so-called mythopoetic
men's movement, and with their reclaiming of "deep masculinity"
through homosocial (but fiercely *heterosexual*) bonding in wilderness settings.[11] For the mythopoetic men's movement, the city has feminized men,
but nature can remasculinize them and facilitate connection among them.
For the fairies, urban gay culture is similarly rejected in favor of uncom-
mercialized queer rituals enacted in the wild. The use of mud in these
"rituals" is also sometimes fetishized by groups of urban men who enjoy
"dirty" erotic play in rural sites (as in the British group called Slosh)—
another sexual culture built around the configuration of particular bodies
with distinct notions of nature.

The fairies' ideas and practices also echo those espoused and lived out
by the better-known lesbian feminist pastoralists who established separatist communes and retreats in the countryside, most notably from the
1960s onward. Explicitly rejecting urban life and lifestyles, all of these
movements mobilize a distinct vision of the country as physically, mentally, and spiritually regenerative, drawing in assorted ecological and New
Age discourses. In the case of the fairies and the "rural lesbians," same-
sex desire and practices are coded as natural, too—away from the oppressive rules of "civilized society," true love can blossom.

*Scene three:* Some men who live in rural areas, it is suggested, engage
in same-sex sexual activity *situationally.* They live and work in all-male environments or in places where moral and/or religious strictures limit op-
posite-sex interactions. This version of rural male homosexuality is well
described in one of the Kinsey reports,[12] and the scenarios it details are
repeated in autobiographical and ethnographic accounts. Indeed, they
have become staples of gay pornography.[13] The gay men's "bear" subculture eroticizes this kind of rural masculinity, for instance, often fetishizing
images of "poor white trash."[14] Moreover, Howard notes that the Kinsey

reports functioned as a kind of pseudo-pornography, as well as a vital source of scarce information about homosexuality, when the two reports were published in the United States in the late 1940s and early '50s. At a time before information about homosexuality was widely available, library copies of the reports became the focus of considerable attention. Public libraries have indeed long been a vital information resource for sexual outsiders—as well as sites for casual sex.[15]

The report on male sexuality details two principal types of rural situational male same-sex activity: that which takes place primarily between boys in remote rural communities, and that which occurs in all-male working environments. Of the first, the Kinsey report says:

> The boy on the isolated farm has few companions except his brothers, the boys on an adjacent farm or two, visiting male cousins, and the somewhat older farm hand. His mother may see to it that he does not spend much time with his sisters, and the moral codes of the rural community may impose considerable limitations upon the association of boys and girls under other circumstances. Moreover, farm activities call for masculine capacities, and associations with girls are rated sissy by most of the boys in such a community.[16]

These archetypal "farm boys" get their teenage kicks off each other (and, as the report also notes, farm animals) because girls are not available to them. Similarly, the second group discussed in the report practices same-sex activities when it has no alternative, but this type is not defined by age. It is described in one of my favorite passages:

> There is a fair amount of sexual contact among the older males in Western rural areas. It is a type of homosexuality which was probably common among pioneers and outdoor men in general. Today it is found among ranchmen, cattle men, prospectors, lumbermen, and farming groups in general—among groups that are virile, physically active. These are men who have faced the rigors of nature in the wild. . . . Such a background breeds the attitude that sex is sex, irrespective of the nature of the partner with whom the relation is had. . . . Such a group of hard-riding, hard-hitting, assertive males would not tolerate the affectations of some of the

city groups that are involved in the homosexual [sic]; but this, as far as they can see, has little to do with the question of having sexual relations with other men.[17]

I have discussed this construction of the rural homosexual in more detail elsewhere, tracking some of its significant representations. Homosexual activity is here coded as natural because it is seen as unrestrained, animalistic, even rapacious—these men just want to fuck, and do not much care who (or what) they fuck with. They are thus naive rather than self-consciously liberated, enjoying same-sex sexual activity because they do not know it is wrong. Thus a powerful notion of rural "innocence" emerges—albeit innocence born of backwoods backwardness.

*Scene four:* In the small town of Laramie, Wyoming, in October 1998, twenty-one-year-old University of Wyoming student Matthew Shepard had been out for a drink at the Fireside Bar. He left with two men he had been seen talking to. A day later, a passing cyclist found him tied to a fence on the edge of town, severely beaten. He died five days later in the hospital without having regained consciousness. Two young local men were later arrested, tried, and sentenced for his murder. As Beth Loffreda writes, Shepard's killing brought to the surface a lot of issues in American sexual politics (and rural politics). Loffreda describes the scene of the murder like this: "[We now know] that Matt Shepard had encountered Russell Henderson and Aaron McKinney late Tuesday night in the Fireside Bar; that he'd left with them; that they had driven him in a pickup truck to the edge of town; that Henderson had tied him to a fence there and McKinney had beaten him viciously and repeatedly with a .357 Magnum. . . . [T]he only spots [of his face] not covered in blood were the tracks cleansed by his tears."[18]

The media coverage of Shepard's murder depicted Wyoming (and therefore rural America more broadly) as "cowboy country," an intolerant place where it is difficult to live as a gay man, and where coping strategies have to be deployed constantly to avoid the day-to-day hassles of homophobia, including (thankfully rare) life-threatening situations. This is, of course, intensely draining and corrosive, so for many "sexual outsiders" born and raised in hostile rural environments, escape to metropolitan gay communities remains the only option, leading to significant rural-to-urban migration.[19] As an image of what gay rural life is like in North America in the late 1990s and early 2000s, the description of Matt Shepard's battered body is powerfully resonant, and has come to assume an iconic status.

These, then, are my four rural male homosexual bodies: Tom of Finland's clones, the radical fairies, Kinsey's cowboys, and Matt Shepard. In the rest of this chapter, I look in more detail at these images, and consider what they have to teach us about the homosexual rural and the rural homosexual. I treat the two separately, before drawing them back together.

## The Homosexual Rural

As already stated, the term "homosexual rural" represents the imaginative construction of the countryside as a particular type of "gay space." Most commonly, it refers to a version of the rural idyll or Arcadia. In this context, Byrne Fone identifies three uses of the homosexual rural in his survey of gay literature:

> 1) to suggest a place where it is safe to be gay: where gay men can be free from the outlaw status society confers upon us, where homosexuality can be revealed and spoken of without reprisal, and where homosexual love can be consummated without concern for the punishment or scorn of the world; 2) to imply the presence of gay love and sensibility in a text that would otherwise make no explicit statement about homosexuality; and 3) to establish a metaphor for certain spiritual values and myths prevalent in homosexual literature and life, namely, that homosexuality is superior to heterosexuality and is a divinely sanctioned means to an understanding of the good and the beautiful.[20]

The natural or wilderness setting here functions as a homosexual Eden, as a precultural site in which homosexual love can flourish, unencumbered by society's moral strictures. Homosexuality is coded as natural, making the natural landscape its perfect backdrop. Across a range of gay cultural texts, from poems to movies, these motifs recur—and we see them in two of my four scenes, Tom of Finland's drawing and the fairies' gatherings. Natural bodies (the fairies' nakedness), natural desires, the natural landscape—rather than seeing homosexuality as a "crime against nature," it is depicted as in harmony with nature; homophobia is located in the sphere of culture.

David Shuttleton argues that we need to think through the contexts in which "gay pastoral" texts originate and circulate, rather than seeing them as a single, transhistorical genre (in the way that Fone perhaps does). That said, there are clear elements that connect them—the fairies explicitly summon up Whitman and Thoreau, for example, and artist and filmmaker Derek Jarman's paintings, movies, and journals contain more than a trace of the Arcadian.[21] Contemporary rural homoerotics bear the imprint of past associations, therefore, even as they rework them—although that reworking may give them new inflections.

Rural folk are sometimes part of this imagining, their lives and bodies connected to nature, the soil, and so on—they are seen as people equally untouched and unbothered by civilization's restraints. Agricultural laborers are particularly fetishized in this context, celebrated for their roughness, manliness, and earthiness. Rural rough trade, as we might say in shorthand, populates this homoerotic landscape, from John Addington Symonds's fascination with shepherd boys to the eroticizing of the cowboy and the lumberjack on the gay clone scene and in gay pornography today—icons Shuttleton refers to as "rural camp."[22] The appropriation of Kinsey's cowboys into rural camp exemplifies the recontextualization process at work, their "situational homosexuality" also coded as natural—if men spend too much time together, freed from society's morals, their lust will find the obvious outlet.

Of course, this eroticizing of the "rural butch" contrasts with the "degaying" strategies of "butching up" or "cowboying up" reported as coping strategies for rural homosexuals anxious about the association of "sissiness" with homosexuality. As respondents in Fellows's *Farm Boys* describe, the performance of manliness is often a necessary defense against outing and harassment in an environment where a hegemonic rural heteromasculinity is omnipresent.[23] Such strategies are also featured in press coverage of Shepard's murder, which stereotype Laramie's politics and lifestyles in the catchphrase "cowboy county." Shepard's murder, some writers argue, reveals a fear of "wussitude" that signals the fragility of hegemonic heteromasculinity. In the writings of gay pastoralists, too, such "effemaphobia" is a common motif, affirming the connection between rural rough trade and manly love, as well as between the sissy and the city: "Pastoral idealism represents and sustains a private, unselfconscious, nonsocially identified and manly notion of homosexuality against which subculturally socialized, gender-transgressive, metropolitan identities are found wanting."[24]

Rural gay masculinity thus often gets figured in particular forms—as natural, manly, rough, and raw. Even the "fairies," many of whom took to the Arizona desert distinctly metropolitan sensibilities, reconstruct themselves in a version of this, drawing on a queered adaptation of "Iron John" deep masculinity that rejects the label "gay" and the culture it has bred: "One of the most remarkable off-shoots of gay liberation . . . has been the emergence of 'radical fairies,' a nationwide, grass-roots movement of gay men seeking alternatives within their own subculture and society at large. Many fairie-identified men see little distinction between the two, arguing that as the gay middle class assimilates into the cultural mainstream, deeper inquiries into the predominant structures of state and spirit are being left unanswered."[25]

Common motifs, then, can be picked out in terms of describing the homosexual rural as a landscape and an identity, both of which have long lineages and varied manifestations. These in turn have complex effects on the rural homosexual; if I can recycle and add to Campbell and Bell's formulation, used earlier, at least some rural folk have looked at Tom of Finland's drawings or read Whitman's poems, alongside seeing *Deliverance,* Marlboro advertisements, and army training manuals. In fact, as John Weir writes in a polemic against urban gay politics, there are plenty of "people with homosexual urges who feel represented more by *Reader's Digest* and *Soldier of Fortune* than by *The Advocate.*"[26] While there are multiple exclusions at work here—concerning class, race, disability, age, and so on—the way *Advocate*-style "metrosexuality" fails to represent and include the provincial (and rural) homosexual is an important point.

What it means to be "gay in cowboy county," then, cannot be separated from the images and ideas about the homosexual rural. Real lives—and real deaths, like Shepard's—assume iconic status too, living on in collective memories as well as in protest songs and charitable acts. These images add to, rework, and transform the constructions of the homosexual rural in an ongoing process of making meaning. As Paul Cody and Peter Welch conclude from their fieldwork in northern New England, "there is a long history of rural gays in this country. It is not as idyllic as Whitman's *Leaves of Grass* implies; however, neither is it as abysmal as urban gay folklore currently suggests."[27] It is to these life experiences—the experiences of the rural homosexual—that I now turn.

## The Rural Homosexual

> Talk to gay men here, and you can begin to draw a secret map of Wyoming, one most of its residents would find unfamiliar. There are particular rest stops and scenic overlooks on certain highways where men can find fleeting companionship; the Cheyenne drag clubhouse without a liquor license that had a short, heady life in the early 1990s; the town parks in Powell and Lander that turn "cruisy" at night; and The Fort, an adult book and video store south of Laramie with private viewing booths. . . . Spend some time at cruisingforsex.com on the Web, and you can find the Wyoming message board, a rather lonely site compared to the heavy traffic on other state boards.[28]

This passage, from Loffreda's *Losing Matt Shepard,* paints a familiar picture of rural gay life duplicated in ethnographic and life-history accounts, as well as in the literature on social service provision for rural gay clients.[29] Social and spatial isolation, everyday homophobia, community underdevelopment, disconnection from "gay meccas," and religious and political intolerance are the themes picked up by the research cited here. As should be clear by now, this does not of course mean there are no possibilities for acting on homosexual desires in the country: "The rural for queer Mississippians was less an escape to the seclusion of nature, than a material ingress to a busy network of men. . . . Homosexual meanings and readings, desires and actions, could surface at most any roadside get-together."[30]

Moreover, a second set of themes emerges in these accounts. As Cody and Welch remind us, for example, there are attractions to rural life for sexual "outsiders," although these may have little to do with sexuality. Among their interviewees, gay men who had chosen to move to the country listed familiar benefits—fresh air, peace and quiet, a slower and simpler pace of life, outdoor recreation, and so on. Others found urban gay culture oppressive, preferring the pleasures of a home-based small-town life. Weighing those positive features against the negatives listed earlier is a version of what Loffreda calls "the daily quick math that accompanies gay life" in rural America—the unending calculation of how to act, who to tell, and the risks involved in being "out."[31] For groups like the fairies, and their lesbian feminist counterparts, the answer is separatism: choosing isolation and self-sufficiency affords the benefits of country life without the costs of homophobia.[32] On a smaller scale, a kind of elective domestic isolation often keeps rural gays closeted, their sexuality privatized—not a uniquely country phenomenon, of course, but one that recurs in accounts of rural homosexual life. Howard's life histories reveal the home as a prime site of sexual experimentation for his Mississippi gay men. Moreover, he warns of simplistically seeing rural space as one big closet, arguing that the countryside offers a mix of opportunity and constraint for same-sex desires. Vincent Bonfitto's work on the Connecticut River valley from 1900 to 1970 also presents a complex picture. He shows that there were plenty of opportunities for gay male sex in this part of Massachusetts, and that gay couples established domestic lives with relative ease. However, fear of exposure limited public *social* intercourse between gay men, and thus no sense of gay "community" developed in the area, at least not until the political upheavals of the 1960s.[33]

Loffreda's "secret map" of Wyoming can also be traced in other accounts, most extensively in Howard's *Men Like That,* which provides a historical cartography of Mississippi gay life. Here the rural homosexual in some cases produces its own version of the homosexual rural, using the countryside in imaginative erotic scenarios: "For those who lived in Mississippi, distinctive features in the rural landscape resulted in particular sexual desires, behaviors, identities, and networks. Queer boys *did it* in abandoned cabins, beside streams, among the trees; in haylofts, in the fields, in ponds; in cars and pickup trucks, at roadside parks, at summer camps; in hotels, bus stations, theaters, bars, city parks, and roadhouses; in prison, in the military; at church, at work, at school, and at home."[34]

Howard's research stresses the importance of mobility and, especially, the car: often the only way to offset the oppressive aspects of rural life is to go somewhere else, if only for a night. Expansive car-facilitated networks can stand in for place-based communities, although they do not readily form the foundation for social and political action (apart from automobile associations!). As Tim Retzloff shows, the car has profoundly reshaped American gay culture: "The car . . . gave men access to gay spaces both local and distant, became a gay space itself, and helped shape stationary gay spaces as they evolved . . . car cruising, car sex, and homosexually active parking lots all became acknowledged sites where gay and bisexual men could claim public spaces as their own. . . . Often far away from urban areas, these various car-centred institutions provided men with possibilities for homosexual encounters and ways to create gay identities."[35]

From Laramie, Wyoming, the nearest place with a recognizable urban gay scene is Denver, an eight- to ten-hour roundtrip away. For many rural gays, however, it is more than worth the drive. For those who choose to make the move permanent, the sense of sexual outsiderness is often swapped for the outsiderness of being rural in the urban, of having to let go of heritage and homeland. Nevertheless, those "farm boys" that had become "city men" in Fellows's work agreed that the gains outweighed the losses, even if some men found urban gay life difficult to get used to.[36] As Allan Berubé remembers, for example, arriving in the great gay "mecca" of San Francisco was a less than utopian moment for him, since the Castro lifestyle was beyond his lowly economic means, and his "trailer trash" background excluded him from gay high culture. The homosexual urban, then, exists as a site as mythological as its rural counterpart, a place made in the imagination and often unmatched in reality.[37]

Of course, as noted in my discussion of Tom of Finland, there is another traffic flow to add in here—urban gay men visiting the countryside. Like Tom's entwined lovers, the bikers in Maurice van Lieshout's Dutch ethnography head for highway rest stops for rural recreational sex. The rest area they visit, known as the Mollebos, is renowned for its "leather nights." Here we have a particular arrangement of Macnaghten and Urry's "bodies in the woods," where the landscape is an erotic backdrop for sado-masochistic leather sex (also fondly depicted in Tom of Finland's work): "The Mollebos proved to be exciting for gay men as an outdoor facility as well as being a wooded territory. It served for many of them as a sexual Fantasia Land where dreams can come true. The woods met conditions for exciting leather and S&M meetings: an erotically experienced space that suggests adventure, threat, and sensation. . . . [M]any leathermen turned out to be regular visitors, on every occasion waiting for the woods to redeem its promises."[38]

As van Lieshout says, urban gay culture in the AIDS era takes an ambivalent stance on public sex activities such as cruising and cottaging, although these practices are becoming woven into the sexual landscape in more positive, less demonized ways, even while they remain subject to surveillance and policing. In many remote areas, of course, they still often have to stand in for urban gay culture. At the highway rest stop, moreover, we can see the potential commingling of two sexual cultures—the urban homosexuals, for whom the woods are a prime site for kinky sex, and the rural homosexuals, for whom the woods might be the *only* site for any sex. In a virtual analogy, Loffreda finds the Wyoming portion of the cruisingforsex.com website populated mostly by "men from out of state, guys with anatomically impressive handles who are jetting into Jackson for a few days of skiing and sex . . . with the occasional plaintive interruption from a local, wondering where all the gay Wyomingites are."[39] Indeed, the internet is often signaled as an important network that has liberated rural homosexuals from place-bound constraints. Chat rooms for rural gays have proliferated, as have sites for those who make a fetish of the rural. As a helping resource, the internet increasingly stands in for the public library, as well as providing opportunities to supply vital social services to isolated rural clients.[40] It also offers new opportunities for social networking, for accessing pornography, for making sexual contacts, and, of course, for having sex.

One area where social services in rural areas have received increased attention is in relation to HIV/AIDS services. Ronald Mancoske summarizes the issues, noting that AIDS cases are currently increasing in number most rapidly in rural areas of the United States. Kathleen Rounds highlights the challenges to care delivery—geographical and social isolation, stigmatization, community intolerance, and so on.[41] Both Rounds and Mancoske focus in particular on the "return migration" of people with AIDS (PWAS) who once left rural areas because of these problems but then returned "home" after diagnosis, reversing the "great gay migration." Homophobia and fear of AIDS are thus brought into the open in communities where they had been hidden by closeting and out-migration. However, moving home can mean having to be re-closeted. Respondents in Rounds's study (from an unnamed southeastern state) report that "in some families the person with AIDS was allowed to move home only if he agreed to cease contact with gay friends and lovers." Mancoske echoes this, writing that "these migration patterns back to rural areas generate unique psychosocial stresses for PWAS and counseling issues for service providers," adding that "rural PWAS seek care less often, later in the illnesses, rely on alternative care providers more often, and experience greater illness-related stigma."[42] In addition, a study by Jonathan Poullard and Anthony

D'Augelli found that volunteers in rural AIDS-prevention programs often harbored homophobic attitudes. To give just two stark examples from their paper, 26 percent of respondents thought "homosexual behavior between two men is just plain wrong," and 21 percent found male homosexuals "disgusting."[43] Clearly, there are significant issues facing the caring professions in rural AIDS work.

All of these studies discuss urban-to-rural return migration as a significant "problem" facing rural America. Meredith Raimondo has written an insightful essay on these "new geographies of AIDS," and in particular on the discourses that emerge in the reporting of these migrations:

> In the late 1980s, a series of stories in major daily newspapers took up the theme of AIDS "coming home" to the American "heartland" through human interest features on the return of white gay sons to rural families of origin. For example, the *Los Angeles Times* ran a story that opened this way: "When David learned that he was going to die, he decided to go home. But when David came home, AIDS came home, too. . . . AIDS is killing in the heartland now. It no longer afflicts only nameless, faceless strangers a long way from Main Street."[44]

As Raimondo shows from her reading of the media, a powerful mythologizing of the rural as maternal "home" emerges here—a rural set against the sexually liberalized but uncaring (and diseased) metropolis these men are now fleeing. Shuttleton, in fact, sees the reprise of nostalgic gay pastoralism as at least in part a response to AIDS.[45] In the narrative Raimondo highlights, gay men seduced by the city's openness—and driven away by the rural—find themselves returning home following HIV diagnosis, back to the place from which they were initially driven. To accommodate these returning sons, a mythological home is created, with a welcoming mother at its door; the incoming men are infantilized and desexualized. A very particular rural idyll thus appears in these accounts, itself perpetuating the idea of the rural as a site of "not-AIDS" and therefore the continuing return migration of ex-rural PWAS.

Raimondo also picks out a familiar "AIDS demon" in the rural United States—the closeted (often married) bisexual man, who is seen as a product of rural closeting and a threat to the rural heterosexual population. A further folk devil can be detected in the form of the so-called AIDS refugee.

These "refugees" were also fleeing the diseased city but not returning home. In this version of the homosexual rural idyll, the country is imagined as a place safe from contamination, where sex is not overshadowed by death. AIDS refugees are driven from the (gay) metropolis by AIDS, but rather than being desexualized in or by the rural, they are migrating to the country on the promise of AIDS-free sex. Some gay male pastoral groups mobilize the same motifs of rural purity against urban disease. The Edward Carpenter Collective, based in Scotland, conjured this image in an advertisement for a week-long retreat: "We will discover an honorable and sustainable way to live intelligent and blissful lives as gay men and to be able to detach from a commercial and predatory gay culture whose death-wish mantra is *Live Fast, Die Young, Be a Beautiful Corpse*."[46]

The closeted bisexual man and the AIDS refugee challenge such "heart-land" idealizations of the country, since they disrupt the link between the rural and "safety" and refuse the desexualization at the heart of the "coming-home-to-die" narrative. As Raimondo writes, these complex discourses and movements force a major redrawing of the geography of AIDS in the United States, which has to acknowledge and address the issue of rural transmission of HIV—something not hitherto considered in either "stories of the compassionate heartland [or] the rural backwater, [both of which] imagined HIV as an urban visitor."[47] What we can see here very vividly, then, is the complex mixing of the rural homosexual and the homosexual rural—the invoking of an imagined "heartland" that can exist only under certain circumstances, and the difficulties this raises for people trying to live under these circumstances. In some instances, maintaining the idyllic homosexual rural means denying certain forms of the rural homosexual, and vice versa.

My aim in this chapter has been to explore what happens when two things come together: the "rural" and the male "homosexual." I began with four scenes where that coming together takes place: in a drawing by Tom of Finland; in the rituals of the radical fairies; in the descriptions of rural "situational homosexuality" found in Kinsey's report, *Sexual Behavior in the Human Male;* and in the victim of homophobic murder, Matthew Shepard. These are useful, if limited, versions of two intertwining motifs of my chapter: the *homosexual rural* (an idyllic place made in the "homosexual imagination" and represented across gay cultural forms) and the *rural homosexual* (the life experiences of men with same-sex desires and/or sexual practices and/or sexual identities who come from and/or live in rural places). As I hope to have shown, separating these two is an act of oversimplification: the homosexual rural and the rural homosexual are densely woven together in complex ways. Ideas like the gay pastoral discussed in Shuttleton's work can be traced through cultural texts and life experiences, folding together and working with and against other notions of the rural—as a site for "natural" love between men, or a dangerous place where intolerance is the norm.[48] This should, in many ways, be unsurprising—we live our lives at the intersection of the material and the symbolic, no matter where we live and what texts we have at our disposal. My concern has been with exploring the particular texts and lives (and texts about lives) that I have at my disposal and that work up their own versions of the homosexual rural and the rural homosexual.

At the opening of the chapter, I made a few observations about exclusivity by noting the exclusions manifest here. I reiterate and add to those exclusions now. My chapter has been about the rural United States but has uneasily totalized that geographical entity. A better Americanist than I could tease out the specificities of the rural West against the rural South, for example.[49] I have also totalized diverse activities and identities (and nonidentities) into the term "homosexual." I should perhaps have been more careful to separate self-identified gay men, men who have sex with men, and so on: Kinsey's cowboys are *not* homosexual in the same way that Matthew Shepard was homosexual. I have also tended to keep clear of other axes of identity that clearly cut across sexuality and complicate the stories I am telling: what about class or race or age, for example? Clearly the middle-class pastoralist has very different experiences from the rural rough he fetishizes, for instance, just as the middle-aged gay couple home-making in the country have a life quite unlike a farm-born teenager who sometimes fucks his male cousins. I should also have spent at least a little time considering the roles of religion, especially Christianity, in shaping both the homosexual rural and the rural homosexual.[50] Moreover, my focus has been on male homosexuality, at the expense of considering the lives and representations of other sexual "outsiders" in the rural. Finally, all this focus on "others" and "outsiders" fails to consider hegemonic sexualities—what are we to make of rural heterosexuality? Given the important work on genderings of the countryside and the role of this book in contributing to that agenda, it would be useful to consider notions of heterosexuality and heteronormativity attached to particular versions of the rural—which in part produce rural sexual others. My hope is that other chapters can do some of that work, and that my chapter can remind readers that rural masculinities include rural gay masculinities, which sometimes confirm and at other times confound our attempts to think through what being a man in the country is all about.

## NOTES

1. Bunce (1994); Cloke and Little (1997); Halfacree (1993); Little (1999); Milbourne (1997); Philo (1992).

2. D. Bell (2000a, 2000b); Bell and Holliday (2000); Bell and Valentine (1995); Bonfitto (1997); Cody and Welch (1997); Dews and Law (2001); Fellows (1996); Fone (1983); Kramer (1995); Phillips, Watt, and Shuttleton (2000); Smith and Mancoske (1997); Valentine (1997); Wilson (2000).

3. Macnaghten and Urry (2000a, 2000b).

4. Howard (1999).

5. Fone (1983).

6. Campbell and Bell (2000, 544). See also Fone (1983).

7. Macnaghten and Urry (2000a, 168). See also van Lieshout (1995).

8. For examples of the artist's work, see, for example, Tom of Finland (1992).

9. Thompson (1987, 275–76).

10. Ibid., 292.

11. For more on the men's movement, see Bonnett (1996); Messner (1997).

12. Kinsey, Pomeroy, and Martin (1948); Kinsey et al. (1953).

13. Cooper (1986); Howard (1999).

14. D. Bell (2000a); L. Wright (2000).

15. Howard (1995).

16. Kinsey, Pomeroy, and Martin (1948, 457).

17. Ibid., 457–59.

18. Loffreda (2000, 1, 5).

19. For discussion, see Cody and Welch (1997); Smith (1997); Weston (1995).

20. Fone (1983, 13). See also Shuttleton (2000).

21. For more detailed discussion, see D. Bell (2000b); Parkes (1996); Shuttleton (2000).

22. Shuttleton (2000, 131).

23. Campbell and Bell (2000); Cody and Welch (1997); Fellows (1996); G. Wright (1999). See also the other chapters in this volume.

24. Shuttleton (2000, 141).

25. Thompson (1987, 260).

26. Weir (1996, 32). See also Binnie (2000).

27. Cody and Welch (1997, 66–67).

28. Loffreda (2000, 69–70).

29. Bonfitto (1997); Cody and Welch (1997); D'Augelli and Hart (1987); Fellows (1996); Howard (1999); Kramer (1995); Moses and Buckner (1980); Poullard and D'Augelli (1989); Rounds (1988); Smith and Mancoske (1997).

30. Howard (1999, 113).

31. Loffreda (2000, 68). See also Moses and Buckner (1980); Smith (1997).

32. For discussion of lesbian rural separatism, see Valentine (1997).

33. Bonfitto (1997).

34. Howard (1999, 123).

35. Retzloff (1997, 243–44).

36. Fellows (1996).

37. Berubé (1996).

38. Van Lieshout (1995, 35). See also Macnaghten and Urry (2000a).

39. Loffreda (2000, 70).

40. Haag and Chang (1997).

41. Rounds (1988); Mancoske (1997).

42. Rounds (1988, 259); Mancoske (1997, 41, 48).

43. Poullard and D'Augelli (1989, 35).

44. Raimondo (2001, 4–5).

45. Shuttleton (2000).

46. Advertisement from *Gay Times*, no date.

47. Raimondo (2001, 9).

48. Shuttleton (2000).

49. Spurlin (2000).

50. Wilson (2000).

# 10

## Embodiment and Rural Masculinity

### Jo Little

This chapter explores the contribution made by work on "the body" to understanding rural masculinity. It argues that masculinity is made and remade through the material practices of the body and that any attempt to examine the performance of masculinity must take account of the expectations, norms, and assumptions that surround the body. The body is not naturally given but socially constructed, reflecting society's values and power relations. It provides a rich source of information on the relationship between sexuality and gender identity. In focusing on the rural body, I also argue that these embodied practices are spatialized—that is, that space is an active agent in the negotiation of bodily practices. The body itself may be seen as a space—the "geography closest in," according to Adrienne Rich (1986)—both a surface on which sexual identity may be inscribed and a factor in the mutual constitution of space and place.

The particular emphasis in this discussion of masculinity is the rural heterosexual body. I argue that rural sexual identity is underpinned by a strong assumption of traditional, family-based heterosexuality. While this heteronormalcy has been apparent in studies of rural gender relations and the centrality of rural women and the family to notions of rural community in, for example, the emphasis on the nuclear family and attitudes toward the division of labor within the household, there has been little discussion of its construction and reconstruction as a dominant set of values in relation to sexual identity. Thus what has been absent from work on traditional rural gender identities has been any attempt to consider how such identities are linked to sexuality and to the actual practices and performances associated with heterosexual relationships. In order to address this absence and look specifically at heterosexual practices as they confirm the power of traditional gender identities, we need to examine the rural body through and within which sexual identity is configured.

Relatively little attention has been paid in rural research to the body, although, as noted below, researchers have recently started to explore the relationship between nature, the environment, and the rural body in the study of farming and also outdoor sport and recreation. Discussions of the relationship between the body and space have usually been limited to the urban body, and in particular to urban performances of sexuality, the creation of "queer spaces," and the disruption of the heteronormalcy of public space (see for example Robyn Longhurst's study of pregnant bodies in the street and Phil Hubbard and Tessa Sander's work on spaces of prostitution).[1] This chapter takes three steps toward understanding the body as relevant to the study of rural masculinity. It starts by providing a context for the study of the rural body by briefly exploring academic approaches to embodiment. It then goes on to draw together the few existing studies on rural embodiment to show where rural social scientists have begun to incorporate the body in work on the rural landscape and environment. Third, it explores three specific examples of rural embodiment: the rural body and the naked calendar; the *Country Living* campaign to find wives for "lonely farmers" in England; and the Middlemarch Bachelor Ball in New Zealand.

In each of these sections I am concerned to demonstrate the relationship between the body and dominant understandings of heterosexuality in rural communities. While sections of the analysis, and two of the case studies, look directly at rural masculinity, I do not restrict the chapter to simply talking about masculine identity but consider masculinity and the male body within the wider context of the relationship between the body, sexuality, and gender identity. Thus, in recognition of the relational nature of gender and sexuality, the chapter includes discussion of femininity and the female body—addressing the same issues and showing how the rural body reflects and creates a dominant idea of heterosexuality that shapes the way gender is constructed and performed for both men and women.

## Embodiment and Gender

This section provides a framework for the examination of masculinity and the body by discussing the development of academic work on embodiment and its contribution to understanding sexuality and gender. Social scientists writing on the recent development of work on the body often begin by questioning what is meant by "the body" and, in so doing, examine different academic approaches to understanding embodiment. Such examinations generally argue that the body—although apparently familiar—is difficult to define and conceptualize. Longhurst, for example, talks about the "bewildering array" of approaches social scientists have developed to the body.[2] We can, however, identify some main theoretical trends within this rich and diverse work.

## Sex and Gender

The main "problem" with defining the body lies in the relationship between sex and gender. Theorists of the body have usually examined this relationship in one of two ways: the "essentialist" or the "constructionist." Early essentialist approaches were developed by feminist theorists who saw women as trapped within their bodies and who interpreted gender inequality as a function of biological difference (while understanding that this biological inequality was maintained by social convention). These feminists felt that equality for women meant reducing the differences between men's and women's bodies, primarily through medical science. More recent essentialist approaches argue for a more positive view of women's bodies—viewing them from a position of strength and seeing women's liberation and sexual equality as stemming from an appreciation of women's bodies and a valuing of their reproductive functions.[3] Such essentialist perspectives have been criticized for maintaining a single fixed, passive interpretation of the body and perpetuating the idea of a "mind/body dualism" (in which the body is simply the physical tool of the mind).[4]

In contrast, constructionist approaches to the body argue that bodies are not essential but are "discursively produced": that is, that the body is a surface on which society "writes" its values, morals, and laws, or, as Longhurst puts it, bodies are "marked, scarred, transformed or constructed by various patriarchal and heterosexist institutional regimes."[5] Constructionist feminists and social scientists, drawing heavily on Foucault, argue that this "inscription" means that the material body reflects social power relations and that bodies are given social meaning through such expression of power.[6] Increasingly, debates on gender identity pay more attention to this type of approach, examining the material practices and social constructions through which the body is "inscribed" or "produced." Early theoretical research on the social construction of the body tended to see bodies simply as "the passive bearers of cultural imprints . . . the blank pages on which meanings are 'inscribed.'"[7] More recently, however, this research has developed a view of the body not as a natural, passive entity onto which society maps gendered characteristics, but rather as a central part of the production, performance, and fluidity of gendered individuality itself.[8]

If we follow this constructionist approach, we can see how the material body helps to produce, reproduce, sustain, and contest dominant social assumptions and expectations. As Raewyn Connell notes in relation to masculinity and the male body: "The materiality of male bodies matters, not as a template for social masculinities, but as a *referent* for the configuration of social practices defined as masculinities. Male bodies are what these practices refer to, imply or address." [9]

These ideas resonate with Judith Butler's discussion of the "naturalization" of certain characteristics in the *performance* of gender. Butler argues that gender is not a series of costumes hung onto a "natural" body[10] but a "continuing performance between bodies and discourses."[11] In this construction, Barbara Brook continues, female bodies become "not the basic ground on which gender is draped, but a field or site created by the interaction of particular discourses which . . . are not only those of gender but also of other cultural markers: ethnicity, age, race class, etc."[12]

Butler develops her ideas of gender performativity to show how biological sex is part of this process, and indeed becomes a regulatory practice that "produces the body it governs."[13] The body is, therefore, central to the repeating processes through which "sex" becomes a material form of "gender."

*Normalizing Heterosexuality*

Butler and others develop these ideas to show how the body is intimately bound up in the normalization of heterosexuality. At the heart of this naturalization, they argue, is the idea of monogamous, procreative sex as the quintessential sexual act.[14] Fundamentally, this (hetero)sexual act is naturalized through the theory that we desire the "other" and thus that "natural" sexual relations originate in "the attraction of opposites," or "difference." This desire for difference operates not only in terms of male and female bodies but also in the emotional responses to sexual activity, in which the male is (theoretically) aggressive and dominant and the female is passive and submissive. Diane Richardson, for instance, notes how important "difference"—particularly bodily difference—is to ideas of attraction and desire: "heterosexuality depends on a view of differently gendered individuals who complement each other, right down to their bodies and body parts fitting together; 'like a lock and key' the penis and vagina are assumed to be a natural fit."[15]

Clearly, the procreative/reproductive sexual act is central to the naturalization of heterosexuality. Hubbard explains how the reproductive meaning of this act "de-eroticizes" heterosexuality because it subordinates sexuality "to a higher purpose."[16] He argues that ideas of morality have served to naturalize the belief that sex must be based on an exchange that is meaningful both materially and emotionally and is based on procreative sexual intercourse. "Heterosex" for any other purpose is thus seen as deviant: "In situating a particular act (and thus individuals) as immoral, and thus on the margins of acceptability, the 'centre' is defined, usually around ideals of family life, the assumption of heterosexual orientation and a related gender identity (i.e., mother and father)."[17] Beyond this center are what Hubbard terms "scary sexualities"—that is, sexual acts that are seen as outside "natural" heterosexual activity and thus as immoral.

Feminists such as Rich see the naturalization of heterosexuality as extending from institutionalized social practices, rituals, and laws, which, through institutions such as marriage, everyday work processes, recreational activities, and domestic life patterns, routinely normalize heterosexuality and thus shut off other avenues of sexual expression.[18] Because normalization is such a powerful force, it can make people (consciously or unconsciously) adopt "normal" sexual identities, even if they are oppressive and restrictive to the individual. If we recognize how all-pervasive the institutionalization of heterosexuality is in our society, however, we can raise questions about the idea of heterosexuality as a preference or a choice and the ways in which it is controlled and kept in place.

## The Body in Space

Thus far I have argued that focusing on the body is central to an understanding of masculinity and femininity. We have seen how the body's materiality is constituted through the performance of the regulatory norms of sex and how "natural" heterosexuality is central to these regulatory norms. Heterosexuality is continually reasserted through the association of "normal" desire with difference and through understanding bodily difference as a condition of attraction. Here we develop these ideas in the context of space and place, showing how space is a factor in the construction and material practices of the body. While the nature of space affects how we use our bodies and the values and assumptions through which we regulate them, bodies also shape the character of space, influencing how it is used and the acceptability of particular actions and activities within it.

How can we relate these arguments to the rural? In the rest of this chapter, I argue that this relationship between space and embodiment needs to inform, and be informed by, our understanding of specifically rural places. For many reasons, the rural provides an excellent (if neglected) space in which to explore the embodied performance of a particular set of gender relations and sexual identities. In contemporary Western society, the rural holds an important place in the cultural imagination, one strongly imbued with associations of naturalness, family, stability, and community. Here I argue that such values are reflected in, and reconfirmed by, values and expectations surrounding the body. In his discussion of sexuality, the body, and space, Phil Hubbard talks of "coding" spaces as homosexual or heterosexual and of the need to recognize different forms of heterosexual space within such broad categorizations.[19] While Hubbard uses these arguments to explore the "scary" heterosexualized urban spaces of prostitution, his idea of space as coded according to a particular version of heterosexuality is also useful in terms of rural spaces. I suggest that rural spaces may be coded as "unscary" spaces, spaces in which heterosexuality has assumed a benign and uncontested form. I now move on to demonstrate how this unscary heterosexuality is played out and reconstituted within the embodied spaces of rural communities and rural landscapes.

## The Body, Rurality, and Nature

Writing on the rural body has tended to focus on the relationship between masculinity and rural nature. Such work concentrates on the association between wilderness and untamed landscapes and constructions of hegemonic rural masculinity. A second, more minor, theme in work on the rural body explores the countryside as a space for performing the homosexual body, again with reference to the importance of nature. Few studies, however, have looked at the rural body in the more "social" spaces of the village, or considered how the body performs sexual identity in the context of the rural community.

Much work on the rural body examines representations of masculinity in agriculture and other land-based professions.[20] Such work identifies the dominant form of masculinity associated with agriculture and how it is reflected in the male body. It shows how men's role in agriculture continues to be underpinned by ideas of dominating nature and conquering the landscape. Thus, a "good" (male) farmer is one who has tamed the elements to produce crops and manage livestock, overcoming nature's vagaries and uncertainties. Such representations of agrarian masculinity are embodied in fitness, strength, and physical stamina. Images of farmers typically display the power of the male body, often emphasizing (as Ruth Liepins points out)[21] the muscular strength of farmers wrestling with their stock. Such images also seem to show a direct correlation between the capabilities of the farmer and the ruggedness of the body, again implying the importance of physical strength in the face of the natural elements.

As Berit Brandth has argued, the embodied representations of agricultural masculinity are now becoming imbued with a technical competence or command over farm machinery.[22] As farm work becomes increasingly mechanized, so the ability to overcome nature in the pursuit of agricultural production requires new skills in understanding and controlling more and more sophisticated machinery. Brandth notes how farm machinery can be seen as an extension of the farmer's body and equates the desire for large, powerful, and sophisticated machines with the importance of bodily strength and competence. Brandth and Marit Haugen also note similar trends in technology's development in relation to forestry work.[23] They observe the endurance of embodied representations of masculinity that, as in agriculture, emphasize the need for physical strength and fitness. They go on to argue, however, that such embodiments are being supplemented (rather than replaced) by images displaying men's technical competence and managerial skills in the face of a changing forestry industry. The need for physical strength has now been augmented by a new requirement for "boardroom" skills and this in turn has been reflected in dominant images of masculinity in the forestry industry.

Other studies focus on the performance (rather than the representation) of masculinity in agriculture. Both Lise Saugeres and Caitríona Ní Laoire note how conversations with male farmers in Ireland and France have shown the enduring association between bodily strength, power, control of nature, and successful agricultural production.[24] In relation to such conventional and lasting embodiments of masculinity, studies have also noted how these ideas reflect persistent binaries in Western philosophy, which associates women with nature and the body and men with science and rationality.[25] Some researchers see male domination of nature as representing a desire to overcome the unpredictability and weakness of the body, for masculinity to control femininity. Interestingly, some research has suggested that the performance of younger farmers, especially those practicing more environmentally sustainable forms of agriculture, demonstrates a shift in dominant forms of masculinity.[26] Such work analyzes the weakening of traditional gender roles among farming families involved in "alternative" forms of agriculture and suggests that this is underpinned by an openness among male farmers, in particular, to alternative models of agriculture and masculinity. This research includes little direct discussion of the body, although Ní Laoire refers to the greater willingness of men participating in sustainable agriculture to admit to bodily weakness in the face of nature.

Outside agriculture, the rural body has also been discussed in work on leisure and recreation in the countryside. Studies on the early "explosion" of outdoor recreation in Britain and North America show how ideas about the importance of the countryside and landscape protection developed from links between health and physical recreation. Such links were clearly embodied in the fit, strong, and capable walker, as authors such as Tim Edensor have observed.[27] According to popular ideas of the time, a fit body indicated a fit mind and an ability to navigate the landscape and survive in the outdoors. As rambling and other forms of rural leisure developed, the fit body was esteemed as somehow more appropriate and "in place" in the countryside, a superior physical condition ensuring a more sensitive appreciation of rural nature. These views also distanced the rural body from the metropolitan body, which by contrast was seen as defensive, passive, and sensually deprived.[28] While countryside recreation was not specifically gendered, the outdoors was characteristically seen as a natural place for the expression of masculinity. Women were thought to be less able to control or discipline their "unruly" bodies and thus less suited for the demands of more serious walking and hiking.

The relationship between the fit body and nature is now discussed in terms of many other, more specialized, forms of rural outdoors activity such as climbing, bungee jumping, white water rafting, and other "extreme" sports.[29] Paul Cloke and Harvey Perkins, for example, discuss the sensual experience of the sporting body and the heightened sensory awareness of nature afforded (exclusively) to the fit body.[30] While, again, the body in such sports is not exclusively the male body, the representations and practices associated with these activities suggests that men who excel are conforming to the expectations of masculinity, while women are stepping outside (beyond) the expectations of femininity. Together with other studies that consider, for example, the body in different spaces of rural nature such as woodlands,[31] such work is important in examining different bodily practices in a rural context and in understanding the values placed on the fit body in that context. These studies, however, rarely focus on the body itself or on the agency of the body within differing views and experiences of the countryside.

Rachael Woodward confronts the relationship between the male body and nature more directly in her discussion of military training in the United Kingdom.[32] Again, Woodward highlights the importance of physical fitness and in particular an ability to survive in inhospitable environments to the construction of masculinity. She notes the way the male body is pitched against the elements in military training and how "success" as a soldier is judged by the body's capacity to withstand harsh, unpredictable wilderness conditions. Woodward also draws attention to the importance of sexuality to embodied constructions of masculinity. The "real" masculine body of the soldier is unequivocally heterosexual; those who are physically weaker are referred to by other recruits as "fairies" or "girls."

Work on the rural body (and the body in rurality) has also focused on sexuality and the gay body. While most work on rural homosexuality looks at the marginalization of gays and lesbians in the social spaces of the village and the rural environment,[33] authors such as David Bell, Will Fellows, and David Shuttleton discuss more positive associations between the gay male body and the rural landscape.[34] Two key themes emerge in this work: first, the notion of the rural as an Arcadian space in gay literature, a place where the purity of the countryside is seen as a "natural" setting for homoerotic relationships and the celebration of the male body; and second, the related idea of the rural as allowing space for the discovery of same-sex relationships. Farming lifestyles in particular are seen to encourage greater freedom to explore homosexual relationships, with the physical development of the male body involved in physical outdoor work holding a particular attraction for urban gay men.

These general, and somewhat limited, themes show where researchers have typically located their work on the rural body. Their emphasis is largely on the relationship between the body and nature, in particular the representation of the male body in the context of overcoming the "natural" elements and enduring wilderness conditions. Very little has been said about the rural body in a social setting,[35] or about the expectations that surround the embodied performance of masculinity and femininity in the spaces of the rural community. I now take my argument into this rich and uncharted area by examining three examples of the rural body that show how hard it is to divorce the body from sexual identity. Here we return to the discussion of heterosexuality and to the assertion that we can see the rural body only through the normalizing "lens" of a particular form of heterosexuality.

## The Rural Body and Community Spaces

To discuss the rural body in the context of the social spaces of the rural community, I draw on three specific examples of embodiment. These three examples include representations of both male and female bodies (although emphasis is placed on masculinity and the male body). The main purpose of the section is to show how the body—as it is represented and performed within the rural community—reflects and reconfirms a highly conventional, benign, and nonaggressive heterosexuality. This is an alternative "reading" of the embodiment of rural masculinity discussed above; it does not assert the conventional relationship between the fit, strong, and powerful male body and the control of nature. Rather, it emphasizes the rural body as homely, unsophisticated, and unthreatening.

### The Rural Body and the Naked Calendar

The first example of the representation of the rural body is the "phenomenon" of the naked calendar depicting men and women in various guises within the rural community and landscape. Although not unique to the United Kingdom, the naked calendars discussed in this chapter are of a particular genre started in the late 1990s as one-off productions organized for charity or to assist particular farming communities. The first and best known of these calendars was produced by the members of the Women's Institute (WI) of the Yorkshire village of Rylstone, England, to raise money for leukemia research following the death of one of the women's husbands.[36] In Rylstone, the calendar's production was highly publicized and raised a considerable amount of money. It also led to some major social and domestic divisions within the community, later documented by one of the venture's prime movers.[37] The Rylstone naked calendar has been followed by many others of a similar style featuring men or women drawn from a particular village, district, or "rural interest group."

The calendars are characterized by their "lighthearted" approach to nudity, and participants have emphasized that they should not be taken seriously and are only a bit of fun. Although the Rylstone calendar was a financial success, raising more than £500,000, the participants and the press treated it as a joke. One article talked of the women as having their "modesty concealed only by the jam-panned, cider pressing paraphernalia of traditional WI pursuits."[38] The jocular tone of the reporting reflects a view of the rural body that is also apparent in the images themselves. The main impression from the Rylstone and other calendars is that the bodies depicted are not conventionally "sexy"; the calendars represent both the women and men as homely and cuddly rather than exciting and dangerous. The bodies are not presented in sexually provocative ways and the models are not pouting, alluring, or suggestive in the manner of other nude calendars. The models are often fuller, rounder, and less physically fit than conventional models—and they are certainly neither aggressive nor racy.

The images contained within these calendars reinforce a view of embodied rural sexuality as controlled, conventional, and uncontested. These people are not overtly sexual and are not "available." Many of the images stress the domestic and family aspects of rural life. In this way, the body is distanced from sexual activity. While part of the message may be that sex in the countryside is more natural, involving bodies of all shapes and sizes, another part also suggests that sex is also distanced from the body, not something governed by uncontrolled and dangerous bodies. As I suggested above, the calendars present a rather different version of the male body from that in classic representations of masculinity seen in the farming press. There are fewer images of rugged, physically strong, "butch" or "buff" bodies, rather an emphasis on jolly, coy, and slightly comic representations. These are not predatory, aggressive, sexy, or threatening images.

The naked calendars provide a useful illustration of how the male body is represented in the rural context and in turn how this reflects a particular

Mr. July: Pre-packed Somerset. Example from *Meat British Beef* calender, 2001.
By kind permission of Nicola de Pulford.

reading of rural masculinity. I do not want to claim that this reading is exclusive to rural society or that it is the only possible reading of rural masculinity. It is important, however, to recognize the power of such representations in the assumptions and values surrounding sexual identities and to acknowledge their role in not only reflecting but also re-creating attitudes toward the male body. The next example takes up the issues raised concerning the embodiment of a dominant form of family-based and traditional heterosexuality as a central characteristic of rural masculinity.

## Country Living: *The Farmer Wants a Wife*

My second example of embodied rurality comes from the farmer-wants-a-wife campaign run by the UK magazine *Country Living,* in which farmers advertise for partners/wives. Each year from 1999 to 2003 the magazine has enlisted fifteen farmers and acted as a dating agency for these men in their search for wives. The magazine prints a picture of each man with a short blurb outlining some basic biographical details and his "requirements" for a wife. Women are invited to write to farmers they are interested in dating and *Country Living* acts as a "broker," selecting a "suitable" partner for each farmer. In 2001, ITV/Carlton television made a television "docusoap" about the campaign, following the fortunes of several farmers and their chosen partners. Here I summarize the magazine articles, interviews with the scheme's main organizer, Emma,[39] and interviews with some of the farmers involved.

I have discussed several themes that emerge from this campaign elsewhere, including the links between highly traditional forms of gender relations, farming, and rurality. Here I want to draw attention to the ways in which the campaign and the expectations of those participating in it convey very conventional ideas of heterosexuality. These ideas in turn embody a rather benign and passive sexuality, reinforcing constructions of rural masculinity similar to those discussed above. The farmer-wants-a-wife campaign was established in response to what the organizer described as a "very real need": the perceived "problem" of unmarried farmers being unable to find suitable wives. As I have noted elsewhere,[40] this construction of the farmers' problem is imbued with strong notions about the importance of the family in agriculture and in particular the securing of the family farm for future generations. Reflecting on previous years of the campaign, *Country Living* couched its success in terms of permanence: "Perhaps you're recently divorced or widowed, or are just too busy—or bashful—to meet the right person. *Country Living* is here to help. Last year our lonely hearts campaign was a phenomenal success, attracting hundreds of single women looking for love in the countryside. Wedding bells are already ringing for three couples and others have found happiness with . . . new partners."[41]

The expectation of permanent relationships articulated in this passage goes beyond the actual campaign, however, and is clearly reflected in the farmers' views. Several spoke of the particular pressures they felt to find a wife and "settle down and have a family." This is not necessarily a surprising attitude, or even a specifically rural or farming-related phenomenon, but reflects the broader expectation of heterosexuality and stable relationships in society generally. The farmers, however, did speak of what they considered additional pressures to form permanent relationships relating to the assumptions of continuity in farming and a need for a "wife" to organize and run the farm household. Farmers who had not achieved permanence in a relationship talked of being viewed as failures. As Emma of *Country Living* explained: "Many of the farmers say 'everyone is on at me, why haven't I settled down, why haven't I got a wife' and it's the accepted thing in their social area that that's what you do—you get married, you settle down, you have children . . . the son takes over the farm and off you go . . . for one reason or another they haven't achieved that."[42]

The campaign also required a committed and serious response from those participating and regarded people who were not looking for a permanent relationship as unsuitable. Each round of the campaign stressed the message that any abuse of the sentiments on which it was based would not be countenanced. In other words, both sets of individuals (the men advertising and the women responding) were expected to adhere to unwritten rules of monogamy, truthfulness, and serious intent. Casual and multiple relationships were frowned on; for example, one of the farmers who was found to be dating another woman outside the campaign, and another who was seeing several women at once, provoked strong disapproval.

In the case of the women responding to farmers' adverts, serious intent was also equated with an understanding of farming and the countryside. The campaign organizer and some of the farmers appeared somewhat scornful of (city) women participants who had no "understanding" of the countryside or, in particular, of a farming lifestyle. Such women were dismissed as potentially flighty, high-maintenance, and disruptive. Only "genuine" country women were considered likely to stay the course, to understand the demands made on them as farmers' wives—demands that appeared to include being willing to adopt traditional gender roles, especially in times of crisis.

Emma related how she could divide the women who responded into two groups: "There are the women who either live in the country and have a very good understanding of what it's about or people who grew up on farms and for one reason or another have moved to towns to get jobs and would always really like to go back to the country way of life and then there's the 50 percent who have absolutely no idea whatsoever and just like the idea of having a horse."[43]

Interestingly, the women's suitability also appeared to be linked to physical characteristics. Farmers who chose their "dates" on the basis of physical attractiveness were seen as unrealistic. Emma talked of having to sit down with the farmers who were "disappointed" with the women chosen for them[44] and explain that the women most likely to understand them and be suitable mates might not be the most "attractive." She concluded that "when they thought about it sensibly they realised this was the case."

In terms of embodiments of masculinity, the farmers advertising did not all conform to the more conventional images of masculinity discussed above. Typically, their photos did not emphasize the physical strength and fitness of farmers in the way other representations have;[45] they were not depicted in macho poses, wrestling manfully with stock or handling powerful machinery. Often they were pictured in domestic situations and with animals—pets or young stock. In describing themselves in the short biographies that accompanied the advertisements, farmers rarely made reference to physical characteristics (in terms of themselves or the partners they sought) but instead drew attention to hobbies and interests. The men are often described as quiet and shy, attaching more importance to loyalty and commitment from their partners than to attraction, excitement, or novelty. This representation of the "quiet, shy country boy" is also central to my third example, the Bachelor Ball in Middlemarch, New Zealand.

## The Middlemarch Bachelor Ball

The third example I consider is from rural New Zealand. It relates to perhaps a rather different "type" of rural community and yet, as I argue below, demonstrates some of the same expectations and assumptions about the nature of rural gender identities and embodiment relations. Like the farmer-wants-a-wife scheme, the Bachelor Ball also engages with concerns over needing to retain the farming family as a central element of rural society.

Middlemarch is a small agricultural community in Central Otago, a region in the lower half of the New Zealand's South Island. In 2001, as part of the annual Agriculture and Produce Show, a ball was organized to provide a social venue in which local single men could meet eligible partners. The idea for the ball had arisen from a study of declining population and services in the small rural town. At the end of a meeting in which the seriousness of the decline was outlined, a member of the community board suggested that one of the solutions would be to "marry off" a local bachelor to a nurse. From there the idea grew into a scheme to organize a special Bachelor Ball and to invite single women to come and meet prospective husbands. Organizers arranged a "love train" from Dunedin, the province's city, to take single men and women to the event (about fifty miles away). The event generated considerable media coverage both locally and worldwide. The Strath Taieri Community Board and local businesses supported the event in the interest of community expansion, as the organizer, Sue,[46] explained: "We are just trying to find additions to the community and we know there's a lot of bachelors around. . . . If we can get some of the bachelors to start a family, all the better."

The Bachelor Ball raises several issues about the problems faced by shrinking rural communities and the provision of services to such communities. Its relevance here is in the constructions of rural masculinity and family life that are both implicit and explicit in the event. Overwhelmingly, the Bachelor Ball implies that the community can be protected from further decline only through the "natural" growth associated with heterosexual family relationships. Interestingly, the problem is seen to stem from a particular form of "typically" rural masculinity in which men are seen as shy and lacking in confidence and hence unable to form relationships with local women: "They are shy, many of them. Farming can be a lonely, difficult life and it's really hard to get to know people."

The representation of the men in the Central Otago farming areas is very much dominated by the "Southern Man": a tough, rugged outdoorsman of few words. The flip side of the "strong, silent" Southern Man, however, is the unsophisticated, vulgar, and socially inept version of masculinity associated with wilderness and extreme environments.[47] The behavior (and indeed the bodies) of these southern men may be seen as inappropriate in terms of attracting women, but this is understandable and excusable given the tough lives they have to endure. As Sue put it, "Some of the social habits are . . . well, I was relieved that we didn't have any 'down-trousers' in the tent. It's one of the party antics that some of them get up to. It gets them the attention they are not getting any other way. A girl can change it just like that."

Women, it seems, need to be able to understand these attributes of masculinity and to "tame" them in the pursuit of stable relationships and family life. The body of the Southern Man is essentially uncontrolled and requires a woman's civilizing influence; once "attached" to a woman, the Southern Man becomes confident and pays attention to his appearance. According to the organizer of the Bachelor Ball, the "revised" Southern Man will take a much more active part in local events and become a more valuable (and valued) member of the rural community. "The guy who is now living with a girl—you can't believe the change in him. He wears a tie to functions and looks tidy. A week after they got together he was down at the golf club—he'd never been there before."

The masculine body here is not threatening or sexy but out of control and rather hopeless. Just as in the advertisements for farmers in the *Country Living* campaign, the men are seen as naive, rather unpracticed, but essentially lovable. Again, this is a rather different version of rural masculinity from the one represented in the farming and sporting press both in New Zealand and worldwide. In this version, men may be in control of their farms but not of their social skills or their bodies. In both the Middlemarch Bachelor Ball and the *Country Living* dating schemes, it is women's job to "socialize" these endearingly ineffectual, underachieving men into acceptable partners and family men.[48] The Bachelor Ball has also led to the production of a "Blokes" calendar (unpublished as this book went to press). The calendar was described as just the blokes of Middlemarch doing what they usually do—that is, a production that definitely does not intend to present the men as sexy or alluring, but simply as rural people with a sense of humor.

This chapter has presented three examples of the embodiment of masculinity in rural communities and argued that these constructions of masculinity underpin, and are underpinned by, the strongly traditional nature of rural gender relations and the importance of the family to the rural community. The examples I have presented reflect a different masculinity from dominant representations in the farming press. I have argued that the rural body here is represented as humorous, fun, and at times uncouth. It is not sexy or sophisticated, and certainly not threatening and aggressive. Unlike images in which male bodies appear to be managing, taming, and controlling nature, the bodies discussed here are more homely, less capable, and even slightly apologetic.

I have also stressed the importance of examining the rural body in the context of sexual identity, and specifically in terms of our society's dominant assumptions of heterosexuality. I have shown that we need to consider the relationship between sexuality and space to appreciate the different types of heterosexual environment that exist. While existing research emphasizes the creation of "queer spaces" or those marked by aggressive or "scary" sexualities, here I suggest that we also need to explore the more conventional sexual identities that normalize heterosexuality and assert the central role of the family in rural communities. As in research on queer or scary sexualities, we can also fruitfully examine the ways in which practices of embodiment and performance create and re-create these more "conventional" heterosexualities.

Although this chapter has been able to present only a very brief discussion of rural embodiment, I have attempted to show how central particular constructions of the rural body are to social and gender relations. These preliminary findings need to be developed in a more extensive and detailed study of the rural body. This chapter has also attempted to go beyond representation to consider the way masculine bodily performance is constantly made and remade in different spaces. While I do not consider these exclusively rural constructions, or the only versions of masculinity and femininity that exist for rural people, they do show particular characteristics that help us to understand more about rural gender identities and the values and assumptions that surround gender roles. In particular, they show clearly that the sexed body is simultaneously part of and also "other" to the assumptions of naturalness that surround the rural family and gender identities. Clearly, there is considerable scope for a deeper analysis of constructions of the rural body, together with its place in the constitution of masculinity and femininity in the countryside.

NOTES

1. Longhurst (2000), Hubbard and Sanders (2003)
2. Longhurst (1997, 489).
3. Rich (1979).
4. See, for example, Firestone (1972).
5. Longhurst (1997, 489).
6. Connell (2000).
7. Ibid., 58.
8. Gatens (1996).
9. Connell (2000, 59).
10. Butler (1990).
11. Brook (1999, 14).
12. Ibid.
13. Butler (1993, 1).
14. Valentine (1993).
15. Richardson (1996, 7).
16. Hubbard (2000, 197).
17. Ibid., 197.
18. Rich (1980).
19. Hubbard (2000, 2002).
20. Brandth (1995); Brandth and Haugen (1998); Bryant (1999); Liepins (2000); Saugeres (2002a).
21. Liepins (2000).
22. Brandth (1995).
23. Brandth and Haugen (2000) and also their chapter in this volume.
24. Saugeres (2002b); Ní Laoire (2002).
25. Rose (1993); Longhurst (2001).
26. Bryant (1999); Ní Laoire (2002).
27. Edensor (2000).
28. Ibid.
29. Cloke and Perkins (1998); N. Lewis (2000).
30. Cloke and Perkins (1998).
31. Macnaghten and Urry (2000a).
32. Woodward (1998, 2000).
33. Bell and Valentine (1995b).
34. D. Bell (2000a, 2000b); Fellows (1996); Shuttleton (2000).
35. Although exceptions include Campbell (2000); Leyshon (2005).
36. Traditionally, Women's Institutes are highly conservative organizations with a generally middle-aged or elderly membership. In the United Kingdom they tend to be associated with rural domesticity and skills such as baking and jam making.
37. Stewart (2001).
38. Barton (2001).
39. Not her real name.
40. Little (2003).
41. "The Farmer Wants a Wife" (2000, 39).
42. Emma (pseudonym), interview by author, London, August 2002.
43. Ibid.
44. From all the letters sent, one woman was chosen as an initial partner to meet each farmer at a function organized by the magazine. Farmers were then given all the letters sent in and left to contact any of the women they wanted to meet.
45. For example, those described by Liepins (2000).
46. Not her real name.
47. Law, Campbell, and Dolan (1999).
48. Little (2003).

# Beer Advertising, Rurality, and Masculinity

*Robin Law*

Recent scholarship on masculinity has stimulated research into how masculinity is represented and constructed in advertising. Within this discourse, beer advertising provides a particularly promising area of study, given that it characteristically draws on (and thus reinforces) stereotypical aspects of masculinities. Beer advertising in New Zealand, for example, draws on the instantly recognizable stereotype of the "Kiwi bloke" whose three main interests in life are rugby, racing, and beer, while, in contrast, Japanese beer advertisements deploy the stereotype of the cosmopolitan, socially successful "modern man." But beer advertising also maintains notions of *regionally specific* masculinities linked to the trademark images of regional beer brands. Thus in Britain the television advertising for Boddington's beer uses a strong north-of-England accent and distinctively "northern" language.

In New Zealand, beer advertisements often mark the distinctiveness of each region by displaying particular kinds of rural landscapes and rural men's work. This chapter looks more closely at such regional and rural constructions of masculinity through the example of the highly successful "Southern Man" advertising campaign developed for Speight's, a popular New Zealand beer. As the name suggests, the campaign presents images of men in a distinctive place (the landscape of a part of New Zealand's South Island), thus generating a version of masculine identity that draws much of its power from the meanings associated with a specific landscape.

Obviously, much beer advertising throughout the world uses similar versions of rural and *regionally specific* masculinity. New Zealand, however, is a particularly interesting site in which to explore this topic, for interest in the nature of masculinity pervades the culture to the extent of constituting what Kai Jensen has termed a "repetitive obsession."[1] This "repetitive

A version of this chapter was originally published as Law (1997). Our thanks to *New Zealand Geographer* for permission to use this version.

obsession" with the nature of men and manhood has generated scholarly texts, many of which are also read by the general public, as well as popular nonfiction. A picture essay entitled *Blokes & Sheds,* for instance, which examines the "kiwi bloke" in his ineffably male workspace, has been one of the top-selling books in New Zealand in recent years.[2] Jensen suggests that a particular tradition of New Zealand manhood, shaped by early novelists and short story writers such as Frank Sargeson, may now be manifesting itself in wider, more accessible media, having been "picked up, amplified and broadcast by popular writers such as [Barry] Crump and Sam Hunt, and cartoonist Murray Ball, as well as by journalists, disc jockeys, politicians, sports writers, advertising agencies, and so on."[3] Regardless of the direction of cultural transmission, however, in New Zealand both consumers and advertising agency copywriters operate within a shared cultural environment rich in ideas about and images of masculinity.

In many ways, New Zealanders define their national identity in terms of rural life. Rural imagery is very common in media representations of New Zealand, despite the fact that a large proportion of the population actually lives in towns and cities.[4] The rural also tends to be coded as masculine (in contrast to the feminine, or effeminate, urban). Contemporary issues of masculine and feminine identity in New Zealand are presented and played out in rural settings in films, television programs, and advertisements.[5] Of these, advertisements for beer are particularly significant, since the practice of drinking beer in this country is laden with gendered meaning. To adopt the catchphrase of another advertising campaign, this time for the Lion Red brand, "what it means to be a man" is intimately bound up with what you drink.[6]

I frame this chapter using Douglas Kellner's recommendation that critical cultural studies should examine production and political economy, engage in textual analysis, and study the reception and use of cultural texts.[7] To this list I add the suggestion that cultural geographers should also investigate how these texts take a material form as objects imbued with meaning within a landscape. These four directives lead to four questions. What conditions create the context for a successful advertising campaign based on local identity? How does that campaign draw on place-specific gender and landscape imagery? How has the campaign altered the environment? And, finally, how has the campaign been received and interpreted?

The research for this chapter was conducted in 1997, in Dunedin, the second-largest city in New Zealand's South Island. Dunedin lies on the southeast coast of Otago, a large, primarily farming region with rugged, sweeping areas of "High Country." The area was originally settled by Scottish immigrants, and in the far south many people still speak with a distinctive rolled "r," an accent known as the "Southland burr." Dunedin itself was originally founded on wool and gold and continues to operate as a center for Otago's rural industries. Its other main industry is provided by the University of Otago, New Zealand's oldest university, with its attendant thriving student population and subculture—the city's modest population (120,000) swells by close to 20,000 during the academic year, and the town advertises itself as offering a highly desirable "campus lifestyle." Like virtually every New Zealand province, Otago and Southland have their own local rugby football team, which is proudly supported by the general population and maintains particular links to the student body. The population also has a much-loved "local beer"—in this case quite literally a local brew, as the Speight's factory has been operating in the city center since 1876.

To study the phenomenon of Speight's "Southern Man" advertising, I drew on both primary and secondary sources of evidence. Wide-ranging face-to-face interviews were conducted with the brand manager for Speight's beer, a marketing consultant involved in the campaign, and—given the strong associations between Speight's, rugby, and the university—the president of the University of Otago Rugby Football Club. Informal telephone discussions were conducted with other individuals with local knowledge, including a product focus group participant and a representative of the public relations agency for Speight's. Published sources consulted included company annual reports, a history of the brewery, and press reports. In addition, a short item was placed in the local community newspaper and in an industry newsletter asking for jokes, anecdotes, and stories about the Southern Man. This chapter discusses the situation in the late 1990s; since then, the Southern Man has continued as the mainstay of Speight's advertising campaigns and has been increasingly adopted as a local symbol by Otago residents.

## Conditions Creating the Context for a Local Identity-Based Advertising Campaign

The two big players in New Zealand's beer industry are Lion Nathan and the DB (Dominion Breweries) Group, which together control about 90 percent of beer consumption.[8] During the 1970s and 1980s, DB dominated the South Island market, especially in rural areas, although Speight's beer (a Lion Nathan brand) maintained a strong local following. In the late 1980s and early 1990s, however, several significant changes to licensing rules and the regulation of alcohol advertising created new conditions within the beer market. Out of these conditions, the Southern Man campaign was born.

By the late 1980s, national beer consumption was declining steadily, thereby intensifying competition for market share. At the same time, Lion Nathan's corporate strategy shifted away from ownership of distribution outlets (mostly pubs) toward more direct marketing to consumers. In 1989 licensing rules that had effectively kept Lion Nathan brands out of some markets changed, and a great many more licensed premises opened, thus increasing the opportunities for expanding market share through consumer-targeted advertising. In 1992 a new regulatory regime governing alcohol advertising was introduced: for the first time, brand advertising for alcohol on television was permitted, subject to a set of voluntary controls over content that limited the choice of pictured scenarios.

There were local as well as nationwide changes. In Otago, three important trends emerged. First, Dunedin Lion Nathan branch managers persuaded their head office to soften the corporate strategy of creating a single national market with national brands, and are thus credited with initiating a later corporate shift toward more local autonomy for branches.[9] Second, the number of university and college students in Dunedin increased dramatically, and—unsurprisingly—Speight's was already strongly associated with a student pub subculture.[10] Finally, from about 1987, the fortunes of the Otago provincial rugby team, the Highlanders (sponsored by Speight's), began to rise, and in 1991 they won the national championship—no small achievement in a country where rugby constitutes, if not a religion, then certainly another "repetitive obsession." Their success was based on an adventurous, team-focused style of rugby, which for many observers epitomized "Otago values" of innovation and integrity.[11] Loyalty to the team among fans was easily transferred to loyalty to the beer.

By the beginning of the decade, therefore, the new deregulated environment meant that the scene was set for a sophisticated marketing challenge from the Lion group of companies for the South Island beer market. One of the main strategies adopted was a strengthening of the regional identification of their brand. The strategy succeeded. Despite a flat market, Lion

Nathan brands continued to grow in volume and share in all South Island regions in the 1990s. Market share grew rapidly to 43 percent in 1992, 48 percent in 1993, and 51 percent in 1994, most of it made up of the regional brands of Canterbury Draught and Speight's.[12] In the Dunedin area, Lion Nathan brands held about a 70 percent share of the market in 1996.[13]

## Place-Specific Gender and Landscape Imagery

The Southern Man campaign was meticulously crafted; even the choice of actors for a brief television commercial was guided by focus-group research. The imagery of landscape and place-specific (masculine) activities was also carefully selected. In the very early version of the campaign, a variety of men in South Island work settings, such as oystermen at work wearing heavy yellow oilskins, were represented. However, this diversity was soon replaced by a consistent focus on a single landscape (the High Country) and a single form of work (sheep mustering).[14]

The implicit attitude toward the subjects of these images is curiously ambiguous. On the one hand, the representation of landscape and men follows conventional Western pictorial norms of "unspoiled" nature and "real" men. On the other, this conventional representation is undercut by a wry, self-deprecating sense of humor. Both halves of the equation, however, serve to reinforce important aspects of the brand image. Most obviously, the depictions of strong, silent "manly men" set against nature's backdrop reinforce the "masculine" aspect of the brand image. This is summed up by a member of the marketing team: "Here's what we think Speight's means: 1. It's honest 2. It's rugged. 3. It's uncomplicated and of course 4. It's quintessential 'Southern.'"[15] This vision is shown in the cornerstone of the campaign: the set of naturalistic photographic images of men at work, which are used in posters, pub signage, and on the sides of delivery trucks. Most images show men accompanied by dogs and horses, herding sheep on golden hillsides. One image in particular—of man, dog, and horse—is universally used in pub signage and has become the iconic Southern Man.

But the heroic element in these images is offset by a dry, self-mocking sense of humor in other components of the campaign. In keeping with this, the marketing staff also describe the brand identity as "quirky," with a "personality" and an attitude of "not taking yourself too seriously."[16] The ironic humor is crucial, since it allows the advertisements to be enjoyed by male (and quite possibly female) readers on two levels: they can identify with the heroic image of the Southern Man but protect themselves from ridicule and feminist challenges by implying that it is all a performance. This humor is most apparent in the suite of television commercials used to advertise the brand, rather than in the naturalistic posters and outdoor media. However, it is also apparent in two popular posters, one of which presents a tongue-in-cheek "Southern Man Identification Chart" ("Right Hand: Holds rugby balls, rifles, shearing equipment, BBQ tongs, tools, and a footy mag in a firm manly grip"), while the other a list of rules on "How to be a Southern Man" ("A Southern Man never eats quiche or beansprouts, uses cellphones or drinks beer out of a stemmed glass").

The television advertisements bring such "Southern Men" to life. In the first and most successful of a series of television commercials, a young man and an older man are resting at dusk by a lake. Both are shepherds, dressed in characteristic slouch hats and musterer's coats. Both also speak with the characteristic Southland burr, using local phrases ("She's a hard road . . ."), and in a laconic style punctuated with many silences. The younger one reveals that he has been seeing a city girl from the North Island who wants him to move to Auckland, New Zealand's "cosmopolitan capital." She can offer a range of sophisticated material comforts such as a yacht and a private box at New Zealand's "home of rugby," Eden Park. But she does not drink Speight's beer, and that clinches it. The younger man's decision is affirmed by the older man's encouraging words: "Good on ya, mate." This advertisement (known in the trade as "perfect girl" after the moment in which the older man glances at the photo of the glamorous blond girlfriend and comments disparagingly that "she's a hard road finding the perfect girl") has won prizes in Australasian competitions and continues to have a powerful impact on viewers.[17] Another advertisement (known as "making tracks") shows the same two characters flipping the switches on railway tracks to divert a train from carrying its load of Speight's beer up north.

Why are these television commercials and billboards so powerful and effective? More particularly, how do they use concepts of masculinity and place? Clearly, the advertisements draw on typical themes in beer advertising in the Western world, and refer to a tradition of idealized representations of masculinity in New Zealand.[18] They show single Pakeha (European) men affirming the importance of male mates, heterosexuality (in the abstract), hard physical outdoor work, the wisdom of older men being passed on to younger ones, and an unselfconscious authority over the animal world.[19] My focus, however, is on the way *place* is incorporated in these advertisements and used to inflect the representations of masculinity. The masculinity on display here is formed and given meaning in part through place. There are four main dimensions to this geographically specific construction of masculinity.

First, at the most general level, the advertisements are placed in *"the rural."* As such, they draw on the cultural tradition that associates nature and the rural with authenticity, and on a particular New Zealand tradition that codes the rural as masculine in contrast to the effeminate urban.[20]

Second, the advertisements are placed in a specific rural setting: the *High Country* of the South Island, and more particularly of Central Otago. This is a place with its own characteristic associations: to some extent, "the High Country is to New Zealanders what the Outback is to Australians, or the Frontier was . . . to Americans."[21] In the Speight's interpretation, the purity and hardness of the High Country landscape are linked to the characteristics of (male) inhabitants and promoted as an ideal model for all New Zealanders. The imagery draws much of its power from the way the local landscape is displayed (and read by New Zealanders) as a distinctive place. This specificity is neatly signified by unobtrusive design elements. All the print and outdoor media images are structured by the steep angle of the horizon and colored with the blue and gold of sky and tussock grass. In the pub signage, the horizon line forms a strong diagonal bisecting the image into two planes of color. These colors not only echo the navy and orange of the beer can but also resonate with the often and proudly displayed blue and yellow provincial and university colors—at any Highlanders rugby game, for instance, the crowd (and indeed the city) becomes a sea of blue and gold. Color and horizon angle thus distill the landscape features of the Central Otago High Country into an easily read visual sign.

Third, the advertisements show a *timeless place*. There are no disturbing modern gadgets among the images of "unspoiled" nature, stripped-down male bodies, companion dogs and horses; we see no farm bikes, two-way radios, or binoculars, not even a plastic bag. Thus, although the advertisements are not explicitly set in the past, their depictions of rurality evoke nostalgia for simpler times and a poignant recognition that this way of life is threatened.

Finally, the advertisements (especially those on television) obliquely refer to the place as an *economically marginal space* that requires masculine strength of character and audacity for its challenges to be met. The "perfect girl" television commercial compares the life available in the south with the material benefits on offer in Auckland. In the "making tracks" commercial, the train symbolically expresses the drain of resources (and people) from the South Island to the North Island. Although the men try to resist this by switching the rail signals, their actions seem bold but are ultimately futile.

The depiction of the south as an economically marginal site and Southern Men as brave resonates with the anxieties of viewers from the South Island about their place in the world. Over the past few decades, the North Island (especially Auckland) has attracted an ever larger share of the country's population, while many places in the South Island have lost both jobs and people. The "perfect girl" television commercial, therefore, speaks to the choice that many young people in the South Island face—especially those completing their tertiary education—of whether to move north in search of a better life. The anxiety about making choices consistent with authentic values is raised and then (humorously) relieved by offering the possibility of staying true to oneself by consuming Speight's beer.

The "making tracks" advertisement identifies a threat to the integrity of the region's resources and shows a creative act of guerrilla defense. In this advertisement, men's traditional role in defending territory is affirmed; yet, according to the marketing team, this advertisement has not been as successful as the first, in part because it contradicts local residents' pride in their beer being a valued commodity in the north.[22] This boosterism, together with what we might call "export pride," is similarly a response to anxiety, in this instance over the precarious economic position of South Islanders in relation to North Islanders. Again, this anxiety is very real: the North Island boasts 75 percent of New Zealand's population (Otago and Southland together constitute about 8 percent) and the two largest cities (Wellington, New Zealand's capital, and Auckland). On a different scale, this economic anxiety is also felt by New Zealanders in relation to Australia, and indeed to the rest of the world. One of the ways the advertisements work is by evoking that anxiety and then appeasing it.

## Environment Altered by the Campaign

These advertisements do not only *represent* an environment, they also *create* one. Shaping the environment takes two forms: on the one hand, urban streetscapes are affected by the placement and design of outdoor advertising such as billboards, while on the other, consumers use advertising products to decorate and create environments, albeit on a much smaller scale.

Since alcohol advertising budgets are large and opportunities to advertise are legally restricted, outdoor advertising for beer is significant. Speight's spends about one-quarter of the amount it lays out for television commercials on outdoor media advertising, a relatively large sum in comparison to other consumer products.[23] In Dunedin, the brewery site near the heart of the city is marked by massive three-dimensional signs that dominate the streetscape from blocks away. Images of the Southern Man also appear outside liquor outlets, at sports facilities, and on the sides of refrigerated trucks. This juxtaposition has the uncanny effect of bringing a rural landscape into the middle of a busy urban setting. The text of the advertisements, moreover, never describes the beer; typically, only the phrases "Southern Man" or "Pride of the South" appear, thus making the meaning of the advertisements particularly open to multiple interpretations. The iconic, often life-size image of Southern Man on a rural hillside is used extensively to advertise pubs, and appears on the street or alongside country roads like a hallucination. It can be read as a promise of an identity accessible through the doors of the pub, or perhaps as a mirror of our true inner selves, like the unexpected reflections of ourselves in shop windows that we sometimes recognize after a moment's confusion.

On a smaller scale, pub interiors are typically decorated with Southern Man posters, as are club bars. Individuals also use the advertising material to mark territory. The exteriors of student housing around the university, for instance, are commonly decorated with Speight's beer bottles, logos, and stickers, while students from outside Otago often "counteradvertise" with stickers for their hometown beer. No other branded consumer product is used in such a public declaration of affiliation.

Bodies also become advertising sites. Clothing emblazoned with the Speight's logo and imagery is given away in promotions and sold in stores devoted to beer memorabilia. At the beginning of the academic year, similar products are used as prizes in student orientation events. The Southern Man image has become interchangeable with other local markers of identity to the extent that, for example, the small gift shop on the university campus sells T-shirts and hats bearing the Southern Man slogan and image alongside mementos bearing the university crest. In these ways,

advertising images become naturalized as part of local culture, and their commercial genealogy and function are obscured.

## Campaign Reception and Interpretation

Advertisements are not closed cultural products but require the participation of readers/consumers to make meaning. There is, therefore, always the possibility of alternative or oppositional readings that subvert the message, rearrange it, and use it to invent a new place and identity.[24] These may coexist with the preferred readings of the advertisement makers; in some cases they may undermine it. The concept of oppositional readings is a useful counterpoint to simplistic models of passive consumers manipulated by advertisement copywriters, but the existence of such alternative readings needs to be discovered rather than assumed.

Although the research for this chapter did not include fieldwork, the investigation did reveal some traces of alternative readings. These tended to do one or more of three things: they questioned the male traits celebrated in this model of masculinity; they challenged the racial and colonizing implications of the advertisements; or they involved a strategy of "invasion" by women resisting their exclusion from this pictured world. The strongest attempt to separate the themes of masculinity and alcohol consumption arises from concern for public health. One health promotion officer writing for the university student newspaper mocks the characters in the Speight's television commercial and calls for a "New Machismo" that says: "I'm a bloke and . . . clever enough to recognise when the alcohol industry is trying to manipulate me."[25]

The association of the Southern Man imagery with Pakeha (European) men has similarly been challenged by direct reworking of the advertising objects. Graffiti on a Dunedin pub sign has blacked out the face of the Southern Man and spray-painted the word "BLACK" over "SOUTHERN." This act links the Southern Man image with two other colonial icons a few blocks away, both similarly embellished. A statue of Queen Victoria had its face spray-painted black, and the slogan "Mana Motuhake"—which means "autonomy" and is the name of a Maori political party—was painted on a portrait of Captain James Cook decorating the outside of the Captain Cook Tavern wall. Like Queen Victoria, Captain Cook operates as a sign of colonization, as the British government of the eighteenth century sent him on several missions to explore and map the coastline of New Zealand. Even more than Queen Victoria, therefore, he stands as the symbolic founding father of white settlement in New Zealand and the subsequent disempowerment of the indigenous Maori.[26]

Like the politically motivated graffiti artist, some women are also challenging their exclusion from the Southern Man myth of local identity, some by refusing to drink Speight's, others by a strategy of appropriating the myth and "invading" the territory. For example, both a candidate in Dunedin local government elections and the mother of a Member of Parliament referred to themselves as "Southern Women"—a clear reference to the advertising campaign.[27] Women's ambivalent relationship with the myth was expressed in a telephone conversation with a woman who responded to my request for anecdotes from the public. She referred to a popular Southern Man pub poster that shows men relaxing outside a hut, apparently at the end of a day's work. She said: "My nickname is Dixie, which is a southern name, I drink at the Southern Tavern, and I used to work at the Southern Orchard in Roxburgh. Once I also used to work as a shearer's cook. Everyone started a joke when I was working at the orchard. They looked at the poster in the pub of the men arriving home at the hut. Everyone kept asking, 'Where's Dixie? Where's Dixie? She's gotta be in there somewhere.' I'd say 'I'm inside the hut.'" I asked, "Cooking?" "No," she replied, "inside the hut having a bottle of Speight's. Cooks get a wee bit hot!"

In this story we hear Dixie claiming her right to enter the imaginary place constructed by the Southern Man advertisements. She looks for her representation on the poster and, undaunted at not finding it, writes herself into the script. While she knows her expected role (as a cook), she refuses it, instead inventing herself not only as a beer drinker but, more important, as a "Southern Woman."

The Southern Man campaign is a product of a particular time and place. It was created within the constraints and opportunities set by the intersection of specific economic, legislative, demographic, and cultural trends, played out at the local scale. The effect of the campaign has been significant. In commercial terms, the campaign has helped to create more Speight's beer drinkers. It has garnered advertising industry awards, generated high brand recognition and loyalty, and contributed to increasing the brand's market share among the target consumer group.

The imagery and text of the advertisements draw on a widely shared set of ideas about masculinity and national/regional identity in New Zealand. In particular, the advertisements work by evoking a distinctive New Zealand landscape, connecting the landscape to a wider set of place-based meanings, and situating a simultaneously heroic and ironic representation of masculinity "in place." The campaign has also had an effect on the South Island environment. The physical manifestations of the advertising (billboards, hotel signage, posters, signs on the side of supply trucks, and so on) have themselves become features in the contemporary landscape of Otago and Southland. Finally, the images and phrases from the campaign have been absorbed into the vocabulary and visual repertoire of New Zealanders. They have been appropriated by people in or connected to Otago, and are used and reworked to support, satirize, and comment on the validity of this construction of regional identity and masculinity.

NOTES

1. The term "repetitive obsession" is used by Jensen (1996). For a review of New Zealand writing on masculinity, see Law, Campbell, and Schick (1999). Among the significant works are books by Phillips (1987); James and Saville-Smith (1994); Jensen (1996); Law, Campbell, and Dolan (1999).

2. Hopkins (1998).

3. Jensen (1996, 17).

4. M. Bell (1996); Carter and Perry (1987); Perry (1994).

5. Campbell and Phillips (1995); Longhurst and Wilson (1999); Liepins (2000).

6. Research on beer drinking in New Zealand includes Campbell (2000); Kraack (1999); Hodges (1984). Beer advertising is analyzed in Honeyfield (1997); Campbell, Law, and Honeyfield (1999).

7. Kellner (1995, 8). For useful sources on interpreting advertising texts, see Goldman (1992); Hall (1993); Williamson (1978).

8. For more detail on the beer industry, see Pawson (1996); Campbell, Law and Honeyfield (1999).

9. Gordon (1993).

10. Kraack (1996, 1999); Hodges (1984); Russell (1999).

11. Fitzharris (1997).

12. *Lion Nathan Annual Reports* (1992–95).

13. *Otago Daily Times* (1996b, 20).

14. Goodwin (1997).

15. Kenrick (n.d.).

16. Goodwin (1997).

17. Cossens (1996).

18. Strate (1992).

19. More specifically, "Pakeha" is the term used in New Zealand for someone of European ancestry, in contrast to "Maori," which refers to someone descended from the indigenous inhabitants.

20. Berg and Kearns (1996); Campbell and Kraack (1998).

21. Fitzharris and Kearsley (1987, 199).

22. Goodwin (1997).

23. Ibid.

24. Hall (1993).

25. Sarten (1996, 6).

26. Kraack (1999) describes drinking practices within the Captain Cook Tavern.

27. *Otago Daily Times* (1996a, 23).

# Changing Masculinity in a Changing Rural Industry: Representations in the Forestry Press

*Berit Brandth and Marit S. Haugen*

Contemporary research on gender recognizes it as a pervasive principle of social organization, operating at multiple levels and across the spaces of work, politics, families, and everyday interaction. Gender is not always easily visible, however, and in many contexts assumptions about gender are taken for granted. Agriculture and forestry are strongly associated with masculinity, and as such may reproduce self-evident meanings of gender, together with its connections to work and organization. But structural changes in the forestry industry and in gender relations as a whole suggest that the meanings of masculinity in these occupations may be changing.

Within the agricultural context, discourse analysis has disclosed two main narratives of hegemonic masculinity—imperatives that Ruth Liepins has termed the "tough men farm" narrative and the "powerful men lead" narrative.[1] While these two types of masculinity can be found in many different rural contexts and countries, they are not immutable: they may come in disparate versions, the power relations between them may differ, and they may change over time. Alternative meanings of masculinity and femininity may gradually emerge, for instance, through the work of new farm women's groups as they produce different narratives of farming and political participation.[2] Similarly, women also influence masculinity when they attempt to enter traditionally male areas of work. A study of female farmers in Norway, for example, showed that when women started to enter men's space by operating tractors in their daily work, other spaces, and thus other types of activity, increased in importance as signs of manhood.[3] This dynamic suggests that the definition of masculinity as different from and superior to femininity tends to be maintained even during reconstructions of masculinity. Likewise, masculinity may be redefined as a result of

A version of this article, entitled "From Lumberjack to Business Manager: Masculinity in the Norwegian Forestry Press," was previously published in the *Journal of Rural Studies;* see Brandth and Haugen (2000).

challenges from other types of masculinity—that is, from within the gender category itself. Because a hierarchy of masculinities exists in which some masculinities dominate other masculinities, the relationships between subordinate and hegemonic masculinities themselves create possibilities for change.[4]

Within rural research, men and masculinity is a young but growing field of study. Berit Brandth's early study on this subject, for example, used tractor advertisements to focus on hegemonic masculinity in farming, showing that hegemonic masculinity shares many of the qualities characteristic of tractors (strength, bulk, power, control, and so on).[5] Because masculinity and technology can thus be seen as mutually constructed, Brandth argues that hegemonic masculinity in farming may be altered as technology changes and the tractor (for example) becomes more computerized and comfortable as a working place. Therefore, as these farm machines are increasingly promoted in terms of their technology rather than their brute strength, the image of the farmer as a strong, dirty, manual mechanic is challenged by a more "businesslike" masculinity. But Brandth also found that while technological and structural changes in farming operate to unsettle traditional hegemonic masculinity, masculine attributes of power and control persist, albeit in other forms. Given the inherent strength of this process, can we locate parallel changes in a related rural industry such as forestry?

In this chapter, we are interested in how masculinities are constituted at the various sites of forestry, and in how masculinities at different sites challenge each other. To examine these concepts, we focus on textually mediated representations of forestry masculinity. Media representations are important because they are not only based *on* social life but have a powerful structuring effect *in* social life. As such, they strongly shape our received meanings of masculinity and femininity. "Media representations tell us who we are, who we should be, and who we should avoid," Michael Kimmel explains.[6] We thus examine a specific forestry magazine to analyze the role of work and its spatial embeddedness in the conceptions and constructions of forestry masculinity.

## Gender Theory and the Invisibility of Masculinity

As many social scientists have pointed out, the apparent solidity and embodiment of gender belies its contingent, unstable, and disputable nature.

To capture the instability of gender, therefore, we will approach it as a social construct in line with the characteristic perspectives in contemporary research on both gender as a whole and men and masculinities in particular.[7] To see gender as a construct means seeing it not only as an attribute or characteristic of people, but more significantly as a relationship, practice, and process of constructing meaning. Such an approach implies a focus on the spatial, cultural, and historical diversity of gender, using the concept of "multiple masculinities" to convey how specific and various forms of masculinity are constructed in relation both to femininity and to other masculinities.[8] To understand the diversity of forms and the changes that occur within masculinity, it is important to "ground" our analysis of it within specific contexts (for example, different workplaces).

In sociology the term "context" is often used to designate the space-time constitution of identity, while in feminist geography the terms "space," "place," and "sites" have proliferated as analytic concepts.[9] In this analysis we use the concept of "sites," by which we mean not only lived realities but also the mental spaces constituted by the locations of family, work, occupation, class, type of industry, organization, and so forth. As might be expected, much criticism about men and masculinities explores masculinities as they are shaped at various sites.[10] Some sites may be strongly associated with gender, while others are more associated with class or status. Sites are also "contested, fluid, and uncertain," and the social practices that define them result in overlapping sites with multiple and shifting boundaries.[11] When multiple sites overlap with one another, gender appears complex and ambiguous.

In this chapter we are interested in the sites of forestry. But "forestry" is not just *one* site where men construct their masculine selves: it includes different types of work in forestry (white-collar jobs versus blue-collar jobs), many occupations, and various classes (forest owners, entrepreneurs, and workers). This multiplicity means that we expect to find multiple representations of men and masculinity. To clarify these multiplicities when reading gender into our chosen text, we have concentrated on three aspects of gender. The first is the *structural* (or spatial) position of power, which shows where men are placed in the social hierarchy of forestry. The second is *practice* (or activity), or what men are pictured doing at the different sites. The third is *display* (or performance), or how men present themselves by means of dress, style, bodily posture, emotions, associations with technology and other people, and so on. To capture the dynamics of gender, all three aspects of gender (structure, practice, display), together with the interplay between them, have to be considered.

The structural/spatial position of power is relatively overt, or visible, in this site. The practice/activity of masculinity, by contrast, relates to the actual activities of the site and to the theoretical conceptions of gender as something men and women do.[12] David Morgan, for instance, has shown the critical and complex significance of work activity for the constitution of masculine identities.[13] It is through activity that gendering processes come into play and individuals express who they are and are not. Thus, in turn, activity may be taken as the material basis of masculinity.[14] In a poststructuralist perspective, however, "doing" is primarily understood as "performance" or "performative."[15] This brings us to our third primary aspect of gender, display/performance. Despite recent theoretical tendencies to define masculinity almost entirely in terms of gender display, in this chapter we regard display as only one of several social demarcations of gender.

Here we examine these three aspects of masculinity through the medium of an occupationally oriented magazine *Skogeieren* (The Forest Owner). We are interested in the way masculinities are constructed through articles, pictures, and advertising in this magazine. Because forestry is traditionally a male bastion, these articles, pictures, and advertisements deal with men and masculinity in a predominantly male space, that is, a space constructed primarily not in relation to femininity but to other men. But there is another aspect of these representations that we need to take into account. Since men and masculinity are usually treated as the "norm" in Western culture, portrayals of men in the media have often been seen as unproblematic—even exemplary. Because masculinity represents the norm, therefore, it does not appear distinctive. Thus the privileged position of men is rendered invisible.[16] By extension, when gender is thus rendered invisible, matters are often assumed to be gender neutral. As Joan Acker explains, "Gender is difficult to see when only the masculine is present. Since men in organizations take their behavior and perspectives to represent the human, organizational structures and processes are theorized as gender neutral."[17]

Pierre Bourdieu uses the term "doxa" to describe the phenomenon of viewing the organizational principles of the social world as obvious, natural, and above all objective or unbiased.[18] Doxa defines an experience that appears not as a result of choice but as something naturally given, a "matter of course," such as the traditional masculine gendering of forestry. Discourse analysis studies doxa to understand not only the processes by which meanings are established as "natural" but also the questions that disrupt the "taken for granted" and therefore admit conditions for change. As theorist Anne Cranny-Francis puts it, speaking of feminist discourse analysis, "The most important role and task of feminist discourse is to challenge this naturalization, this obviousness, this common sense. And to challenge it feminist discourse has to make it visible."[19]

In line with both feminist research and the new discourse of men's studies, we view masculinity as a problematic gender construct. We assume that the gendered character of this construct tends to be taken for granted, and thus we take up "gender lenses" to study how gender is represented in the forestry press. According to Michael Messner, using "gender lenses" means "unpacking the taken-for-granted assumptions about gender . . . showing just how central assumptions about gender continue to be to the organization of the social world, regardless of their empirical reality."[20] Our analysis of *Skogeieren*, therefore, renders visible the invisible or "taken-for-granted" masculine gendering of forestry in order to identify the construction and dynamics of hegemonic masculinity.

## The Text

*Skogeieren* is the official magazine of the Norwegian Forest Owners' Federation. The magazine was first published in 1914, appears monthly, and is distributed to all members (forest owners) of the federation. Accordingly, articles aim not only to present the members' interests but also to open up issues for discussion and differences of opinion. The magazine is an important source of information for, and a link between, the members. The federation was established in 1913 to protect forest owners' economic interests, building on cooperative principles, membership democracy, and local self-rule. The organization is large—in 2003 it boasted 56,000 members—and is organized into district and local associations throughout the country. These associations are predominantly autonomous. Because organizational activity and politics (in addition to practical forestry work) are increasingly important aspects of the industry, a large part of the federation's activity involves business politics directed toward issues such as increasing competition and market regulation. Perhaps unsurprisingly, given its power, in many of these matters the federation's practice with central price negotiations and cooperation over prices is in conflict with free market ideals and international trade regulations.

We base our analysis on all forty issues from three years, 1976, 1986, and 1996—a twenty-year period encompassing great changes in society and gender relations. We believe that these three anthologized volumes are sufficient to inform us of the broad patterns and trends of change. Our point of departure is 1986, the year in which the women's network organization Girls in Forestry (JiS) was founded to motivate women to participate more closely in forestry. As our study was originally concerned with the possible effects of this initiative on the representation of masculinity, we chose to focus on the volumes ten years before and after the founding of JiS.[21] For the purpose of this chapter, however, we have focused on the representations of men and masculinity during the whole twenty-year period.

Initially, we simply counted the number of male and female writers and the number of men and women appearing in pictures as a way of establishing the gendering of the magazine. We found that male dominance was numerically clear in all three volumes. With few exceptions, all the journalists and writers in the magazine were men, the illustrations were mainly of men, and all the editorials and readers' letters were written by men. This overwhelming numerical superiority underlines not only the dominance of male readers but, more important, the masculine character of the discourse and the site. As the magazine articles represent men talking to men, they function to define and redefine masculine work identity and pride, constantly reaffirming what men find central and important and demonstrating how men see themselves in relation to colleagues.

## Forestry: A Man's Job

The overwhelming masculinity of forestry discourse represented by this initial numerical survey reflects forestry's history as one of the most masculine of rural activities. Even today, forestry is a man's job. According to the 1989 Census of Agriculture and Forestry,[22] 85 percent of Norwegian private forest owners are men.[23] Even though many of these forests have two formal owners—one representative study indicates that as many as 80 percent of married farm forest owners share property rights[24]—women are typically recruited to different tasks within the industry than men. As we have shown in a previous article, and as an American study of the diversification of forest service jobs similarly demonstrates, women are overrepresented in clerical and administrative jobs and underrepresented in professional and technical positions.[25]

When it comes to ownership, the socialization of boys and the transfer of knowledge and skills from father to son have functioned to exclude women from forestry. Traditionally, although women carried out many tasks, such as bringing home firewood and animal feed, forestry has always been regarded as a male workspace.[26] While it was not unusual for daughters and wives to accompany fathers and husbands to debark and haul timber, lop off twigs, and gather fodder, men seldom talked about this work because of the sense of shame associated with being able to afford help only from "womenfolk."[27] More usually, forest work meant that men had to stay away from the farm for long periods in the winter to log and transport the timber. In the absence of their husbands, wives had the responsibility for more domestic concerns, such as the small forestry farm, animal husbandry, and raising children.

As *Skogeieren* illustrates, mid-twentieth-century technical developments and changes in the organization of forestry work inevitably altered these traditional conditions and led to a differentiation of roles for forest owners. By the 1960s, for example, forestry increasingly became year-round work, a transition accelerated by the introduction of Timberjack machines (purpose-built fellers, bunchers, skidders, log loaders, and harvesters). One of the most important changes brought about by this type of machinery was the transition from individually based work to teamwork.[28] More automated and advanced machinery also made roundwood cutting and transportation easier, which in turn promoted specialization of forest work. To a decreasing extent, therefore, forest owners, forestry cooperatives, and farmers cut the roundwood themselves, preferring to defray the cost of expensive machinery by hiring contractors to do this work. During the 1980s the use of new and bigger machines owned by entrepreneurs expanded to the extent that, by the end of the decade, forest owners logged only one-third of their total volume themselves, focusing instead on managing property and optimizing resource use. In contrast, by the 1990s attitudes toward heavy machinery changed, as the industry started to question its suitability for Norwegian forestry and its compatibility with emerging environmental concerns. Naturally, these technological and organizational changes imply parallel changes to the meaning of masculinity within forestry, changes that can be summed up in the transformation of the lumberjack into a business manager.

## From Lumberjack to Business Manager

In this second half of our study, we consider Liepins's two masculine imperatives, "tough men farm" and "powerful men lead," in terms of the two most distinct areas of forestry: practical forestry work and managerial/organizational activity.[29] By examining how these two sites are represented in *Skogeieren*, and how these representations have changed over time, we analyze what kinds of masculinities are constructed at the different sites and how their relative positions have changed.

### *"Tough Men Log"*

The site given most attention in *Skogeieren* is practical forestry work. This "hands-on" site may be characterized as heavy, dirty, dangerous, and connected with dominant narratives of rural masculinity.[30] Numerous articles deal with different aspects of work in the forest, such as clear felling, thinning, planting, cleaning, pruning, transporting, and road building—all, except for planting, activities dominated by men.[31] Not all these activities, however, are equally important as signs of masculinity. In *Skogeieren*, logging operates as the most important site of "tough man" masculinity.

Traditionally, working hard and being seen as a good workman have been sources of status in farming societies.[32] In keeping with this, the magazine presents many individual forest workers, all of them represented as outstanding foresters in one way or another. Articles also point to the importance of their rural identity, thus placing these men firmly within the "tough men farm"—or, in this case, "tough men log"—narrative. These men are described as resilient, hardworking, and able to endure harsh natural conditions like rain, snow, storms, and frost. They are "lads with muscles and snuff," smelling of resin and sweat, with strong backs and a resilient work ethic.[33] While independence and freedom are important to these rugged workers, comradeship—belonging to a community of forest workers as in the old days—is also valued. Several pictures thus illustrate male bonding in different settings.

The forest workers do not boast about their physical strength; it is taken for granted, a "naturalized" part of their masculine identity. More typically, the journalist contrasts himself and his work (his "tools" of pen and paper) with the brawny forest workers and their machines, and lets the readers understand that the work is physically tough and demands the vigor of manhood. Typically, the journalist emphasizes not only the masculine taciturnity of the forest worker but also his harsh environment: "'The forest is fine. I enjoy myself here. I am my own boss and do not need to clock in,' says J. R. through the icicles in his beard."[34] The magazine also contrasts the advantages of outdoor forestry work with the disadvantages of other types of work, such as office work and even farm work, stressing that such forestry work is free and easy, independent and individual, and takes place outdoors in fresh air against the dramatic backdrop of nature. Although the magazine does acknowledge that forestry is a risky occupation, it also implies that competently handling risk is an attribute of masculinity.[35]

At this site, men constantly put themselves in danger, effectively participating in many "battles" to master nature and conquer difficult natural environments like steep slopes, marshy terrain, and, in the winter, deep snow and frost. Men working in the forest at −20° C, for example, claim that they do not mind the cold, for their work keeps them warm. Again, journalists contribute to this rugged masculine image by focusing on the inhospitable conditions—one journalist, for example, begins his story: "One grey December day when one snowdrift replaced the other, we met A. L. who faced the weather and was in full activity with lumbering."[36] While this mastery of nature is in many ways the primary focus in *Skogeieren,* the magazine also recognizes a different relationship with nature, one that involves respect for and care of the natural landscape for future generations. As well as a site of "battles" against nature, therefore, the forest also operates as a site for masculine recreational activities such as hunting and fishing.

Mastering machines is a central aspect of the mastery of nature required by forest work, and thus also a central aspect of this form of masculinity. Judging by the number of articles picturing men at work with machines, this goes to the very heart of masculine identity in forestry. These men are active and competent in practical, technical matters, and their knowledge of the forest is highly valued. Mastery over this technology, therefore, bestows power on these men, particularly in relation to other men and women who lack mechanical expertise.

Within the "hierarchy" of technological skill, heavy machines rank highly as displays of masculinity. As one might expect, most of the advertisements in *Skogeieren* are for machinery and other equipment. Such advertisements usually contain a plain description of the item's advantages and qualities (for example, power, efficiency, security, low running costs, and environmental considerations) and a picture of it, frequently against a background of trees, rocks, thunder, or lightning. As previous research on tractor advertisements has shown, when metaphors are used in this type of advertisement they overwhelmingly relate to qualities important to men and masculinity, and so it is with the advertisements in this forestry magazine directed at the working logger.[37] One power saw is described as "king of the woods," another as "a great, strong hulk of a fellow without weight problems." A hoisting apparatus is called "the power packet," a belt-driven transport vehicle with a winch is characterized as the "iron horse," and a pickup truck is "a rough and rugged working car with real power to pull." In our survey, we found that the association of the macho image of the forest worker with technology was exceptionally strong in 1986. In neither of the other years studied do we see so many images of strong, vigorous men posing with their power saws, ready to bring down the forest. Likewise, in neither of the other years do we find so many interviews with men "in action," conquering new land by building roads through virgin forest to facilitate the use of big machinery.

Plainly, the 1980s can be seen as the decade of machine entrepreneurs in forestry. Across the twenty-year span of our study, however, we noticed signs that the hegemonic "tough men log" narrative was gradually challenged, as new skills became needed in forestry work. For instance, computers have become increasingly important as a tool in forestry planning. In 1986 an advertisement for a personal computer apparently shows the traditional working skills central to hegemonic masculinity in forestry on the defensive. The advertisement pictures a forester (a man with a helmet) saying, "Practitioners should be listened to. There are too many wiseacres in agriculture."[38] But the defense of "hands-on" forestry is nevertheless linked to technological advancement, and the advertisement as a whole suggests that "new" technology needs to be combined with practical knowledge. This advertisement, and others like it from this decade, show that while control may be achieved by different means, the importance of control itself remains central. That is to say, while the display of hegemonic masculinity might be changing, its social position of power is not. Moreover, practical forestry cannot completely dismiss new technology, as being in command of the very latest developments signifies being involved in the future.

The 1980s also saw a new generation of women who wanted to work in forestry, and thus traditional or hegemonic forestry masculinity found itself challenged by a new feminization. Attracted by nature and the environment, these women fought the view that females were unsuited for forest work, effectively contesting the discourse of the rugged and physically strong male forest worker.[39] When Girls in Forestry was founded in 1986 to encourage more women to enter forestry, *Skogeieren* particularly addressed the issue of women in forestry in its 1986 issues. The simple fact that women were about to enter the site as active forest owners raised questions about male dominance and, by extension, the corresponding discourse of hegemonic masculinity. We speculate that the introduction of women into forestry work may have prompted the magazine's expressly macho representation of masculinity in 1986. During this year, the magazine celebrates the "tough man" image of masculinity by persistently stressing fundamental signs of masculine status and self-esteem—manual labor and machinery, physical endurance, and mechanical skills.

Certainly, the twenty-year span covered in our study of *Skogeieren* demonstrates an evolution of the forest worker's masculinity. While in 1976 the magazine made a great point of men struggling with nature, in 1986 the focus was much more on mastering machinery. In keeping with this shift, the mild-mannered old workmen with furrowed, weather-beaten faces on the cover pages in 1976 tended to be replaced by young, dynamic men with power saws and heavy machinery in 1986. By 1996, in turn, the "macho" aspects were less visible, and the advertisements within tended to be more sober. As with the shift from "traditional" to "mechanized" forestry, this change suggests that the discourse of hegemonic masculinity in forestry is again being opened up to alternative discourses, and that attention is shifting to a different site. Could it be that within the discourse of late twentieth-century forestry, "physical" masculinity is slowly giving way to "organizational" masculinity?

*"Powerful Men Lead"*

The second site in *Skogeieren* that we studied was the managerial organization of the Forest Owners' Federation, as the magazine has given this site increasing attention over the years. While the narratives of this site are presented as gender neutral, men are nevertheless the actors who disseminate knowledge, discuss policy, negotiate, comment on issues, and give statements. The men pictured at this site are men of political power and influence within the organization. Their titles indicate their middle- to high-level positions—director, chief executive, chairman, trade policy adviser, and so on—in other words, they are men of status and authority who hold significant managerial positions. Men are, furthermore, depicted as very dynamic and visible at this site, actively pushing cases and aiming to locate themselves at the core of organizational and political debates. They are pictured at meetings, at rostrums, and around conference tables. They are shown formally dressed in white collar and tie, overt signs of managerial authority. At this site, therefore, we are presented with a version of masculinity based on managerial decisiveness, assertiveness, authority, oratorical strength, and diplomatic skill. The closer a man is to the top rung of the federation, the more important skill in this form of masculinity becomes.

Organizations are characteristically sites of competition between men, particularly in terms of organizational restructuring and politics. When it comes to these areas within the federation, *Skogeieren* presents us with an internal discourse describing men battling between themselves for recognition and power. Over the twenty-year period studied, increased international competition and new regulations created needs for a solid central office and strong, professional management. Accordingly, being a federation representative (*tillitsmann*)[40] increasingly demands special qualities because of expanded managerial activity and new types of organizational tasks.

As early as 1976 the federation anticipated that being a representative would become more difficult because of such increased activity. It stressed that demands on the representatives had become greater because of the need for professionalization and the federation's increased industrial and international engagement, as it had become the largest owner of forest industry in the country. Representatives participating in the organizational discourse produced by such activity were mostly recruited from forest owners. While previously their knowledge about forestry was enough to hold an organizational position, today managerial skills have almost become a profession in themselves, as a statement from a 1986 interview illustrates: "Much more is demanded of a representative today than previously. It is not enough to know all about forestry and one's own organization. Knowledge about industry, its products and structure is also demanded. It is essential that one is able to see forestry as a part of the country's economic life, and know a certain minimum about international affairs." [41]

In 1996 the magazine explicitly expressed a great need for a clearer structure of power within the federation, questioning what should constitute power in the organization and where it should reside. In this year the federation's managing director resigned after fourteen years in office (the previous director had held his position for thirty-three years), recognizing that he had not succeeded in keeping the organization together. Although his resignation was not presented as dramatic—as other scholars have pointed out, control of emotions is part of the culture of the "rational man"—one can easily imagine the underlying conflicts, particularly given that managerial hegemonic masculinity at this site is typically represented by metaphors that refer to fighting and battle. [42] One 1996 article, for example, described the federation's top management as "castrated male cats," lacking the power to fight or to execute their tasks. [43] Similarly, another article claimed that the members of the committees ought to behave more like "commanders of an army" than "weathercocks." [44] When a committee (of eleven men) was set up to propose a restructuring of the organization, its purpose was to create "a modern, future directed, and hard-hitting organization." [45] It is important to note that there are practically no women to be seen at this organizational site, and there is no discussion about a need for increased representation of female forest owners. In 1996 there was one female representative on the central body, but in 1997 she was no longer a representative—and no other woman took her place.

As noted above, over the twenty-year span covered, the magazine's content became increasingly occupied with organizational and managerial matters. In keeping with this shift, as the organizational site has increased in importance, it has provided a new visual locus for the demonstration of masculinity. Almost without exception, all the articles from our survey period are accompanied by pictures of middle-aged managerial men. In 1976 these pictures tended to be group pictures, but by 1996 they were mostly individual portraits. This pictorial shift reflects a growing emphasis on individualism and assertiveness—characteristics that parallel the "new achiever" type of corporate man.[46]

In the earlier survey years, the most respected men appear to be those who can display masculinity at both the forestry and managerial sites, men for whom the power saw and the filofax are equally important symbols. A 1986 issue of *Skogeieren,* for example, shows the federation's manager with a lumberman's gear, explaining in the accompanying text that "[G. R.] is not only an organizational man. He also knows the practical work."[47] This image exemplifies the representative with strong roots in forestry work, who simply puts on a tie when attending meetings. His legitimacy depends on other forest owners' approval. By 1996, however, there was less overlapping between practical and managerial sites. This increasing autonomy of sites may indicate that organizational masculinity is in the process of gaining legitimacy in itself, and that the professional business manager as a "type" is becoming more important and focused in the magazine. Unlike his rugged predecessors, whose performances were judged by their control of harsh nature and heavy machines, the professional manager's success depends mainly on economic results, efficiency, and managerial competence.

We have seen that at the sites of practical forestry work and managerial activity, men see and relate only to other men, and that the gender relations within forestry are constructed, reconstructed, and maintained within this overwhelmingly male domain. But while articles in *Skogeieren* are about men, they do not explicitly focus on men *as gendered beings.* As we have explained, without "gender lenses" masculine gendering is invisible because it is not openly discussed. By assuming "gender lenses" to investigate these two sites, therefore, we have deconstructed the two hegemonic narratives of masculinity operating within them—the "tough man" and the "powerful man"—and shown how these narratives are played out through structural (spatial) organization, activity (practice), and performance (display).

These two models of masculinity differ in terms of degree of power, type of work performed, and manner of display. The forestry worker's power is based on the bodily strength required in "battling" the natural environment and is displayed by means of work clothes and machinery. The organizational man's power, by contrast, is based on control over economic resources, managerial acumen, and political skill, and is displayed by means of "power look" business suits, conference tables, and rostrums. Paradoxically, while the "powerful man" is positionally contrasted to the "tough man" in forestry, the two roles are actually mutually dependent and draw on similar or parallel qualities. Both masculinities, for instance, are constructed through control and "battle." While the forestry worker must battle the elements, the organizational man must battle markets, deregulation, and internal controversies.

In this chapter we have contrasted the "tough" man and the "powerful" man as versions of masculinity the magazine represents in a predominantly coherent and unified manner. Even within these categories, however, there are signs of ambiguity. The "tough man"—the forest owner—is no longer also the rugged logger, as entrepreneurs increasingly take over much of this activity. Likewise, the sturdy old working man who monopolized the magazine's focus in 1976 is replaced in the 1980s by the energetic young man wielding new, efficient, and powerful machinery. In keeping with this shift, the 1986 issues concentrate on entrepreneurial representations of masculinity that promote technological ability and control over such new machinery. This "macho" representation of masculinity in 1986 may be seen in connection as a result of the founding of Girls in Forestry and the impact of women's entry into forest work. The emphasis on "macho men" at this time may also indicate a competition for hegemony between the "tough" and "powerful" positions of masculinity; when the "tough man" narrative is challenged, it responds by defining itself in a more extreme form. Threats from both women and a managerial type of masculinity, therefore, combined with the introduction of new, heavy, "hypermasculine" machinery, may have motivated this reassertion of a waning form of masculinity.

A decade later, however, this modernist paradigm of the technologically skilled "macho man" has weakened: now the practical "tough man" is unarguably retreating before the managerially "powerful man." But there is diversity even within the discourse of the "powerful man" and his position within forestry. On the one hand we have the professional managers of the industry, on the other the representatives of the federation, men who to a large extent are (or have been) forest owners themselves. Those representatives whose identities are based on their ties to forest work seem to occupy a position similar to that of the professional, and thus the diversification of this position supports its continuation.

While the practices and displays of masculinity in *Skogeieren* are spatialized, the spaces themselves are not fixed or static. This dynamic helps us understand the relationship between the two types of masculinity, particularly if we interpret the constant attempts at reaffirmation from the site of practical forestry—"practitioners should be listened to"—and the overlapping of sites as an overlapping of discourses. The overlapping of working site and organizational/managerial site suggests that the "powerful" man needs to gain legitimacy from the "tough" man. Similarly, the overlapping of organizational site and practical site implies an increasing emphasis on updating knowledge, training, and organizational engagement among "hands-on" forestry workers. Given these "spillovers," we can say that mutuality and competition for hegemony operate simultaneously in the "tough" and the "powerful" narratives of forestry masculinity.

By illustrating the dynamics of masculinity through variation and change, we have attempted to show that logger culture is changing. At the same time, the practical forestry in which such logger culture is founded is itself giving way to a managerial culture. The center of gravity is shifting, a shift that parallels wider changes in Western labor markets, which show a decline in blue-collar and an increase in white-collar jobs. White-collar professionals and managers define masculinities differently from skilled workers, even if these definitions typically overlap at various critical points. The changing models of masculinity in forestry, therefore, result from technical and organizational changes at different sites.

NOTES

1. Liepins (1998b).
2. Liepins (1998a).
3. Brandth (1994a, 1994b).
4. Connell (1987).
5. Brandth (1995).
6. Kimmel (1992), xii.
7. West and Zimmerman (1991); Morgan (1992, 1996); Lorber (1994); Hearn and Collinson (1994); Collinson and Hearn (1996); Kvande (1999).
8. Carrigan, Connell, and Lee (1985); Connell (1995a).
9. Giddens (1984, 1985); Women and Geography Study Group (1997).
10. Craig (1992); Mac an Ghaill (1996).

11. McDowell (1999, 4).
12. West and Zimmerman (1991); Kvande (1999).
13. Morgan (1992).
14. Collinson and Hearn (1996).
15. Butler (1990).
16. Hanke (1992).
17. Acker (1991).
18. Bourdieu (1989).
19. Cranny-Francis (1990, 2).
20. Messner (1997).
21. Brandth and Haugen (1998, 427).
22. Central Bureau of Statistics (1989a, 1989b).
23. Forest owners who own twenty-five hectares or more of productive forest

area (Central Bureau of Statistics 1989a). Altogether 78 percent of the productive forest land in Norway is privately owned (Central Bureau of Statistics 1989b). Most of the private forest properties are a combination of agriculture and forestry.

24. Strupstad (1991).

25. Thomas and Mohai (1995).

26. Alfnes (1990); Johansson (1989); Kaldal (1998).

27. *Skogeieren* (1999, no. 11:14).

28. Krogstad (1998).

29. Liepiens (1998a, 371).

30. Brandth (1995, 123); Liepins (1998b, 371).

31. Lidestav (1998, 66–73).

32. Johansson (1989, 200).

33. *Skogeieren* (1986, no. 4:41).

34. *Skogeieren* (1986, no. 1:22).

35. Morgan (1992).

36. *Skogeieren* (1976, no. 1:6).

37. Brandth (1995).

38. *Skogeieren* (1986, no. 4:4).

39. Halberg (1993, 543).

40. The Norwegian term for representative, *tillitsmann*, is gendered, translating as "man of trust."

41. *Skogeieren* (1986, no. 2:21).

42. Kanter (1977); Kvande (1999).

43. *Skogeieren* (1996, no. 9:13).

44. Ibid., 5.

45. *Skogeieren* (1986).

46. Barthel (1992).

47. *Skogeieren* (1986, no. 11:8).

# 13

## Warrior Heroes and Little Green Men: Soldiers, Military Training, and the Construction of Rural Masculinities

*Rachel Woodward*

This chapter is about soldiers, military masculinities, and rurality. My argument here is that soldiers are not born but made. Military training molds recruits into soldiers and draws on models of military masculinity in the process. This process does not just happen, however. Rural space and rurality are absolutely crucial to how the soldier is made. In this study I examine how rural space, rural place, and concepts of the rural influence one such model of military masculinity, that of the "warrior hero."

This chapter looks at how masculinity and rurality intersect in the making of the soldier by looking at the British army in the United Kingdom. There is nothing new, of course, in looking at the ways in which gender identities—what it means to be male or female—impinge on soldiers and military life. What is less obvious is the significance of place and space in the development of those gender identities, and that military masculinities are rural masculinities. Recruits become soldiers, and construct their identities as military men, in the countryside.[1]

## Examining Rurality and Gender in Military Masculinity

This argument—that military masculinities draw on constructions of rurality—evolved gradually as a result of research projects on issues such as military land use, the politics of military environmentalism, and the construction of gender identities in the British army.[2] The sources I draw on are eclectic. I examined recruitment material produced by the army for regiments and corps in combat arms, combat support arms, and supporting services. This material tends to be information on the various careers open within the army and the relevant selection criteria. This is the material sent to potential recruits, who tend to be male, white, aged sixteen to twenty-four, and educated to secondary-school level. I pored over publicity material produced by the army and the Ministry of Defence about military

training—press releases, *Soldier* ("the magazine of the British Army"), and
the video *Room to Manoeuvre,* which sets out the army's case for the military use of land for training.[3] I watched videos used by the army in recruit
training, like *Train Green* (about the need for environmental responsibility
when out on the ranges) and *It's Plain Sense Too* (about needing to look
after training ranges such as the army's holdings on Salisbury Plain in the
south of England). I devoured mass-market paperbacks telling tales, both
factual and fictional, of military exploits in the army. This genre, marketed
to a young male readership, explains much about military life to the novice
and sets out an aspirational model of military masculinity.[4] I watched television documentaries about military life and fly-on-the-wall series about
army training.[5]

   These were my sources, my "texts," if you like. According to the meth-
odology of discourse analysis (the approach followed in this research), texts
can be dissected and studied to determine how meaning is given to objects
and actions—how events and things are interpreted. My task in this research was to look at these texts and work out how discourses about military training, gender identities, and rurality were constructed.[6] A starting
point in this kind of approach is that both masculinity and rurality are
socially constructed; the meanings we give to masculinities and ruralities
are made, not innate. Feminist scholars have argued for decades that our
gender identities—what it means to be male or female—are made, the
tangible outcome of conscious human action, not biologically prescribed.
Second, and following from this, gender identities are fluid and change-
able; we have the capacity to endorse, reproduce, change, and subvert
norms of behavior prescribed by social convention. Third, our abilities to
do so are often enabled or constrained by the contexts in which our gender
identities are played out. Fourth, these gender identities are not monolithic
but show infinite variety according to the contexts in which they are produced and reproduced. Fifth, they are also relational; some are dominant,
others subordinate. Sixth, gender identities are constructed in space, with
reference to place and through the relationship of the body to space. Finally, gender identities are both culturally and temporally specific.[7]

## Military Masculinity and the Warrior Hero

Armies and military activities have long been recognized as important
sites for the social and cultural construction of masculinities. Militaries

are seen by many sociologists as masculine, patriarchal, and androcentric, and there is a large and diverse literature on the relationships between masculinity and military activity.[8] Here, I want to stress three specific points that come from this literature.[9]

First, there are many forms of military masculinity; that is, there is not just one way of being a man in the military. Furthermore, much in military life is predicated on the relationships between different models of military masculinity. Raewyn Connell, for example, notes how in contemporary Western military culture a masculinity celebrating a capacity for physical violence, yet subordinate to orders, may be dominated by a masculinity celebrating organizational competence.[10] Second, different cultures celebrate or deride different models of military masculinity at different times. Thus military masculinities are time- and space-specific. Therefore, although there may be parallels between, say, masculinities in the British army and in the U.S. Army, we cannot assume they will be the same. Similarities and differences have to be looked for, not assumed.

Third, there are parallels and connections between what we might term "hegemonic masculinity"—the culturally dominant ways of being male—and the dominant model of military masculinity that is discussed here, what we could term the "warrior hero." Values such as controlled aggression, a capacity for violence, and aggressive heterosexuality are celebrated in both.[11] The warrior hero is physically fit and powerful. He is mentally strong and unemotional. He is capable of both solitary individual pursuit of his goals and a self-denying contribution to the work of the team. He's also a bit of a hero with a knack for picking up women. He is resolutely heterosexual. He is brave, adventurous, and prepared to take risks. He has the physical ability to conquer hostile environments, to cross unfamiliar terrain, and to lay claim to dangerous ground. He appears, for example, as a poster-sized centerfold in a recruitment packet sent out by the British army to aspiring infantrymen. He wades waist-high through a river, leading a patrol of followers, weapon at the ready, and camouflaged against the reeds and branches. The caption endorsing the picture says, "ACTION / YOUNG / ON-THE-MOVE / SORTED / WELL-TRAINED."[12] He is a warrior hero, and he is the model of military masculinity I use as a starting point in this chapter. As a cultural icon, he informs the production of many of the ways of talking about masculinity in the texts I discuss.

## The Countryside and Rurality in the Construction of Military Masculinities: Military Recruitment Literature and Training

Nothing in the relationship between masculinity and rurality is automatic. The connections I draw between the two appear through circumstance and are reinforced by social practices, that is, the things people do in day-to-day life. A useful place to start looking at this relationship is in the literature the British army gives potential recruits in response to their inquiries about joining up, and how the images of rural masculinity presented within this literature are reflected in military training. The purpose of recruitment literature is simple: to present a picture of army life that is attractive to those with the potential and attributes suitable for being molded into an identified finished product, the professional soldier. The purpose of military training is equally simple: to create these professional soldiers. The recruitment literature I consider is for the infantry—other occupations within the army have different emphases. The infantry was chosen because of the quantity and quality of information available on training practices, and because of the ties between infantry training and rural sites; it is in the infantry that the connections between rurality and masculinity are most explicit. To be sure, they exist elsewhere in the army, but they are most visible within infantry units.

As a civilian, one thing that always strikes me as I look at this literature is the emphasis placed on the totality of the military life experience. Being a soldier is all-encompassing. Becoming a soldier requires complete commitment and determination. The trade-off, according to the recruitment leaflets, comes in the rewards for such commitment. In the words of one brochure, joining up brings "training for life, unbeatable rewards, excitement and adventure, a great lifestyle, a job worth doing." Being a soldier entails a whole new lifestyle. "Training for life" is central to producing the military masculinities that mirror the warrior hero model. It involves the transformation from civilian to soldier, which happens through the process of military training.

Military training is a process by which soldiers gain and develop the skills and attributes, both mental and physical, that they need to wage war. It is a process in which individuals are shaped and molded according to a uniform template, their appearance, behavior, and attitude conforming to a single set of expectations.[13] The countryside as a location and rurality as a social construction are fundamental to developing the requisite physical and mental attributes.

Rural areas provide the location for and backdrop to most infantry training in the British army. All recruitment literature makes use of this backdrop. An Army Recruiting Group brochure, for example, combines text describing the routine of infantry training with a series of photographs in which trainee soldiers load mortars on a hillside, crouch camouflaged in woodland, and run at full tilt down a moorland fell.[14] Another brochure, *Getting Fit for the Army,* uses similar illustrations. As the text explains, "Being a soldier is an active, outdoor life whichever part of the Army you join. You have to be able to think fast, keep going and do your job even when you're tired and working in difficult conditions."[15]

The rural location provides the backdrop, but is also portrayed as a challenging location against which the recruit is pitted. It is at this point that we see different constructions of rurality being drawn on in the representation of the training process. Artillery firing, camouflage use exercises, and cross-country running, for instance, take place in a bleak moorland landscape spread out under lowering gray clouds.[16]

To deal with the challenges of training and its location, the recruitment literature emphasizes the particular physical attributes that are needed. First and foremost, the soldier has to be, quite literally, "fighting fit": "The Army operates in all sorts of climates and terrains around the world and its men and women have to be ready to take up that challenge at a moment's notice. From steamy jungles to snowy mountains, you will be trained to carry out your specialist and military roles quickly and effectively. You will become fitter and stronger than you have ever been and you will learn to think on your feet and respond to rapidly changing circumstances."[17]

This physical fitness, then, is a quality needed for mastery of a variety of terrains. Again, images of rurality creep in: note how fitness is needed for jungle and mountain terrain. Presumably, training for foot patrols on the streets of Sarajevo or Baghdad does not have the same allure. Above all, this physical fitness is central to the type of masculinity promoted as a desirable attribute of the infantry soldier. Clearly, physical fitness is absolutely essential to the role of the foot soldier. Therefore, being "fitter and stronger than you have ever been" is celebrated as a defining attribute within this particular model of military masculinity. This is not the controlled physical exercise of the gym or health spa. It is a physical necessity developed in order to master the environment in which soldiers find themselves. This attribute is valued as highly for the model of the warrior hero as it is for the real soldier.

In order to work toward this peak of physical strength, recruits go through their basic training. The rural location for this is important; this process is not just fitness training on an athletics track but fitness to tackle the challenges of nature. Recruitment literature draws heavily on the rural as location and as construction in spatializing, or grounding, this element of training. After a first week of drill skills, map reading, and instruction in health and hygiene, a second week of fieldcraft puts recruits straight out into the open air of an army field training center in order to get to grips with the countryside: "You'll learn camouflage techniques and have your first taste of night training. That means using your eyes and ears in a different way—exploring how to identify noises at night, and how to see more clearly using off-centre vision. On your first night exercise, you and your battle partner operate in a buddy/buddy team. You'll build a shelter, which you'll sleep in, you'll cook your rations, and look out for each other."[18]

Training is about developing both physical and mental attributes. In this passage we see how such training includes acquiring a new way of being in the countryside, which involves using camouflage and night vision and relying on the senses. For many recruits, this will involve a fundamental shift: senior military personnel frequently complain about the lack of outdoor experience among a largely urban-based army intake.[19] But the rural, in the passage quoted above, is about more than just physical location. The rurality constructed here is matched to the task: the great outdoors is a place for survival, not pastoral contemplation, and a place of potential hazard and danger, not a landscape of leisure. It is certainly not the rural idyll of community and nature in harmony that a largely urban body of recruits may imagine.

## Constructing New Visions of the Countryside: Seeing and Being

### Seeing

A new way of being in the countryside requires a new way of seeing that countryside. The inculcation of environmental awareness in recruits is entirely necessary given that many of them come from urban backgrounds, may have attained only low levels of education, and may thus lack affinity for the natural environment. One task of training videos, therefore, is "to turn a recruit with a disregard for the environment into someone with a stake in the countryside."[20] One such video, *It's Plain Sense Too* (about the Salisbury Plain Training Area), sets up a vision of the countryside as the object of legitimate military concerns. This vision is carried forward in a discourse that establishes the scope of military activities in the rural training estate as a balance between effective training and environmental disturbance.[21] The idea of environmental protection is made more palatable to the conceivably disparaging recruit through the use of humor, provided by the actor Tony Robinson (the Baldrick character in the *Blackadder* television series and the presenter of the archaeology television program *Timeteam*) dressed up as (variously) ancient Briton, Roman legionnaire, Civil War royalist, and World War I recruit. In these assorted personas, he comments on historic uses of Salisbury Plain to provide parallels and contrasts with present military uses, as the following example shows:

> Us Ancient Brits were very fond of [Salisbury Plain]. We always had respect for the environment though, even in the heat of battle. Once I was locked in mortal combat with the local bully, Snogbag the Swine. I was just about to deal him a deathly blow with my club when he shouts out, "Look out! An orchid," and there beneath my feet was a rare and delicate flower that we were about to trample on. Forgetting our blood lust for a moment, I bent down to savour the beauty and fragrance of this tiniest of nature's miracles. Snogbag, a warm smile creasing across his fearsome face, then stabbed me in the leg, the bastard. Still, those were the days. We led a simple life, harvesting our crops, raising our cattle, shagging anything that moved, which more often than not was our cattle. But they do say that whatever you take out of nature you should put back in again, so that was probably quite a green thing to do really.[22]

Military discipline, to follow the video's logic, thus includes the soldier's having the necessary discipline to consider the impact of military training on the natural environment. As the video's final caption states: "Train and Preserve, Preserve and Train."

## Being: The Embodied Experience of Landscape

This new way of being in the countryside also requires new ways of being in a group. Again we see the values attributed to a model of military masculinity being developed as part of the training process. We can also see the role played by the rural in this process. The tension between individualism and teamwork is one of the hallmarks of the warrior hero model of military masculinity: the warrior hero needs both, but he also needs to judge when one or the other is appropriate.

Teamwork is required to enable group survival in hostile environments. In their accounts of Special Forces training, soldiers Adam Ballinger and Sarah Ford emphasize this point when they describe the rosters for sleeping, guard duty, and eating required during night patrol: on this course, the mistakes of one individual can mean failure for the whole group.[23] Therefore, individualism outside its appropriate context is discouraged; the warrior hero needs to support his or her mates. The importance of developing teamwork as a soldierly attribute is also evident in the passage quoted above describing fieldcraft. The key point here is the portrayal of teamwork not only as necessary ("you'll look out for each other") but as fun: cooking, eating, and sleeping in a "buddy/buddy" team are activities associated with camping as much as with military training. Thus the rural location here not only represents novelty and excitement but also a place for survival against the elements. While survival in the great outdoors is obviously important as a test separating the men from the boys, the rural location in which this testing occurs means it is also exciting and adventurous.

This model of military masculinity also celebrates individualism and independent endeavor. Again, these are qualities required by the soldier and thus trained for by the recruit. By week nine of basic training, when "adventurous training" begins, the recruits face several emotional as well as physical challenges—now their ability and aptitude for solitary work are developed and tested: "You travel to one of the camps in Wales, Scotland or on the South coast. Whilst much of the focus of the previous weeks has been on teamwork, this week is about your individual development. Through exercises such as hill walking, orienteering, canoeing, and abseiling, you'll face excitement, fear and challenge, and learn how to control and use your emotions effectively."[24]

The rural as rugged adventure playground is celebrated in the accompanying photography as both backdrop to these activities and part of the necessary context for training. It is the latter that is particularly striking in this example: the rural is the setting for circumstances in which emotions—specifically excitement, fear, and a sense of challenge—can be stimulated and then overcome through the acquisition of the necessary mental attributes. Again, visual images of a bleak, open, inhospitable moorland landscape accompany the text, and again, I would argue, we can see the rural as the medium through which specific values associated with the model of military masculinity are transmitted to the soldier.

## Mastering Emotions: Excitement, Fear, and Challenge

The three emotions highlighted above—excitement, fear, and a sense of challenge—figure strongly in soldiers' accounts of the military training process. Excitement, like the other two emotions, can be highly productive when managed appropriately—and, of course, being "master" of one's emotions is a strong characteristic of masculinity. Narratives of adventure and resourcefulness, therefore, help "disarm" potentially dangerous training activities in an unfamiliar landscape. Ballinger's account of the selection procedure for recruitment into the Special Forces, for example, clearly illustrates the sense of excitement when he talks about survival training in terms of a boy's own adventure story.[25] I know from my fieldwork the palpable sense of adventure and fun that flows from young recruits as they get to grips with the reality of training on army ranges. This is a highly gendered discourse: a high-ranking British general talks in his memoirs of organizing adventurous training weekends along army lines for his son and friends and defines them as strictly boys' activities, excluding his daughter from participation.[26]

Fear, the second emotion, is critical in training. While being afraid is a natural reaction to battle, it has to be conquered if the infantry soldier is to perform his tasks on the battlefield. Much of the army's justification for using large training ranges, rather than relying on simulated landscapes, rests on the need to inculcate in soldiers both fear and an ability to transcend physical discomfort. As one publicity video puts it: "If they are to perform the tasks we ask of them with any confidence, our soldiers must get dirty, wet, tired, and scared. This is the absolute bottom line of all military training."[27]

Being afraid of that landscape and of one's security within it are prominent themes in soldiers' accounts of their training and, again, conquering those fears is an essential step for these would-be warrior heroes. Fear is experienced but controlled. In this model of military masculinity, the soldier admits fright but conquers it to his advantage. As Andy McNab's *Bravo Two Zero* illustrates, humor helps, with sick jokes cracked at tense times. The book's heroes—like the professional soldier—laugh in the face of danger.[28]

The third emotion (or more accurately, skill) central to adventurous training is that of facing up to or meeting a challenge, be it physical or mental. Ballinger articulates well the sense of sheer physical and emotional challenge faced by trainees, be they raw seventeen-year-old civilian recruits or hardened elite soldiers. He talks of punishing weekends spent out on the hills. "We walked, climbed and ran in our squadrons for nine hours without a break. We rarely used paths and never roads. We went from A to B, usually on a compass bearing. At the end, high up in the hills of North Wales, Scott [an officer] stopped us and each man sat on his bergen [pack], grateful for the rest. We sat in a curve, two or three rows deep, around him. The wind whistled over the ridge, and our smocks, soaked with sweat, flapped against our skin."[29]

Spence describes one such thirty-kilometer (nineteen-mile) hike at Penn-y-Fan in the Brecon Beacons, Wales: "These things are done at a hell of a lick and are, frankly, gut-busters."[30] The recruits become exhausted, cold, wet, hungry, and injured, but still they carry on. Throughout, urged on by their superior officers, their identities as men are made. The sheer physical challenges of route marches and mountain running are presented as tests of manhood. The warrior hero must be fit enough to conquer landscapes; indeed, he is literally made in the landscape of the army's training areas.

This process of meeting a physical challenge is coupled with developing mental aggression sufficient to drive the soldier forward. Aggression, a hallmark of the warrior hero model of military masculinity, is cultivated on the wide moorland landscapes of military training areas. During fieldwork, my colleague and I watched in awe as recruits were deliberately psyched up and then led up a gully in the North Yorkshire hills to stab dummies with bayonets, yelling all the while. Reflecting on his training experiences, Ballinger recalls one conversation in which he and his fellow recruits realize what is happening:

"Are you enjoying the course, Avery?" I asked.

"I wouldn't say I was enjoying it, exactly," he said, ". . . but it does give you a chance of distinguishing yourself physically.". . .

"Besides," he added, after a pause, "Selection has totally changed my outlook on life."

"What, already? In what way?"

"Bullshit," he said. "I can't take bullshit anymore. Also I am much more aggressive."[31]

Ballinger also comments on the verbal abuse used to "toughen up" recruits as they face physical and emotional challenges, and the gendered nature of this abuse. As we know, gender identities are relational: they are often defined in opposition or relation to other masculinities or femininities. The oppositional ideas drawn into the construction of this model of military masculinity show what the warrior hero is and is not. For the warrior hero, to falter is female. Ballinger tells of insults shouted by superior officers to recruits unable to finish elements of the selection and training course, couched in terms equating failure with effeminacy. "What's this? The Girl Guides?" shouts one officer. Aggressive heterosexuality accompanied by a fierce homophobia matches this fear of the female and is also a hallmark of this model of military masculinity: "Are you queer? Are you a fairy?" shouts a sergeant major at faltering recruits.

Femininity is also despised when encountered in the landscape. Ballinger explains one recruit's failure to climb a mountain in terms suggesting that the recruit's downfall results from his being seduced by the landscape's beauty. In another section of his book, he quotes a commanding officer's description of the darkness of a moonless moorland landscape in Wales through the use of the crude simile, "As black as a witch's tit." The labeling of attributes as female, and the subsequent denial of their place in the soldier's world, are key components of this model of military masculinity.

In summary, the rural as constructed in military training is matched to the masculinities exemplified in the strong, brave, "hard" warrior hero. Training takes place in dangerous territory. This is not a green and pleasant idyll but a bleak, hostile wilderness of nature red in tooth and claw, where only the tough survive. This is not to say that the green and pleasant land does not exist anywhere in military narratives: in fact, the army constructs the bucolic, pastoral rural as the object for military protection. In contrast, the harsh, bleak rural is constructed as the "tough" location that makes the soldier. By dominating this formidable landscape, by meeting the physical and emotional challenges set by it, the recruit passes the selection process and the soldier is made.[32]

## The Significance of Rurality to Military Masculinity

Why is rurality so important to the construction of this model of military masculinity, as I suggest it is? Modern warfare is, after all, a technological affair relying more on a soldier's ability to master complex equipment than on sheer physical prowess. (This technological mastery is itself a site for the creation of further military masculinities.)[33] With the exception of some of the British army's activities in Northern Ireland and the Falklands/Malvinas, the military activities the army has engaged in over the past fifty years have characteristically been in environments far removed from the uplands and heath where this training takes place. So why is rurality so important in the construction of military masculinity?

I offer three explanations. First, as I have argued, rural locations are chosen specifically to construct and mold the soldier in specific ways. According to the army, training happens in cold, wet hillsides for very good reasons: namely, army officers believe that the challenges of this process produce better soldiers. Better soldiers, according to the value systems in operation in the British army, are those who mirror at least in part the attributes of the ideal type, the warrior hero.

Second, rural space is central to much military activity in the United Kingdom. Most of the land owned or used for military purposes in the UK is rural. It is typically remote from urban centers, sparsely populated, devoid of pressures for urban development or intensive agriculture (although farming does take place on training areas), or marginal in some other way. Although many central military administrative functions are located in towns and cities (the Ministry of Defence, for example, is located in the heart of London), the daily organizational and training functions that go toward maintaining a standing army are mostly carried out in rural areas. The British army's status as a predominantly rural institution, therefore, is a consequence of its using vast areas of rural estate. This is a reflection of historical requirement and necessity, and a result of social expectations that the majority of the population remains undisturbed by the sights and sounds of military activity, particularly military training.

Third, a rural inheritance is woven into the very fabric of the armed forces. There would never be any possibility (even if there were the unlikely suggestion) that these lands should be relinquished in exchange for the acquisition of training grounds more closely suited to the theaters of combat in which the army engages. Safety, expense, and lack of available territory preclude this. It is also possible, given the persistence of the British class system, that the landed elite from which the officer class is still largely drawn would be reluctant to shift base to unknown territory.[34]

Ultimately, discourses of militarism and rurality legitimate the location of soldiers in the British countryside. These discourses operate on many levels within British (or often exclusively English) cultural life. For example, the rural is constructed as the legitimate place for the bearing of arms; in this narrative, authorized weapons such as farmers' shotguns or soldiers' rifles are contrasted with the illegitimate weapons of the urban criminal or terrorist. Similarly, in the United Kingdom and many other nations, there is a strong symbolic link between rurality and nationhood (for example, in the case of England, "England is the country and the country is England," in Stanley Baldwin's well-worn phrase),[35] where national defense is constructed with explicit reference to rural imagery. In short, the rural as location and the rural as social construction are fundamental to military cultures and to the gender identities those cultures produce.

## Consequences of Rural Military Masculinity

What are the political consequences of this model of rural masculinity? Obviously, these are complex and wide reaching and can be examined on local, national, and international scales. Two of the most immediate concerns in terms of this argument, however, concern the implications of this model for rural communities and for women in the armed forces. While space prevents discussion of these concerns in depth, it is important to summarize some of the effects rural military masculinities have in the specific places in which they are constructed and for the specific gender they exclude.

One set of implications is the impact of this military masculinity on daily life for those in rural communities dominated by the major army field training centers and other large training establishments. In quantitative terms, this is not a huge problem for the majority of those living in rural Britain, as the areas affected are relatively small. Qualitatively, the impact of the military per se, rather than that of military masculinities, is most often cause for comment. But in those areas dominated by military training, there are occasional concerns. For example, one resident of a village adjacent to the Otterburn Training Area, in the northeast of England, confided to me during fieldwork there her fears for the social structure and "balance" of the village, given the army camp, with its transient military population, up the road. Otterburn, she said, was "too macho" as a result. She has a point. Jacky Tivers examines such sociocultural attributes of a garrison town in her study of the military landscapes of Aldershot.[36]

The second set of implications is the effect on women in the armed forces. I have implied in this chapter that the British army is a masculine institution, its members molded by social constructions of masculinity. I have also presented the warrior hero as one hegemonic model of masculinity among many. This model may be open for subversion as well as reproduction, but the point remains that it exists, it is dominant, and it is resolutely male.

Women in the military are thus left in an unenviable position. There are only about 8,000 women in the army, around 7.5 percent of a total force of about 112,000. In 1998 an ongoing recruitment crisis, combined with a social climate demanding equal employment opportunities for women, resulted in many hitherto closed trades in the army "opening up" to women. This has pushed up the intake of women to the army to 14 percent of all new recruits. Even so, the proportion of women in the army will not reach 10 percent until at least 2006. Meanwhile, military culture remains dominated by a model of military masculinity that at times is extremely hostile to the idea of gender integration and cooperation. The warrior hero (and indeed the British secretary of state for defence) does not want women in the troops, viewing gender integration in combat as detrimental to operational effectiveness.[37] There are signs that some of the worst excesses of rampant, militarized masculinities in the army—physical and verbal harassment on the basis of sex and gender—are being dealt with, not least because of the negative impact such activities have on the fighting unit. A range of equal opportunity and diversity management strategies are in place in an attempt to counter such behavior and to assure civilian onlookers that the British army takes seriously its aim of promoting gender equity.[38] However, inducing cultural change is difficult at the best of times. Strategies for dealing with behavioral excesses vary. As Sarah Ford notes in her account of training and action with the Special Forces, there seemed little point in trying to challenge an ingrained, deeply misogynistic culture from the inside; it seemed better to ignore it or quietly subvert it.[39] For a woman officer in charge of a recruitment office, change was the consequence of persistence, of chipping away at the collection of activities and practices that limited women's military participation, whatever they might be, from policy to practice.[40] The point is that cultural change is slow, generational. Furthermore, many soldiers benefit (and recognize that they benefit) from this model of military masculinity and the status and privileges that its exclusionary practices confer. Cultural change may not be impossible, but it certainly takes time.

## NOTES

1. In the British army, the infantry and armored corps are all male. Only 70 percent of all army jobs are open to women. Around 7.5 percent of army military personnel are female (January 2004 figures). See Defence Analytical Services Agency (2004).

2. Woodward (1996, 1998, 1999, 2000, 2001, 2003, 2004, 2006); Woodward and Winter (2004).

3. In England, space is at a premium and conflicts between different potential land users often arise.

4. For example, Ballinger (1992); McNab (1993); Ramsey (1996); C. Ryan (1995); Spence (1997, 1998); Lukowiak (1993, 2000); J. Lewis (1997). In addition, *Combat and Survival* makes a monthly contribution to this genre.

5. For example, Carlton Television (1999); British Broadcasting Corporation (1999, 2000).

6. Fairclough (1997); Mills (1997); Van Dijk (1997).

7. Butler (1990, 1993); Connell (1995a, 1995b, 2000); De Beauvoir (1973); Rose (1993); Women and Geography Study Group (1997).

8. Goldstein (2001).

9. Addleston and Stirrat (1996); Barrett (1996); Cohn (1995); Connell (1993, 1995a, 1995b), Cooke and Woollacott (1993); Donaldson (1993); Enloe (1993); Elliott (1996); Herbert (1998); Morgan (1994); Yuval-Davis (1997). See also the September 2002 special issue of *Current Sociology* on gender and the military (Kummel 2002).

10. Connell (1995b). See also Barrett (1996) on this point.

11. See Connell (1995b) on hegemonic masculinity, and Dawson (1994) and Newsinger (1997) on the warrior hero.

12. Army Recruiting Group (1998a).

13. Beevor (1991); British Broadcasting Corporation (1999).

14. Army Recruiting Group (1998a).

15. Army Training and Recruiting Agency (1999, unpaginated).

16. Army Recruiting Group (1998b).

17. Army Recruiting Group (1998a, unpaginated).

18. Army Recruiting Group (1998b, 15).

19. British Broadcasting Corporation (1999); Beevor (1991).

20. Coulson (1998).

21. See Woodward (2001) for a critique.

22. Army Department (1996).

23. Ballinger (1992); Ford (1997).

24. Army Recruiting Group (1998b, 15).

25. Ballinger (1992).

26. De la Billière (1994). See also Woodward (1998).

27. Services Sound and Vision Corporation (1995).

28. McNab (1993).

29. Ballinger (1992, 57).

30. Spence (1997, 14).

31. Ballinger (1992, 65).

32. The idea of wilderness is relative, of course. North American readers will equate wilderness with rather a different landscape (one that is untouched, unpopulated, and unfarmed) from the wilderness that British ruralities denote as bare, tree-free moorland landscapes used only for extensive sheep farming, grouse shooting, and military training.

33. See Barrett (1996) for examples of this in the U.S. Navy.

34. Strachan (1997).

35. Stanley Baldwin was Britain's prime minister between 1923 and 1929.

36. Tivers (1999).

37. A policy announcement on this was made in May 2002, when the secretary of state announced that women would continue to have access to only 70 percent of available posts in the army.

38. Woodward and Winter (2005).

39. Ford (1997).

40. Senior British army officer, interview by Trish Winter, Tri-Service Equal Opportunities Training Centre, UK, summer 2002.

# PART 3
## Changes

The rural is the unchanging, the seat of tradition and routine—or so we have long imagined. In this view, progress and innovation are the features of urban life. Cities are where the young and innovative go, happily leaving behind the old, the social detritus of unchallenged custom and habit, the boredom of convention and settled lives, and the constraints of community solidified by isolation. Against the restless pulse of the city, however, we maintain a mental picture of a "home" we can return to—an "old country" that is always there, where neighbors still know each other, where families meet for picnics, where nature and *Gemeinschaft* remain to comfort the overwrought and heal those battered, bent, and dented by urban artifice. As an old Appalachian song, the *Blue Ridge Mountain Blues*, puts it,

> When I was young and in my prime
> I left my home in Caroline
> Now all I do is sit and pine
> For all those folks I left behind

Like the idealized and immutable rurality of this vision, the masculine is often similarly conceived as rock-solid and unchanging. What is the toughness and self-reliance of the real man but a kind of gendered obdurateness in the face of the trials of life and what they fling at the self? In this conception, masculinity is not compliant, nor does it vacillate; it makes no errors and therefore never has to correct the self; it takes no input from others because it needs none—it is already done, complete, finished and everlasting; rock not plastic, nature not nurture.

Given the persistence and power of these conceptions, it may seem culturally paradoxical to consider not just the rural in the context of change, but rural masculinities—apparently a double immutability. But rural masculinities are plural, not singular, and in that plurality we find both the means and the evidence of rural masculine change. In these final chapters of the book, two experienced observers of the rural and the masculine consider the methods and the indications of this change, and ponder the possibilities and constraints for future directions in rural masculinities.

Raewyn Connell gives us a largely historical vision of this apparent double obdurateness, showing how intellectuals from ancient Rome to modern Australia have found much more than singular and unchanging masculinity in the rural. Connell opens by reminding us of the Roman poet Virgil, whose writing is steeped in the conservatism we so strongly associate with the male farmer and his countryside, before moving to sketch out a history of rural radicalism. From the late nineteenth-century Australian magazine *The Bulletin,* with its sense of the rural as a site of a cleansing masculinity capable of exposing the corruptions of capital, to the commune movements of the sixties, to contemporary counterculturalists, Connell shows us how intellectuals have long envisioned the rural as a place to start anew, to experiment with alternative gender relations, and to resist the depredations of mammon.

In our final chapter, Linda Lobao points her overview of the book toward a focus on change in rural masculine (and masculine rural) practices of a different sort: the agenda of social science research. She begins by bringing together the threads of a theme prominent throughout the volume—the symbolic and physical contingencies of space and place that are so central to rural masculinities. Lobao uses this spatial perspective to review how the contributors to the book demonstrate the social significance of rural masculinities, how the rural and the masculine intersect, and how these significant intersections also provide openings for change. But she also points out that there is much more to be done, not only for the development of social science but also for social science's broader moral agenda to give capacity to society's potentials—in this case in terms of the gendered boundaries of both rural and urban power.

Rurality is not unchanging, and masculinity is not a fact of nature. Indeed, while we live in the world and interact with it, nothing can be final and unchanging. Nothing, therefore, is a fact of nature, if by a "natural fact" we mean something final and unchanging. It is a sign of rural masculinities' continuing hegemonic hold that we so often still see them as singular and complete—and our developing ability to engage rural masculinities in their own reconstitution is perhaps equally a sign that this hold is now slipping. Increasingly, we are gaining the ability to consciously examine rural masculinities specifically as what they have always been: multiple and emergent in a relational world. Perhaps more important, we are also now able to study what they could become: sources of empowerment with others, instead of sources of power over others.

# 14

## Country/City Men

*Raewyn Connell*

The country has always been a force in the imagination of city people. In the early days of urbanism, of course, the link was intimate and unavoidable. I remember once walking through the ruins of a Minoan-era town in Crete, impressed both by how sharp the rural/urban distinction was and by how direct the urban/rural relationship was. There was a line around the city, a sharp boundary, even though there was not the defensive wall that most ancient cities had. Step over that line, and you were immediately in the agricultural and pastoral countryside. Many of the town dwellers must have taken that step each day.

Even a metropolis, like Rome at the end of the republic, had intimate links with the countryside. Much of its swollen population was made up of rural/urban migrants, and its victorious and all-important army, until the early empire at least, was largely recruited from the Italian peasantry. It is not surprising, then, that even in the Roman ruling class there was a supportive audience for the celebration of rural life by that most establishment of poets, Publius Vergilius Maro. Before getting round to challenging Homer with the *Aeneid,* Virgil wrote a famous set of pastoral poems, generally known as the *Eclogues,* and a concentrated celebration of rural life and labor and the cycle of the rural year, the *Georgics.* At the end of Book II of the *Georgics,* in passionate verses, Virgil denounces the madness of the city and the violence of its politics:

> Others trouble unknown seas with oars, rush on
> their swords, enter the gates and courts of kings.
> This man destroys a city and its wretched houses,
> to drink from a jewelled cup, and sleep on Tyrian purple:
> that one heaps up wealth, and broods about buried gold:
> one's stupefied, astonished by the Rostra: another, gapes,
> entranced by repeated applause, from people and princes,
> along the benches

Virgil immediately contrasts this feverish life with the peaceful, rhythmic, and productive life of the country man:

> The farmer has been ploughing the soil with curving blade:
> it's his year's work, it's sustenance for his little grandsons,
> and his country, his herds of cattle and his faithful oxen.
> There's no rest, but the season is rich in fruit
> or his herd's produce, or Ceres's wheat sheaves
> burden the furrows with their load, and fill the barns . . .
> Meanwhile his dear children hang on his lips,
> his chaste house guards its purity, the cows drop
> milky udders, and the fat kids butt each other,
> horn against horn, on the pleasant grass.[1]

Virgil was not the originator of pastoral poetry, but he was far and away the most influential practitioner of it. These verses mark the insertion into the European tradition of an idealization of country life, seen from an urban perspective, which remained influential as a frame of literary thought for the next two thousand years. Very specifically, this was couched as the picture of the life of a country man, an owner of land and patriarch of a family, with the implication that this was the best possible way for a man to live.

Of course the reception and use of rural imagery changed, especially with the transition to capitalism and empire of the past few centuries. By the late nineteenth century the "rural" antithesis to the dark satanic mills of the industrial city included not only the green and pleasant land of the peasant hinterland in Europe—the setting for the "rooted" masculinities described by Ní Laoire and Fielding (Chapter 6 in this volume)—but also the blood-drenched frontier of empire and settlement overseas.

Some of the most important studies in the recent surge of research on masculinities have traced the construction of specific forms of masculinity on the imperial frontier. Jock Phillips opened up the issue by tracing a sequence in public constructions of masculinity in colonial New Zealand, and tracing its connections with the economics of settlement, the stabilization of the colonial state, and its integration into the geopolitics of the British Empire.[2] Robert Morrell, in a very detailed study, traced the construction and institutionalization of a collective masculinity among the white colonists of Natal, the interweaving of this gender project with the maintenance of race and class hierarchies, and the positioning of the colony in the international economy.[3]

The experience of empire fed back to the metropole, as John MacKenzie has shown by tracing the role of the "imperial pioneer and hunter" in the reconstruction of the ideology of manhood in Britain by entrepreneurs such as Baden-Powell.[4] One of the reasons why such exotic material about "scouting" and big-game hunting took hold in the metropole, I would suggest, is that it reworked the familiar literary figure of rural virtue and urban decadence. In popular texts ranging from *The Last of the Mohicans* (1826) to *Tarzan of the Apes* (1912), via *King Solomon's Mines* (1885), the Man of the Frontier became a model of many virtues—physical strength, survival skills, autonomy, and moral strengths ranging from bravery to incorruptibility to unshakable male friendship.

In colonial Australia the last of these was accounted the most important, and was named—perhaps adapting a Dutch word—"mateship." Men's friendship became a theme song of the nationalist/laborist literary movement of the 1880s and 1890s, centered on the radical magazine *The Bulletin,* which used the moral virtue of country life to exalt the bushman and pour scorn on the British connection. With the popular success of that movement, the archetypal bearer of mateship, the male pastoral worker, soon became an icon of Australian identity.

Feminist researchers have uncovered the gender dimension of "the Australian legend" but have not focused on the specific issue of rurality.[5] This, however, is essential to the model of masculinity being constructed. In the very popular 1889 poem "Clancy of the Overflow," celebrating the life of a drover, A. B. ("Banjo") Paterson wrote lines that could almost have come from Virgil—whom Paterson had certainly read as a pupil at Sydney Grammar School. He imagines Clancy riding along behind the sheep, singing:

> And the bush has friends to meet him, and their kindly voices
> greet him,
> In the murmur of the breezes and the river on its bars,
> And he sees the vision splendid of the sunlit plains extended,
> And at night the wondrous glory of the everlasting stars.

> I am sitting in my dingy little office, where a stingy
> Ray of sunlight struggles feebly down between the houses tall,

And the foetid air and gritty of the dusty, dirty city,
Through the open window floating, spreads its foulness over all.[6]

And so on, in a splendid denunciation of the city's squalor. In Paterson's even more popular poem "The Man from Snowy River"—a best-seller as a book of verse in 1895, and still holy writ in Australia, despite being made into a Hollywood film—Paterson abandons the contrast with the city and tells the story of an anonymous bushman's triumphant ride. The Man is a youth who joins the hunt for an escaped thoroughbred and outdoes all the famous riders in bravery and endurance:

> When they reached the mountain's summit, even Clancy took a
>     pull—
> It well might make the boldest hold their breath;
> The wild hop scrub grew thickly, and the hidden ground was full
> Of wombat holes, and any slip was death.
> But the man from Snowy River let the pony have his head,
> And he swung his stockwhip round and gave a cheer,
> And he raced him down the mountain like a torrent down its bed,
> While the others stood and watched in very fear.

The Man triumphs over the other riders by triumphing over the mob of wild horses, and he defeats them by triumphing over the dangerous landscape. He is able to do that because he comes from the wildest part of the land, the Snowy River country:

> Where the hills are twice as steep and twice as rough;
> Where a horse's hoofs strike firelight from the flint stones every
>     stride,
> The man that holds his own is good enough.

Bodily skill, bravery, and a good mountain pony are the fruits of this environment. Though equally virtuous, this is a different version of rurality from Virgil's husbandman, who came equipped with land and family and would not have dreamed of galloping around the Campanian hillsides. It is, however, a classic version of what we might call the frontier-pastoral picture of masculinity—good tough men growing from a tough, remote, rural environment.

The idea of rural virtue and the cleansing power of the bush remained active in Australian life for generations. A reactionary twist was given it by the Country Party, created in the 1920s with a radical element but eventually captured by rural capital and conservatism. In the 1970s a radical twist was given to these ideas by the counterculture that developed in the wake of the New Left, acquiring a geographical center in northern New South Wales. A loose network of rural communes, country town businesses, and individual settlements developed in the region, providing a base for an environmental movement and a range of New Age enterprises, festivals, and so on.[7]

We met some men from this milieu in the course of the project that became *Masculinities*.[8] Peter Streckfuss, a psychologist working for a public-sector agency, had moved to the area from the city five years before we interviewed him. The move was part of a remaking of his life that involved a change from a technical to a humanistic occupation, and more sexual freedom (he called it an "open marriage"). In some ways Streckfuss's picture of his rural environment is very familiar. For instance, he describes himself hanging around his workmates and engaging in a lot of small talk, "because I see that that is the way that you get accepted in a country town. You have just got to be one of the folks, and to sit yourself away in your ivory office is not the way to get anybody's respect."

But unlike the picture of gender relations in, say, Sharon Bird's account of rural small business,[9] Streckfuss sees this environment as allowing gender reform:

> I do more traditionally female things. I clean, I wash, I cook, I wash up—but I think most males do that anyway—and these things like our open marriage have been negotiated. It's not finished because there are some areas of resentment that I experience. I think that I have learned, and taken on a lot of the actual tasks that women, that my mother performed and that my father wouldn't dream of performing. I don't see Ann, as quite an ardent feminist, as having made the same effort to perform the equivalent male tasks.

The acknowledged resentment suggests the limitations of the change. So does his further reflection on the move to the country. But he likes the area: "the gap that I experience at the moment is that in Brigg's Inlet it is hard to find people that you can really talk to. In particular it is hard to find couples that you can talk to . . . I feel lonely, emotionally lonely."

The break from city life made by Peter Geddes, a former journalist, was more dramatic. Geddes had been a successful yellow journalist with a fast-lane lifestyle. In words that again recall Virgil, he contrasted this with a vision of rural peace:

> It was very competitive, it was a really exciting place to work. I never expected to have a better life than I had then as a reporter, because I had a pocket full of credit cards and a big leather bag full of Nikons, and I used to just rage around. If my suit was dirty I would race in and buy another one, just leave the other one, it wasn't important. It *was* really important to be able to pick up the phone and file a story ahead of the other newspapers. . . . I was really fat and lardy and out of condition, drinking very heavily. . . . I was constantly having bad things happen, you know, car accident, fight in a pub. . . .
>
> I met a guy who had bought—who was a dropout high school teacher, who had run off with a PE teacher. And they were living on one of those little islands. He built a traditional Swedish-shaped cottage, beautiful place surrounded by cherry trees and apple trees. I rang up my wife, said, "I've just bought this thing." She was pretty stunned.

Thus Geddes resigned from his job and they went off, with five children, to live in the wilderness: "A complete change. Like there was no one out there, no one to drink with, no other blokes, so all of a sudden I was—had all these children which I never really noticed before. . . . It sort of brought us back into some sort of real values. We had a gas stove, but we didn't have a real lot of money, so we couldn't buy bottles of gas. We had heaps of firewood so I used to be sawing up firewood and chopping firewood and we would cook a lot on the wood stove." It did not last. The small business Geddes tried to set up failed. The family began an oscillation between countryside, country town, and city, in the course of which the marriage ended and the family began to break up under the stress of poverty. Geddes drifted into other relationships and deeper into the counterculture,

continuing his personal quest for "real values" and his rejection of the
conventional masculinity of his career days.

This was not his first city/country move. At the age of fifteen he had
run away from an unhappy home and school situation to get a job in a
shearing shed. Hauled back, he persuaded his parents to send him to technical college, where he trained as a wool classer, and then worked in the
wool industry as a young man. Starting in journalism, he was sacked from
his first job (on his account, for screwing the boss's daughter), and was
only able to survive by moving upcountry and learning journalism hands-
on from a small-town editor, soon becoming the editor of a country newspaper himself. The move into countercultural rurality, in Geddes's life,
was thus continuous with an older pattern of escaping from urban problems into rural life and returning from time to time.

The Geddes family's brush with poverty points to another dimension
of rural life, which was largely ignored by Banjo Paterson but was highlighted by other writers who contested the literary idyll of the bush. Paterson was no social radical. Many of the *Bulletin* authors were, and their
accounts of the bush gave much more attention to poverty, class inequality,
and the power of the banks.

A famous controversy in verse was staged in 1893 between Paterson
and Henry Lawson, the other leading light of the nationalist literary movement, with the representation of rural life as the theme. Paterson accused
Lawson of selling doom and gloom, while Lawson called Paterson a "city
bushman" and accused him of ignoring injustice and romanticizing country life:

> It was pleasant up the country, City Bushman, where you went,
> For you sought the greener patches and you travelled like a
>     gent . . .
> Ah! We read about the drovers and the shearers and the like
> Till we wonder why such happy and romantic fellows strike.
> Don't you fancy that the poets ought to give the bush a rest
> Ere they raise a just rebellion in the over-written West?

The bushmen of Lawson's short stories, in books like *While the Billy
Boils* (1896), went on foot, not on horseback, struggled with unemploy-
ment, loneliness, and drink, and sometimes died of industrial accidents

and other unromantic causes. Lawson's stories are as much the products of literary craftsmanship as Paterson's ballads, but they are a lot more profound and strike much deeper into the experience of settler colonialism.

Lawson writes mainly about the casualized itinerant workforce associated with pastoral capitalism in regions occupied by European settlement for little more than fifty years. Some of the men strike it lucky (for instance, through gold mining) and become small property owners, but most never do. These workers have an ambiguous relationship with the land. It is the site of their hopes, the basis of their skills and subsistence. But the land is also an enemy, the site of their exploitation and—through distance, drought, and heavy labor—the site of the destruction of their bodies.

In a different context, this reinforces the point made by Hugh Campbell (Chapter 5 in this volume) that for rural working-class men there is an intimate connection between the structure of a local labor market and the symbolic construction of masculinity. The much-trumpeted "mateship" was, in Lawson's writing, an expression of both class solidarity and gender segregation. The distinctive pattern is epitomized in one of his most famous stories, "The Union Buries its Dead," where fourteen men in a far outback town form a funeral procession in the midday sun for a young laborer drowned while working. He is nobody's particular mate, but he has a union ticket and respect is due.

Lawson himself grew up in midwestern New South Wales and tramped some outback tracks, though he spent most of his adult life drinking himself to death in the city. He was not the only intellectual to come from the country. Antonio Gramsci, the most influential twentieth-century theorist of intellectuals, was also a country boy who had grown up in poverty in Sardinia before going as a young man to university in the city of Torino. His great essay "The Southern Question" (1926) sets out a striking theory of the role of intellectuals in traditional rural society where the mass of the population are peasants. Broadly, the intelligentsia, mediating between the peasantry and the large landowners, weld an unstable, even disintegrating, social structure into a political bloc.

Plainly, such analyses do not apply directly to settler colonies such as Australia, New Zealand, the United States, and the southern cone of Latin America. Certainly in these settings there are people who, like Gramsci and Lawson, moved from rural origins to an intellectual milieu in the city. I could cite Miles Franklin, a young woman whose first novel, *My Brilliant*

*Career,* a comic account of settler life combined with a sharp critique of the stifling pressures on young women, was sponsored for publication by Lawson.[10] Or, to move outside the Anglophone world, I could cite the poet Pablo Neruda, who wrote memorable descriptions of the southern forests and his early life in a remote country town, but became a citizen of the world after a stint in urban bohemia.[11]

Not all moved to the city. There were others who remained, organic intellectuals of settler rurality. A notable example is E. A. Partridge, an Ontario country boy who became a grain farmer in Saskatchewan. In the early part of the twentieth century, as Murray Knuttila's biography recounts, Partridge became a key activist in Canadian grain farmers' movements, pushing farmers toward cooperative marketing, breaking the power of the big grain companies.[12] He increasingly turned against urban capitalism and developed a vision of the Canadian west, the region of recent settlement, as the home of a far-reaching experiment in humane socialism. Knuttila argues, I think with justice, that Partridge meets the definition of a classic intellectual—someone who, while a farmer and not a professional brain worker, generated ideas, took a broad view of history, and tried to articulate the humane possibilities in the society around him.

All forms of rural life give rise to cultural alternatives. In some circumstances they give rise to intellectuals who can articulate them. Images of rural masculinity are not just urban products—not only the work of pastoral poets, or of slick advertising agents, as in Robin Law's agreeable tale of the "Southern Man" beer campaign (Chapter 11 in this volume). They also grow from local experiences of gender relations and can be locally articulated. Gender relations are never monolithic, and forms of masculinity coexist in the same social space, as David Bell's engaging account of the "rural homosexual" reminds us (Chapter 9 in this volume). Intellectuals in rural life have a double significance here: they articulate rural identity and they also embody diversity, themselves representing alternative practices and identities.

Intellectuals also, by their work of articulating and circulating ideas, link rural settings to urban audiences, and vice versa. In this discussion I have sketched some of the ways in which the cultural interplay of rural and urban is significant for ideas of manhood and even for ideas about gender change. For this, as for many other problems, the relational character of gender is fundamental.

NOTES

1. Quotations from Virgil are translated by A. S. Kline. See Virgil (2002).
2. Phillips (1987).
3. Morrell (2001).
4. MacKenzie (1987).
5. Lake (1986).
6. See Paterson (1956) for this and following quotations.
7. Smith and Crossley (1975).
8. Connell (1995a).
9. Bird (2003).
10. Franklin (1966).
11. Neruda (1978).
12. Knuttila (1994).

# 15

## Gendered Places and Place-Based Gender Identities: Reflections and Refractions

*Linda Lobao*

I'm a man.
I can change.
If I have to.
I guess.

This volume brings together the ways in which we experience and conceptualize the social world through two lenses: that of gender, in this case masculinity, and that of place, in this case rurality.[1] Although gender and place tend to be seen as disparate phenomena in the academic and popular eye, this volume shows how they intersect and create often mutually reinforcing experiences, social statuses, and representations. As Doreen Massey noted some time ago, gender relations, like other social relations, are not inseparable from space but occur in space, and we experience them from a spatial vantage point.[2]

The conceptual roots of studying the intersection of gender and place are found in a number of literatures, as noted in Campbell, Bell, and Finney's introductory chapter and below. But existing literature provides only limited understanding of the subject addressed in this volume. By drawing from fragmented conceptual perspectives, extending them to the intersection of masculinity and rurality, and highlighting empirical examples, the authors of this volume are carving out a new social science research area: rural masculinities.

In this concluding chapter I summarize how *Country Boys* has examined rural masculinities, together with how it goes on to suggest further study of rural masculinities, under three general headings: "the social significance of rural masculinities," "intersections between the masculine and the rural," and "openings for change." My first section shows how the social implications of rural masculinity range from popular representations of rural men as "manly men" to the actual lived experience of men in rural areas and occupations. If we examine issues such as the specific contexts, times, and places in which rural masculinity is played out, or the types of negotiations involved in establishing rural male behavior, we can identify the importance of rural masculinity studies to both academic research and to wider concepts of social change. Specifically, the process of examining these issues involves identifying points at which the rural and the masculine intersect. In my second section I outline two "scales" of social action that can be mobilized to observe these intersectionalities, and summarize the questions raised in these chapters as they analyze different aspects of connection between the rural and the masculine. The final section extends these questions into potential "openings for change" in three significant areas: representations, experiences, and scholarly work, where I suggest further avenues of research in this fertile subject.

## The Social Significance of Rural Masculinities

The intersection of rurality with masculinity is a significant topic for several reasons. Most broadly, place, location, and gender are major sources of social identity and structural positions, and have implications both for society at large and for particular individuals.

As the authors discuss, the intersection of rurality with masculinity gives rise to popular representations that influence behavior and ideology. Many of these representations center on occupations commonly associated with rural spaces, such as cowboy, farmer, coal miner, woodsman, and fisherman. These salt-of-the-earth manual jobs in the primary economic or extractive sector once characterized much of the developed world. Although this has not been true for at least the past hundred years, the representative power of these characterizations lives on, most vividly in societies that once had large frontiers, including many parts of the Americas, Australia, and New Zealand. It is much more difficult to consider how urban spaces are linked to occupational legacies in the popular mind, and when one does, the less heroic occupations such as gangster and gang member typically occupy center stage. Only more recently—and possibly temporarily—do any urban occupations come close to capturing the respect accorded to traditional rural occupations, and this is primarily due to the role played by firefighters in New York City on September 11, 2001.

For particular individuals, occupational representations provide self-identity and a way of interpreting the social world. Also, as the authors note, rural occupational and general "country boy" representations are often appropriated by individuals for self-serving political and commercial purposes. Like the banners of God and flag, rural "salt-of-the-earth" occupations confer widespread legitimacy.

As noted throughout this volume, place and masculinity are linked in the popular imagination through the long-standing association of rural areas with a certain type of masculinity—specifically, with being a "man's man." Such imagery pervades much of the Americas and other developed nations in the West. More recently, in U.S. cities a distinct and contrasting type of place-based masculinity has also emerged: the "meterosexual" (also termed "metrosexual"), or heterosexual man who likes urban pursuits such as shopping, gourmet cooking, and decorating. The term "meterosexual" has struck a chord with the media and the public, in part precisely because it provides such a stark mirror image of representations of rural men.

The association of rurality with traditional forms of masculinity is brought into sharper relief when seemingly spatially gendered incongruities are made visible. David Bell portrays these incongruities most clearly in his chapter on rural gay men's lives, while Will Courtenay also highlights them as he challenges the popular imagery of healthy, robust rural men with empirical findings about their poor health status. These incongruities are often portrayed in literature, film, and other media. One well-known example is the character of Atticus Finch in *To Kill a Mockingbird*: a progressive, sensitive rural man, attorney, and single father, but also a skilled marksmen and hunter. That such men are seen as exceptional to those around them plainly points to the power of traditional representations.

The subject of rural masculinities is also important for understanding the lived experiences of rural men. Part I of this volume highlights dimensions of social life where rural masculinity is constructed through social practices of farming (Peter et al., Barlett), other locally oriented business and employment (Bird, Campbell), right-wing politics (Kimmel and Ferber), and health (Courtenay). These and other chapters make several key observations. First, that there is a gap between practices and popular representations. Rural men are not a homogeneous category; rather, there are wide variations in their behavior. Only in some cases (such as conventional farming), and in certain communities (such as isolated agricultural centers), does rural men's behavior come closer to that of popular imagery.

Second, the chapters in this volume point out that rural men's behavior is negotiated within their constrained set of local reference groups, networks, and community and regional contexts. For example, roles, practices, and worldviews vary between local conventional farmers and those using sustainable agriculture (Peter et al., Barlett) and even within conventional farm settings (Barlett). Regional and national differences also amplify or inhibit certain behaviors.

Third, there are real social costs to the status intersections of rurality and gender. Courtenay's chapter on health and Kimmel and Ferber's chapter on political mobilization by right-wing militias highlight how the interplay of the rural and the masculine result in behaviors that have social as well as individual costs.

Fourth, there are distinct time-space paths associated with rural masculinities. Public places, particularly the local tavern, become a key part of daily activity. Hugh Campbell's chapter, for instance, illustrates the daily time-space path of men in a small New Zealand community: from home to work site; from work site to tavern at the end of the working day; and then (often considerably later) from tavern to home once again.

Fifth, the subject of rural masculinities is significant for academic research. In particular, intersections of place and gender are not well understood from a conceptual or empirical standpoint. Certainly, focus on this topic varies by academic discipline, with geographers (for example) devoting comparably more explicit attention than sociologists to how gender relationships work out spatially. Gender itself also operates as a variable, in that studies that do pay attention to intersections of place and gender tend to focus on women. In their introduction to this volume, Campbell, Bell, and Finney note that since patriarchy entails men's relatively greater power, prestige, and privilege, men tend to be ubiquitous both socially and spatially. Because of this ubiquity, a standard of male normalcy prevails from macrolevel structuring of social institutions to microlevel day-to-day physical movement, especially outside the household. Thus, as the authors point out, in a sense men are like air—everywhere but not plainly visible or necessarily problematic for researchers.

In contrast, some well-developed bodies of work exist on women and place that specifically attend to rural women. Most notably, Ester Boserup's work in the 1970s constituted the first step in an ever-increasing corpus of literature on women in international agricultural development. Initially concerned with general cross-national differences in women's statuses, this literature has also moved downward in spatial scale to consideration of local, subnational spatial differences, and has broadened outward beyond early concerns with material status to examine an array of issues about women's lives and worldviews. A smaller but still coherent literature also exists on farm women and the spatial division of labor in developed countries. In a similar way, the topic of rural masculinities is now opening up a new area of scholarly investigation, one that has previously been invisible precisely because it is so omnipresent. In this way the study of rural masculinities contributes to broader scholarly understanding of the intersection of gender and place.

Finally, the subject of rural masculinities is important for social change. As I discuss below, creating a more progressive, socially just society requires making gender rigidities visible, raising consciousness, and enabling public choice and action.

## Intersections Between the Masculine and the Rural

In order to make rural masculinities more visible and to highlight potential opportunities for change, it is useful to examine two scales of social action where the rural and masculine connect: the individual and the place. Both involve the social construction, and subsequent consequences, of rural masculinity.

As Campbell, Bell, and Finney note, "rurality" and "masculinity" are socially constructed via the symbolic meaning that social actors attach to these concepts. Individuals believe that the "rural" is real and act accordingly, whether this involves behavioral changes such as in-migration to a "rural" area or studying the "rural" as a ontological part of one's academic discipline. A similar observation can be made about the concept of masculinity: individuals believe that a practice, behavior, or experience reflects masculinity and likewise act accordingly. From this view, the rural, the masculine, and their intersection have real consequences for individual social actors' behavior.

This volume pays slightly less attention to another way in which rural masculinities are socially constructed: through the creation of distinct places. Uneven development processes involving changes in the organization of production and social relations wash across territories, creating variations across place. In the wake of these changes we find industries, firms, and jobs, forms of government support and public services, local infrastructure, and social organizations—all of which may favor one gender over another. Gendered places are thus socially created, in part, by macrolevel social forces. The skewed sex ratios in rural areas in many parts of the world exemplify this inequality. In addition, as several chapters in this volume point out, gendered places are created from the bottom up, for instance, by the routine behavior of people in bars, on farms, and in small towns. The result is often a great deal of gender rigidity in both men's and women's roles, particularly in highly masculinized rural places. In these places, as Ní Laoire and Fielding, Bell, and Campbell demonstrate, women may suffer de facto exclusion (at least) from important areas of social life. As a consequence, women may vote with their feet and migrate. Such highly masculinized rural places also tend to have detrimental consequences for men, not only narrowly circumscribing their sexuality, occupational choices, worldviews, and life experiences, but also—as Courtenay shows—impairing their health.

In sum, the chapters in this volume raise several different but interconnected questions as they examine scales of social action. How do individual social actors appropriate and use markers of rural masculinity in order to "do gender"? How do rural places themselves become gendered through both external, or macrolevel, forces and internal, more microlevel, behaviors? What are the social consequences of both types of gendering?

## Openings for Change

As the Possum Lodge pledge with which I began suggests, changes in rural masculinities are possible, but they are likely to be incremental. This volume suggests the potential for change in three main areas: representations, practices, and scholarly work.

### Representations

The authors of this volume suggest that shifts in the ideological hegemony of rural masculinities are occurring—at least incrementally—in two primary ways. First, worldviews appear to be changing for some segments of rural men. The chapters by Peter et al. and Barlett show that farmers more oriented toward sustainable agricultural production tend to have a broader, more progressive vision of their roles and place in rural society. As older generations of farmers cease farming owing to attrition and competitive forces, therefore, new generations are emerging in which hegemonic masculinities are less entrenched.

Change is also arising owing to those who adopt lifestyles that conflict with the dominant masculine model—a change most clearly portrayed in Bell's chapter on rural gay men's lives. Even though the flouting of social norms still unarguably has negative repercussions, rural communities are opening up to wider public scrutiny and choice. The death of Matthew Shepard may have hastened this change, but even irrespective of this very public event the resilience of other gay men who make their home in rural communities provides a constant reminder of alternative sexualities.

Other sources also show that hegemonic rural masculinities are losing legitimacy. Recent articles in the *New York Times* (among other media), for example, have challenged the traditional representation of farmers. In contrast to hard-working individualists of humble means, these articles portray agribusinessmen as affluent, underemployed, and dependent on corporate welfare.[3] While obviously not an accurate description of most farm men, this characterization challenges the popular image of farmers as vocationally and morally "superior" to other Americans. Other recent articles challenge representations of rural men in order to break the grip of right-wing ideology. Ted Williams, for example, argues that sportsmen (like himself) need to stop supporting George Bush.[4]

*Experiences*

The lived experiences of men whose self-images are connected to rural masculinities are also undergoing change. Most of the occupations discussed in this volume are in rapid decline. Kimmel and Ferber, for instance, aptly describe the massive economic downturn in many communities in the U.S. heartland and how jarring this decline is to men's self-image. At present, the lack of alternatives for the rural working class in the United States has made military service a major path to upward mobility—unsurprisingly, we learn that many of the dead in the war on Iraq have come from small towns and rural America. The continuing economic marginalization of rural men in developed nations, therefore, constitutes a major axis of social and behavioral change.

Several of the authors in this volume also suggest that rural women may be a catalyst for change. Women who refuse to accept social marginalization, together with those who nurture progressive gender relations among family members, can break the hold of hegemonic masculinities.

## Scholarly Work

In terms of scholarly work, this volume itself creates change by identifying a previously "invisible" research area and opening up a new window on social life, but there is obviously much future work to be done. First, as the subject of rural masculinities matures, changes in theory—including greater theoretical development as a whole—will follow. In the introduction the volume editors point to several theoretical literatures that can inform the subject. Currently, building on theories of third-world women and ecofeminist theory may be most useful, given that in addition to their attention to gender, these theories tend to be place-based and sensitive to the rural.

Second, the scope of topics that can be viewed through the lens of rural masculinities extends beyond the present volume. Domestic violence, treatment of animals, and environmental issues would seem to be particularly fertile areas for future research.

Third, attending to rural masculinities will inevitably influence other literatures. For example, existing literature on farm women indicates that gender roles on farms appear to be extremely rigid over time. During the last farm crisis, midwestern women tended to report not only decreasing farm work but also moving into off-farm work, and some researchers have asked whether women's exodus from the family farm has been, in part, a reaction to entrenched male control.[5] Understanding how rural masculinities operate can help explain such findings on farm women.

Finally, more comparative work will be needed to build theory and to make a stronger case for the distinctiveness of the subject of rural masculinities. Within a nation, comparisons between urban and rural areas, as well as between men and women, can strengthen portrayals of rural masculinities. The meaning and significance of rurality varies cross-nationally and intra-nationally, as does the intersection of rurality with gender and with certain forms of masculinity. Female out-migration from rural areas, for example, typifies much of the Americas but not other continents, such as sub-Saharan Africa. Even in the United States, in specific rural areas such as parts of the South, the number of exclusively women-headed households remains high. In other nations, hegemonic masculinities may also be less clearly tied to urban-rural difference—for instance, in the case of "machismo," the Latin American counterpart to many of the masculinities described in this volume. In short, by striving to be spatially and gender comparative, future research will help clarify and advance theory and research findings.

To create progressive social change, we also need to look beyond the specific subject of rural masculinities. The title of this concluding chapter, I think, addresses the larger issue of where research, policy, and political action are needed—that is, in the persistence of gendered inequalities across place, and in the appropriation of these inequalities by some individuals and groups who seek to maintain their power over others.

NOTES

1. The epigraph is taken from the Possum Lodge Members' Pledge of *The Red Green Show*, a cult comedy series set "way up north" in "Possum Lodge," Canada. The all-male cast explores fundamental aspects of the masculine psyche through bonding, adventuring, and experiencing the great outdoors, and offers helpful handyman hints involving the comprehensive use of duct tape—a man's best friend—in the understanding that "If women don't find you handsome, they should at least find you handy."

2. Massey (1994).

3. "Welfare Reform for Farmers" (2003).

4. T. Williams (2004).

5. Lobao and Meyer (1995a).

# About the Contributors

**Peggy F. Barlett** is a professor of anthropology at Emory University. She is the author of two books on agrarian life—*Agricultural Choice and Change: Decision-Making in a Costa Rican Community* (1982) and *American Dreams, Rural Realities: Family Farms in Crisis* (1993). Her early work in economic development was part of a social science cohort that focused on decision making, summarized in *Agricultural Decision-Making: Anthropological Contributions to Rural Development* (1980). Her recent work—*Sustainability on Campus: Stories and Strategies for Change,* edited with Geoffrey W. Chase (2004)—has shifted to the sustainability challenge to higher education. Most recently she has written on local food systems, bioregionalism, and the impact of place-based grassroots efforts in *Urban Place: Reconnecting with the Natural World* (2005).

**Donna Bauer** has farmed in southwest Iowa since 1977. She received her B.A. in sociology, with an emphasis on environmental studies, from Iowa State University in 1994. She is a longtime member and one-time board member of Practical Farmers of Iowa. She remains involved in many local rural-entrepreneurial projects.

**David Bell** is senior lecturer in cultural studies at Manchester Metropolitan University, UK. His research interests include rural and urban cultures, sexuality, consumption and lifestyle, and science and technology. His recent books include *Ordinary Lifestyles* (2006, edited with Joanne Hollows) and *Science, Technology, and Culture* (2005).

**Michael Mayerfeld Bell** is associate professor of rural sociology at the University of Wisconsin–Madison and a part-time composer. He is particularly interested in dialogue, democracy, and unfinalizability in social, ecological, and musical life. He is the author, along with Gregory Peter, Susan Jarnagin, and Donna Bauer, of *Farming for Us All: Practical Agriculture and the Cultivation of Sustainability* (The Pennsylvania State University Press, 2004). The second edition of his *Invitation to Environmental Sociology* (1998), written with Michael Carolan, appeared in 2004.

**Sharon Bird** is associate professor of sociology at Iowa State University. Her research and teaching center on issues of inequality (race, gender, class), with particular emphasis on men and masculinities, gender inequality in small business, and in science, math, engineering, and technology careers. Her recent publications include "Gendered Socio-Spatial Practices in Public Eating and Drinking Establishments in the United States," in *Gender, Place, and Culture* (2005, with Leah K. Sokolofski). She is also editing a special volume of the *Gender Studies Journal* on men and masculinities with Sergei Zherebkin.

**Berit Brandth** is a professor in the Department of Sociology and Political Science at Norwegian University of Science and Technology in Trondheim, Norway. She is also affiliated with the Norwegian Centre for Rural Research. Her research focuses on gender in agriculture and forestry. She has also published widely on gender, working life, and care politics.

**Hugh Campbell** is associate professor of social anthropology at the University of Otago in New Zealand. He obtained his Ph.D. in rural sociology in 1995 from Charles Sturt University, Australia, after completing a study of the impacts of agricultural deregulation on farm families in New Zealand. He has long-term research interests in sustainable agriculture, rural restructuring, and rural masculinity. Together with Michael Bell, he co-edited a special edition of *Rural Sociology* on rural masculinities, a project that formed the basis of this volume.

**Raewyn Connell** is University Professor at the University of Sydney, and author or co-author of nineteen books, including *Ruling Class, Ruling Culture; Making the Difference; Gender and Power; Schools and Social Justice; Masculinities; The Men and the Boys,* and most recently *Gender* and the co-edited *Handbook of Studies on Men and Masculinities.* She contributes to journals in sociology, education, political science, gender studies, and related fields. Her current research concerns social theory, gender justice, globalizing masculinities, and the world sociology of intellectuals.

**Will H. Courtenay,** Ph.D., LCSW, director of Men's Health Consulting in Berkeley, California, graduated from the University of California, Berkeley. He is a clinical faculty member with the department of psychiatry at Harvard Medical School and the University of California (San Francisco) Medical School, and editor of the *International Journal of Men's Health*. As a researcher and writer, he examines psychological, behavioral, and social factors influencing men's health and develops evidence-based interventions. He maintains a psychotherapy practice in Berkeley, California.

**Abby L. Ferber** is the director of women's studies and associate professor of sociology at the University of Colorado, Colorado Springs. She is the author of *White Man Falling: Race, Gender, and White Supremacy;* co-author of *Hate Crime in America: What Do We Know?* and *Making a Difference: University Students of Color Speak Out;* she is co-editor, with Michael Kimmel, of *Privilege: A Reader*. She most recently edited *Home-Grown Hate: Gender and Organized Racism*.

**Margaret Finney** works as an editor for the Center for the Study of Agriculture, Food, and the Environment at the University of Otago, New Zealand, and also as a lecturer in the English Department there. Her research interests include gender, the social construction and performance of identity, twentieth-century literature, and the strategies of effective writing.

**Marit S. Haugen** is Dr. Polit. in sociology and works as a director and senior researcher at the Centre for Rural Research in Trondheim, Norway. She has mainly published on gender issues in farming and in rural communities and is currently focusing on changing ruralities and young people's images of the rural.

**Susan Jarnagan** has a master's degree in agronomy and a Ph.D. in rural sociology. She works in the Graduate College at Iowa State University, teaches English to immigrants, works on environmental protection in Mexico, and tends her garden.

**Michael Kimmel** is a professor of sociology at SUNY, Stony Brook. His research and teaching interests focus on the sociology of masculinity, and his co-edited textbook, *Men's Lives* (now in its sixth edition), has been adopted by the majority of courses dealing with men and masculinity throughout the United States. He has published several books in this area, his most recent being *The Gendered Society* (2000), together with many articles in scholarly journals, newspapers, and magazines. He has fre-

quently appeared on television to discuss issues of masculinity and has acted as an expert witness in this area for the U.S. Department of Justice.

**Robin Law** was a woman of *mana*, a geographer, and a feminist. Her work is filled with care and commitment. She died in Dunedin, New Zealand, on March 29, 2003. Her courage in a long battle with breast cancer won her many admirers and no little affection. Her ashes rest in university ground—across the river, in a grove of trees.

**Jo Little** is a professor of gender and geography and a member of the Nature, Society, Rurality Geography Research Group at the University of Exeter. Her main research and teaching interests are in rural communities, social identities, and gender and geography.

**Linda Lobao** is a professor of rural sociology, sociology, and geography at Ohio State University. Her research interests are stratification processes across localities and regions, political sociology, and gender. In addition to publishing two books and numerous articles, she is co-editor of a forthcoming book on spatial inequality. She was president of the Rural Sociology Society in 2002–2003.

**Caitríona Ní Laoire** is currently a postdoctoral research fellow in the department of geography, University College, Cork. Her research interests revolve around migration, gender, and rurality, with specific interests in narratives of recent return migration to Ireland, rural masculinities, and children and migration.

**Gregory Peter** is assistant professor of sociology at the University of Wisconsin–Fox Valley. He earned a B.A. in East Asian studies, with an environmental studies minor, at the University of Wisconsin–Madison, and an M.S. in rural sociology and Ph.D. in sociology at Iowa State University. He is co-author of *Farming for Us All: Practical Agriculture and the Cultivation of Sustainability,* as well as other publications in rural sociology, sustainable agriculture, and the interface between the environment and society. He is also an applied sociologist conducting fieldwork and consulting for governmental and nongovernmental agencies.

**Carolyn Sachs** is a professor of rural sociology at The Pennsylvania State University. Her research and teaching interests are found within the areas of women in agriculture, rural women's work, sustainable agriculture, gender and the environment, international development, and the sociology of agriculture. She is currently completing a volume examining rural women, feminist theory, and the environment, which speaks to inadequacies in the ways in which rural theories and feminist theories have addressed rural women's issues.

**Rachel Woodward** is a senior lecturer in the School of Agriculture, Food, and Rural Development at the University of Newcastle, UK. She is the author of a number of articles on military masculinities, a book on "military geographies" (2004), and co-author (with Trish Winter) of articles on gender and the British army.

# A Note on the Photographs

The photographs that accompany each chapter opening in the book were all taken by Cynthia Vagnetti, the noted documentary photographer of rural and agricultural life. Vagnetti has traveled the length and breadth of the United States, recording the varieties and realities of the lives of rural men and women, in the tradition of Dorothea Lange and Russell Lee. She is also a documentary video producer and is at work on a series of videos of women farmers entitled *Voices of American Farm Women*, several of which have already been released.

We include Vagnetti's photos of rural masculinities without captions, for several reasons. Foremost, each one tells its story powerfully enough on its own, undirected by words. Captions would amount to a constraint on what they might tell. In addition, we do not intend her photographs to be directly illustrative of the individual chapters. Vagnetti's work is all based in the United States, to begin with, while our chapters are based on case studies from some six countries: Australia, Britain, Ireland, New Zealand, and Norway, as well as the United States. Moreover, one can discover a kind of argument through looking for connections between her work and the case studies from countries other than the United States. Despite differences in the inflections of their speech and their societies, there is much that all country boys would recognize in one another's lives.

# References

Acker, Joan. 1990. "Hierarchies, Jobs, Bodies: A Theory of Gendered Organizations." *Gender and Society* 4 (2): 139–58.
———. 1991. "Hierarchies, Jobs, Bodies: A Theory of Gendered Organizations."
In *The Social Construction of Gender,* ed. Judith Lorber and Susan A. Farell,
162–79. Newbury Park, Calif.: Sage Publications.
Ackland, Leopold G. D. 1930. *The Early Canterbury Runs.* Christchurch: Whitcoulls.
Adams, Jane H. 1988. "The Decoupling of Farm and Household: Differential Con-
sequences of Capitalist Development on Southern Illinois and Third World
Family Farms." *Comparative Studies in Society and History* 30 (3): 453–82.
———. 1994. *The Transformation of Rural Life: Southern Illinois, 1890–1990.* Chapel
Hill: University of North Carolina Press.
Addleston, Judi, and Michael Stirrat. 1996. "The Last Bastion of Masculinity: Gen-
der Politics at the Citadel." In *Masculinities in Organizations,* ed. Clifford
Cheng, 54–76. Beverley Hills, Calif.: Sage Publications.
Aho, James A. 1990. *The Politics of Righteousness: Idaho Christian Patriotism.* Seat-
tle: University of Washington Press.
Alexander, C. S., M. R. Somerfield, M. E. Ensminger, Y. J. Kim, and K. E. Johnson.
1995. "Gender Differences in Injuries Among Rural Youth." *Injury Preven-
tion* 1 (1): 15–20.
Alfnes, Aslaug Marie. 1990. "Kvinner og Praktisk Skogsarbeid" (Women and Prac-
tical Forestry Work). Master's thesis, Agricultural University of Norway, Ås,
Department of Forest Sciences.
American Academy of Dermatology. 1997. "It Can't Happen to Me." In *Americans
Not as Safe from the Sun as They Think They Are.* Schaumburg, Ill.: American
Academy of Dermatology.
American Cancer Society. 1994. *Cancer Facts and Figures: 1994.* Atlanta: American
Cancer Society.
American Heart Association. 1994. *Heart and Stroke Facts: 1995 Statistical Supple-
ment.* Dallas: American Heart Association.
Ankney, R. N., J. Vizza, J. A. Coil, S. Kurek, R. DeFrehn, and H. Shomo. 1998.
"Cofactors of Alcohol-Related Trauma at a Rural Trauma Center." *American
Journal of Emergency Medicine* 16 (3): 228–31.
Appadurai, Arjun. 1996. "The Production of Locality." In *Modernity at Large: Cul-
tural Dimensions of Globalization,* 178–99. Minneapolis: University of Min-
nesota Press.
Army Department (UK). 1996. *It's Plain Sense Too.* Training video C1908.
Army Recruiting Group (UK). 1998a. *Experience Life as a Soldier.* Recruitment bro-
chure CP(A)96.
———. 1998b. *The Modern Army: A Job with a Future.* Recruitment brochure
CP(A)99.

Army Training and Recruiting Agency (UK). 1999. *Getting Fit for the Army*. Recruitment brochure CP(A)140.

Bachman, Ronet. 1992. "Crime in Nonmetropolitan America: A National Accounting of Trends, Incidence Rates, and Idiosyncratic Vulnerabilities." *Rural Sociology* 57 (4): 546–60.

Bakhtin, Mikhail M. 1981. *The Dialogic Imagination: Four Essays*, ed. Michael Holquist, trans. Caryl Emerson and Michael Holquist. Austin: University of Texas Press.

———. 1986. *Speech Genres and Other Late Essays*, ed. Caryl Emerson and Michael Holquist, trans. Vern W. McGee. Austin: University of Texas Press.

Ballinger, Adam. 1992. *The Quiet Soldier: On Selection with 21 SAS*. London: Orion.

Barlett, Peggy F. 1991. "Status Aspirations and Lifestyle Influences on Farm Survival." In *Household Strategies: Research in Rural Sociology and Development*, vol. 5, ed. Daniel C. Clay and Harry K. Schwarzweller, 173–90. Greenwich, Conn.: JAI Press.

———. 1993. *American Dreams, Rural Realities: Family Farms in Crisis*. Chapel Hill: University of North Carolina Press.

Barlett, Peggy F., and Katherine Jewsbury Conger. 2004. "Three Visions of Masculine Success on American Farms." *Men and Masculinities* 7:205–27.

Barrett, Frank J. 1996. "The Organizational Construction of Hegemonic Masculinity: The Case of the US Navy." *Gender, Work, and Organization* 3 (3): 129–42.

Barthel, Diane. 1992. "When Men Put on Appearance." In *Men, Masculinity, and the Media*, ed. Steve Craig, 137–53. London: Sage Publications.

Barton, L. 2001. "A Village Affair." *The Guardian* (25 October).

Bayne-Smith, Marcia, ed. 1996. *Race, Gender, and Health*. Thousand Oaks, Calif.: Sage Publications.

Beevor, Antony. 1991. *Inside the British Army*. London: Corgi.

Bell, Claudia. 1996. *Inventing New Zealand: Everyday Myths of Pakeha Identity*. Auckland: Penguin Books.

Bell, David. 2000a. "Eroticizing the Rural." In *De-Centring Sexualities: Politics and Representations Beyond the Metropolis*, ed. Richard Phillips, Diane Watt, and David Shuttleton, 83–101. London: Routledge.

———. 2000b. "Farm Boys and Wild Men: Rurality, Masculinity, and Homosexuality." *Rural Sociology* 65 (4): 547–61.

Bell, David, and Gill Valentine, eds. 1995a. *Mapping Desire: Geographies of Sexualities*. London: Routledge.

———. 1995b. "Queer Country: Rural Lesbian and Gay Lives." *Journal of Rural Studies* 11 (2): 113–22.

Bell, David, and Ruth Holliday. 2000. "Naked as Nature Intended." *Body and Society* 6 (3–4): 127–40.

Bell, Michael M. 1992. "The Fruit of Difference: The Rural-Urban Continuum as a System of Identity." *Rural Sociology* 57 (1): 65–82.

———. 1994. *Childerley: Nature and Morality in an English Country Village*. Chicago: University of Chicago Press.

———. 1995. "The Dialectic of Technology: Commentary on Warner and England." *Rural Sociology* 60 (4): 623–32.

―――. 1998a. "Culture as Dialogue." In *Bakhtin and the Human Sciences: No Last Words*, ed. Michael M. Bell and Michael Gardiner, 49–62. London: Sage Publications.

―――. 1998b. "The Dialogue of Solidarities, or Why the Lion Spared Androcles." *Sociological Focus* 31 (2): 181–99.

―――. 1998c. *An Invitation to Environmental Sociology*. London: Pine Forge Press.

―――. 1998d. "The Social Construction of Farm Crises." Paper presented at the annual meeting of the Rural Sociological Society, Chicago, 5 August.

Bell, Michael M., with Donna Bauer, Susan Jarnagin, and Gregory Peter. 2004. *Farming for Us All: Practical Agriculture and the Cultivation of Sustainability*. University Park: The Pennsylvania State University Press.

Belyea, Michael J., and Linda M. Lobao. 1990. "Psychosocial Consequences of Agricultural Transformation: The Farm Crisis and Depression." *Rural Sociology* 55 (1): 58–75.

Bennett, John W. 1982. *Of Time and the Enterprise: North American Family Farm Management in a Context of Resource Marginality*. Minneapolis: University of Minnesota Press.

Berg, Lawrence D., and Robin Kearns. 1996. "Naming as Norming: 'Race,' Gender, and the Identity Politics of Naming Places in Aotearoa/New Zealand." *Environment and Planning D: Society and Space* 14 (1): 99–122.

Berlet, Chip, and Matthew Lyons. 1995. "Militia Nation." *The Progressive* (June): 22–25.

Berubé, Allan. 1996. "Intellectual Desire." *GLQ* 3:139–57.

Binnie, Jon. 2000. "Cosmopolitanism and the Sexed City." In *City Visions*, ed. David Bell and Azzedine Haddour, 166–78. Harlow, UK: Prentice-Hall.

Bird, Sharon R., and Stephen G. Sapp. 2004. "Understanding the Sex Gap in Small Business Success: Rural and Urban Comparisons." *Gender and Society* 18 (1): 5–28.

Blackwell, Tony. 2001. "The Rural Men's Health Program." *Health Promotion Strategies* 2 (2): 3.

Blair, Aaron, and Sheila H. Zahm. 1991. "Cancer Among Farmers." *Occupational Medicine* 6 (3): 335–54.

Bly, Robert. 1990. *Iron John: A Book About Men*. Reading, Mass.: Addison-Wesley.

Bonanno, Alessandro, Lawrence Busch, William Friedland, Lourdes Gouveia, and Enzo Mingione, eds. 1994. *From Columbus to ConAgra: The Globalization of Agriculture and Food*. Lawrence: University Press of Kansas.

Bonfitto, Vincent. 1997. "The Formation of Gay and Lesbian Identity and Community in the Connecticut River Valley of Western Massachusetts, 1900–1970." *Journal of Homosexuality* 33 (1): 69–96.

Bonnett, Alastair. 1996. "The New Primitives: Landscape and Cultural Appropriation in the Mythopoetic Men's Movement." *Antipode* 28:113–22.

Bourdieu, Pierre. 1989. *Outline of a Theory of Practice*. New York: Cambridge University Press.

―――. 2001. *Masculine Domination*. Stanford: Stanford University Press.

Boyd, Todd. 1996. "A Small Introduction to the 'G' Funk Era: Gansta Rap and

Black Masculinity in Contemporary Los Angeles." In *Rethinking Los Angeles,* ed. Michael J. Dear, H. Eric Schockman, and Gregg Hise. Thousand Oaks, Calif.: Sage Publications.

Brandth, Berit. 1994a. "Changing Femininity: The Social Construction of Women Farmers in Norway." *Sociologia Ruralis* 44 (2–3): 127–49.

———. 1994b. "Teknologi og Mannlighet i Forandring: Gården som Arena for Konstruksjon av Kjønn" (Technology and Masculinity in Transition: The Farm as an Arena for the Construction of Gender). *Sosiologisk tidsskrift* 3:185–203.

———. 1995. "Rural Masculinity in Transition: Gender Images in Tractor Advertisements." *Journal of Rural Studies* 11 (2): 123–33.

Brandth, Berit, and Marit S. Haugen. 1998. "Breaking into a Masculine Discourse: Women and Farm Forestry." *Sociologia Ruralis* 38 (3): 427–42.

———. 2000. "From Lumberjack to Business Manager: Masculinity in the Norwegian Forestry Press." *Journal of Rural Studies* 16 (3): 343–55.

British Broadcasting Corporation. 1999. *Soldiers To Be.* Television documentary.

———. 2000. *Guns and Roses.* Television documentary.

Brod, Harry, ed. 1987. *The Making of Masculinities: The New Men's Studies.* Boston: Allen and Unwin.

———. 1994. "Some Thoughts on Some Histories of Some Masculinities." In *Theorizing Masculinities,* ed. Harry Brod and Michael Kaufman. Thousand Oaks, Calif.: Sage Publications.

Brod, Harry, and Michael Kaufman, eds. 1994. *Theorizing Masculinities.* Thousand Oaks, Calif.: Sage Publications.

Brook, Barbara. 1999. *Feminist Perspectives on the Body.* London: Pearson Education.

Brown, Terence. 1995. *Ireland: A Social and Cultural History, 1922–85.* London: Fontana.

Brueggemann, John. 2000. "The Power and Collapse of Paternalism: The Ford Motor Company and Black Workers, 1937–1941." *Social Problems* 47 (2): 220–40.

Bryant, Lia. 1999. "The Detraditionalization of Occupational Identities in Farming in South Australia." *Sociologia Ruralis* 39 (2): 236–61.

Bunce, Michael. 1994. *The Countryside Ideal: Anglo-American Images of Landscape.* London: Routledge.

Burris, Beverly H. 1996. "Technocracy, Patriarchy, and Management." In *Men as Managers, Managers as Men: Critical Perspectives on Men, Masculinities, and Managements,* ed. David L. Collinson and Jeff Hearn, 61–77. London: Sage Publications.

Burroughs, Edgar Rice. 1912/1990. *Tarzan of the Apes.* New York: Penguin Books.

Butler, Judith. 1990. *Gender Trouble: Feminism and the Subversion of Identity.* New York: Routledge.

———. 1993. *Bodies That Matter: On the Discursive Limits of "Sex."* New York: Routledge.

Campbell, Hugh. 1994. "Regulation and Crisis in New Zealand Agriculture: The Case of Ashburton County, 1984–1992." Ph.D. diss., University of Otago.

————. 2000. "The Glass Phallus: Pub(lic) Masculinity and Drinking in Rural New Zealand." *Rural Sociology* 65 (4): 562–81.

Campbell, Hugh, and Emily Phillips. 1995. "Masculine Hegemony in Rural Leisure Sites in Australia and New Zealand." In *Communications and Culture in Rural Areas,* ed. Perry Share, 107–25. Wagga Wagga, Australia: Centre for Rural Social Research, Charles Sturt University.

Campbell, Hugh, and Anna Kraack. 1998. "Beer and Double Vision: Linking the Consumer to the Rural Through New Zealand Television Beer Advertising." In *Proceedings of the Agri-Food Research Network Conference: Monash University, July 1996,* ed. Roy Rickson. Melbourne: Department of Geography, Monash University.

Campbell, Hugh, Robin Law, and James Honeyfield. 1999. "What It Means to Be a Man: Hegemonic Masculinity and the Reinvention of Beer." In *Masculinities in Aotearoa/New Zealand,* ed. Robin Law, Hugh Campbell, and John Dolan, 166–86. Palmerston North: Dunmore Press.

Campbell, Hugh, and Michael M. Bell. 2000. "The Question of Rural Masculinities." *Rural Sociology* 65 (5): 532–46.

Carlton Television. 1999. *Soldier Town.* Television documentary.

Carrigan, Tim, Robert W. Connell, and John Lee. 1985. "Hard and Heavy: Towards a New Sociology of Masculinity." *Theory and Society* 14:551–604.

Carrington, William J., and Kenneth R. Troske. 1994. "Gender Segregation in Small Firms." *Journal of Human Resources* 30 (3): 503–33.

Carter, I., and N. Perry. 1987. "Rembrandt in Gumboots: Rural Imagery in New Zealand Television Advertisements." In *Te Whenua Te Iwi: The Land and the People,* ed. Jock Phillips, 61–72. Wellington: Allen and Unwin.

Caspersen, C. J., and R. K. Merritt. 1995. "Physical Activity Trends Among 26 States, 1986–1990." *Medicine and Science in Sports and Exercise* 27 (5): 713–20.

Centers for Disease Control. 1993a. "Prevalence of Sedentary Lifestyle: Behavioral Risk Factor Surveillance System, United States, 1991." *Morbidity and Mortality Weekly Report* 42 (29): 576–79.

————. 1993b. "Use of Smokeless Tobacco Among Adults: United States, 1991." *Morbidity and Mortality Weekly Report* 42 (14): 263–66.

Central Bureau of Statistics. 1989a. *Census of Agriculture and Forestry 1989,* vol. 2. Oslo: Central Bureau of Statistics.

————. 1989b. *Census of Agriculture and Forestry 1989,* vol. 7. Oslo: Central Bureau of Statistics.

Cerhan, James R., James C. Torner, Charles F. Lynch, Linda M. Rubenstein, Jonathon H. Lemke, Michael B. Cohen, David M. Lubaroff, and Robert B. Wallace. 1997. "Association of Smoking, Body Mass, and Physical Activity with Risk of Prostate Cancer in the Iowa 65+ Rural Health Study (United States)." *Cancer Causes and Control* 8 (2): 329–38.

Chiappe, Marta B., and Cornelia Flora. 1998. "Gendered Elements of the Alternative Agriculture Paradigm." *Rural Sociology* 63 (3): 372–93.

Chodorow, Nancy. 1978. *The Reproduction of Mothering: Psychoanalysis and the Sociology of Gender.* Berkeley and Los Angeles: University of California Press.

Citizens Project. 1998/1999. *Freedom Watch* (December/January). Colorado Springs: Citizens Project.

Clark, Thomas A., and Franklin J. James. 1992. "Women-owned Businesses: Dimensions and Policy Issues." *Economic Development Quarterly* 6 (1): 25–40.

Clatterbaugh, Kenneth. 1997. *Contemporary Perspectives on Masculinity: Men, Women, and Politics in Modern Society.* 2d ed. Boulder: Westview Press.

Clifford, James. 1986. *Writing Culture, the Poetics and Politics of Ethnography: School of American Research Advanced Seminar.* Berkeley and Los Angeles: University of California Press.

Cloke, Paul, and Harvey Perkins. 1998. "Representations of Adventure Tourism in New Zealand." *Environment and Planning D: Society and Space* 16 (2): 185–218.

Cloke, Paul, and Jo Little, eds. 1997. *Contested Countryside Cultures: Otherness, Marginalisation, and Rurality.* London: Routledge.

Clough, Patricia. 1992. *The Ends of Ethnography: From Realism to Social Critics.* Newbury Park, Calif.: Sage Publications.

Clover, Carol J. 1992. *Men, Women, and Chainsaws: Gender in the Modern Horror Film.* Princeton: Princeton University Press.

Cody, Paul, and Peter Welch. 1997. "Rural Gay Men in Northern New England: Life Experiences and Coping Styles." *Journal of Homosexuality* 33 (1): 51–67.

Cohn, Carol. 1995. "Wars, Wimps, and Women: Talking Gender and Thinking War." In *Men's Lives,* 3d ed, ed. Michael Kimmel and Michael Messner, 131–43. Boston: Alleyn and Bacon.

Collier, Jane F. 1986. "From Mary to Modern Woman: The Material Basis of Marianismo and Its Transformation in a Spanish Village." *American Ethnologist* 13 (1): 100–107.

Collins, Patricia Hill. 1990. *Black Feminist Thought: Knowledge, Consciousness, and the Politics of Empowerment.* London: Routledge.

Collinson, David, and Jeff Hearn. 1994. "Naming Men as Men: Implications for Work, Organization, and Management." *Gender, Work, and Organization* 1 (1): 2–22.

———. 1996. "'Men' at 'Work': Multiple Masculinities/Multiple Workplaces." In *Understanding Masculinities,* ed. Máirtín Mac an Ghaill, 61–76. Buckingham: Open University Press.

Conger, Rand D., and Glen H. Elder Jr. 1994. *Families in Troubled Times: Adapting to Change in Rural America.* Hawthorne, N.J.: Aldine de Gruyter.

Connell, Raewyn [R. W.]. 1987. *Gender and Power: Society, the Person, and Sexual Politics.* Cambridge: Polity Press.

———. 1993. "The Big Picture: Masculinities in Recent World History." *Theory and Society* 22 (5): 597–623.

———. 1995a. *Masculinities.* Cambridge: Polity Press.

———. 1995b. "Masculinity, Violence, and War." In *Men's Lives,* 3d ed., ed. Michael Kimmel and Michael Messner, 125–30. Boston: Alleyn and Bacon.

———. 2000. *The Men and the Boys.* Cambridge: Polity Press.

Cook, John R., and John D. Tyler. 1989. "Help-seeking Attitudes of North Dakota Farm Couples." *Journal of Rural Community Psychology* 10 (1): 17–28.

Cooke, Miriam, and Angela Woollacott, eds. 1993. *Gendering War Talk*. Princeton: Princeton University Press.

Coombes, Brad, and Hugh Campbell. 1996. "Pluriactivity in (and Beyond?) a Regulationist Crisis." *New Zealand Geographer* 52 (2): 11–7.

Cooper, Emmanuel. 1986. *The Sexual Perspective: Homosexuality and Art in the Last 100 Years in the West*. London: Routledge.

Cooper, James Fenimore. 1826/1986. *The Last of the Mohicans*. New York: Penguin Books.

Corcoran, James. 1997. *Bitter Harvest: The Birth of Paramilitary Terrorism in the Heartland*. New York: Penguin Books.

Cornwall, Andrea, and Nancy Lindisfarne, eds. 1994. *Dislocating Masculinity: Comparative Ethnographies*. London: Routledge.

Cossens, John (senior lecturer, Department of Marketing, University of Otago). 1996. Interview by Robin Law, 17 October.

Cott, Nancy F. 1977. *The Bonds of Womanhood: Women's Sphere in New England, 1780–1835*. New Haven: Yale University Press.

Coulson, Martin (video consultant). 1998. Personal communication with Rachel Woodward.

Courtenay, Will H. 1998a. "Better to Die than Cry? A Longitudinal and Constructionist Study of Masculinity and the Health Risk Behavior of Young American Men." Ph.D. diss., University of California, Berkeley. Dissertation Abstracts International, 59(08A), publication number 9902042.

———. 1998b. "College Men's Health: An Overview and a Call to Action." *Journal of American College Health* 46 (6): 279–90.

———. 2000a. "Behavioral Factors Associated with Disease, Injury, and Death Among Men: Evidence and Implications for Prevention." *Journal of Men's Studies* 9 (1): 81–142.

———. 2000b. "Constructions of Masculinity and Their Influence on Men's Well-Being: A Theory of Gender and Health." *Social Science and Medicine* 50 (10): 1385–401.

———. 2000c. "Engendering Health: A Social Constructionist Examination of Men's Health Beliefs and Behaviors." *Psychology of Men and Masculinity* 1 (1): 4–15.

———. 2001a. "Counseling Men in Medical Settings." In *The New Handbook of Psychotherapy and Counseling with Men: A Comprehensive Guide to Settings, Problems, and Treatment Approaches*, vol. 1, ed. Gary R. Brooks and Glenn E. Good, 59–91. San Francisco: Jossey-Bass.

———. 2001b. "Men's Health: Ethnicity Matters." *Social Work Today* 1 (8): 20–22.

———. 2002. "A Global Perspective on the Field of Men's Health." *International Journal of Men's Health* 1 (1): 1–13.

———. 2003. "Key Determinants of the Health and Well-Being of Men and Boys." *International Journal of Men's Health* 2 (1): 1–30.

Courtenay, Will H., and Richard P. Keeling. 2000. "Men, Gender, and Health: Toward an Interdisciplinary Approach." *Journal of American College Health* 48 (6): 1–4.

Courtenay, Will H., and Don Sabo. 2001. "Preventive Health Strategies for Men in Prison." In *Prison Masculinities*, ed. Don Sabo, Terry A. Kupers, and Willie London, 157–72. Philadelphia: Temple University Press.

Courtenay, Will H., Donald R. McCreary, and Joseph R. Merighi. 2002. "Gender and Ethnic Differences in Health Beliefs and Behaviors." *Journal of Health Psychology* 7 (3): 219–31.

Craig, Steve, ed. 1992. *Men, Masculinity, and the Media*. Newbury Park, Calif.: Sage Publications.

Crandall, C. S., L. Fullerton, L. Olson, D. P. Sklar, and R. Zumwalt. 1997. "Farm-Related Injury Mortality in New Mexico, 1980–91." *Accident Analysis and Prevention* 29 (2): 257–61.

Cranny-Francis, Anne. 1990. *Feminist Fictions*. Cambridge: Polity Press.

Crawford, M. 1995. *Talking Difference: On Gender and Language*. Thousand Oaks, Calif.: Sage Publications.

Crawford, Robert, and Devin Burghart. 1997. "Guns and Gavels: Common Law Courts, Militias and White Supremacy." In *The Second Revolution: States Rights, Sovereignty, and Power of the County*, ed. Eric Ward. Seattle: Peanut Butter Publishing.

Danbom, David B. 1979. *The Resisted Revolution: Urban America and the Industrialization of Agriculture, 1900–1930*. Ames: Iowa State University Press.

Dandeker, Christopher, and Mady Wechsler Segal. 1996. "Gender Integration in the Armed Forces: Recent Policy Developments in the United Kingdom." *Armed Forces and Society* 23 (1): 29–47.

Dansky, Kathryn H., Diane Brannon, Dennis G. Shea, Joseph Vasey, and Riad Dirani. 1998. "Profiles of Hospital, Physician, and Home Health Service Use by Older Persons in Rural Areas." *Gerontologist* 38 (3): 320–30.

D'Augelli, Anthony, and Mary Hart. 1987. "Gay Women, Men, and Families in Rural Settings: Toward the Development of Helping Communities." *American Journal of Community Psychology* 15:79–93.

Davenport, Stephen. 2000. "From Big Sticks to Talking Sticks: Family, Work, and Masculinity in Stephen King's *The Shining*." *Men and Masculinity* 2 (3): 308–29.

Davidson, Osha Gray. 1996. *Broken Heartland: The Rise of America's Rural Ghetto*. Iowa City: University of Iowa Press.

Davidson, P. M., P. N. White, D. J. Smith, and W. A. Poppen. 1989. "Content and Intensity of Fears in Middle Childhood Among Rural and Urban Boys and Girls." *Journal of Genetic Psychology* 150 (1): 51–8.

Dawson, Graham. 1994. *Soldier Heroes: British Adventure, Empire, and the Imagining of Masculinity*. London: Routledge.

De Beauvoir, Simone. 1973. *The Second Sex*. Harmondsworth: Penguin Books.

Dees, Morris. 1996. *Gathering Storm: America's Militia Threat*. New York: Harper Perennial.

Defence Analytical Services Agency. 2004. *UK Defence Statistics*. London: H. M. Stationery Office.

Degler, Carl. 1980. *At Odds: Women and the Family in America*. New York: Oxford University Press.

De la Billière, Peter. 1994. *Looking for Trouble: SAS to Gulf Command: The Autobiography*. London: HarperCollins.

Department of Health and Human Services. 1997. *National Household Survey on Drug Abuse: Main Findings, 1995*. Rockville, Md.: Substance Abuse and Mental Health Services Administration.

———. 2000. "Deaths: Final Data for 1998." In *National Vital Statistics Reports* 48 (11). DHHS publication number [PHS] 2000–1120. Hyattsville, Md.: National Center for Health Statistics.

Department of Statistics. 1986. *New Zealand Census of Population and Dwellings*. Wellington.

Dews, Carlos, and Carolyn Law, eds. 2001. *Out in the South*. Philadelphia: Temple University Press.

Dillman, Don A., and Daryl J. Hobbs. 1982. *Rural Society in the U.S.: Issues for the 1980s*. Boulder: Westview Press.

Donaldson, Martin. 1993. "What Is Hegemonic Masculinity?" *Theory and Society* 22 (5): 643–57.

Donnermeyer, J. J., and D. S. Park. 1995. "Alcohol Use Among Rural Adolescents: Predictive and Situational Factors." *International Journal of the Addictions* 30 (4): 459–79.

Dudley, Kathryn Marie. 1994. *The End of the Line: Lost Jobs, New Lives in Postindustrial America*. Chicago: University of Chicago Press.

———. 2000. *Debt and Dispossession: Farm Loss in America's Heartland*. Chicago: University of Chicago Press.

Dyer, Joel. 1997. *Harvest of Rage: Why Oklahoma City Is Only the Beginning*. Boulder: Westview Press.

Eaton, C. B., A. N. Nafziger, D. S. Strogatz, and T. A. Pearson. 1994. "Self-reported Physical Activity in a Rural County: A New York County Health Census." *American Journal of Public Health* 84 (1): 29–32.

Edensor, Tim. 2000. "Walking in the British Countryside: Reflexivity, Embodied Practices, and Ways to Escape." In *Bodies of Nature*, ed. Phil Macnaghten and John Urry, 81–106 (special issue of *Body and Society* 6 [3–4]).

Edwards, Tim. 1997. *Men in the Mirror: Men's Fashion, Masculinity, and Consumer Society*. London: Cassell.

Eisler, Richard M. 1995. "The Relationship Between Masculine Gender Role Stress and Men's Health Risk: The Validation of a Construct." In *A New Psychology of Men*, ed. Ronald F. Levant and William S. Pollack, 207–25. New York: Basic Books.

Elder, Glen H., Jr., and Rand D. Conger. 2000. *Children of the Land: Adversity and Success in Rural America*. Chicago: University of Chicago Press.

Elliott, Lorraine. 1996. "Women, Gender, Feminism, and the Environment." In *The Gendered New World Order: Militarism, Development, and the Environment*, ed. Jennifer E. Turpin and Lois Ann Lorentzen, 13–34. London: Routledge.

Enloe, Cynthia. 1993. *The Morning After: Sexual Politics at the End of the Cold War*. Berkeley and Los Angeles: University of California Press.

Fairclough, Norman. 1997. *Critical Discourse Analysis: The Critical Study of Language*. London: Longman.

Fairweather, John R., and Hugh Campbell. 1990. *Public Drinking and Social Organisation in Methven and Mt. Somers*. Research report no. 207. Lincoln: Agribusiness and Economics Research Unit, Lincoln University.

"The Farmer Wants a Wife: Calling All Single Countrymen." 2000. *Country Living* (September).

Farrell, Warren. 1994. *The Myth of Male Power: Why Men Are the Disposable Sex*. Berkeley, Calif.: Berkeley Publishing Group.

Fellows, Will. 1996. *Farm Boys: Lives of Gay Men from the Rural Midwest*. Madison: University of Wisconsin Press.

Felton, Gwen M., Mary A. Parsons, Russell R. Pate, Dianne Ward, Ruth Saunders, Robert. Valois, Marsha Dowda, and Stewart Trost. 1996. "Predictors of Alcohol Use Among Rural Adolescents." *Journal of Rural Health* 12 (5): 378–85.

Ferguson, Kathy E. 1984. *The Feminist Case Against Bureaucracy*. Philadelphia: Temple University Press.

Fielding, Shaun. 1998a. "Can the Swaledaler Speak? The Cultural Identity of Marginal Peoples." Master's thesis, University of Wales, Lampeter.

———. 1998b. "Indigeneity and Identity: Perspectives from Swaledale." In *Migration into Rural Areas: Theories and Issues*, ed. Keith Halfacree and Paul Boyle, 151–65. Chichester: Wiley.

———. 2000. "The Importance of Being Shaun: Self-Reflection and Ethnography." In *Ethnography and Rural Research*, ed. Annie Hughes, Carol Morris, and Susanne Seymour, 66–80. Cheltenham: Countryside and Community Press.

Fink, Deborah. 1987. "Farming in Open Country, Iowa: Women and the Changing Farm Economy." In *Farmwork and Fieldwork: American Agriculture in Anthropological Perspective*, ed. Michael Chibnik, 121–44. Ithaca: Cornell University Press.

———. 1992. *Agrarian Women: Wives and Mothers in Rural Nebraska, 1880–1940*. Chapel Hill: University of North Carolina Press.

Firestone, Shulamith. 1972. *The Dialectic of Sex*. London: Paladin.

Fitzharris, B. (president, University of Otago rugby football club). 1997. Interview by Robin Law, University of Otago, 9 January.

Fitzharris, Blair B., and Geoff Kearsley. 1987. "Appreciating our High Country." In *Southern Approaches: Geography in New Zealand*, ed. Peter Holland and W. Johnston, 197–217. Christchurch: New Zealand Geographical Society.

Foley, D. J., R. B. Wallace, and J. Eberhard. 1995. "Risk Factors for Motor Vehicle Crashes Among Older Drivers in a Rural Community." *Journal of the American Geriatrics Society* 43 (7): 776–81.

Fone, Byrne. 1983. "This Other Eden: Arcadia and the Homosexual Imagination." *Journal of Homosexuality* 8 (3–4): 13–34.

Ford, Sarah. 1997. *One Up: A Woman in Action with the S.A.S*. London: HarperCollins.

Franklin, Miles. 1901/1966. *My Brilliant Career*. Sydney: Angus and Robertson.

Friedburger, Mark. 1988. *Farm Families and Change in Twentieth-Century America.* Lexington: University Press of Kentucky.

―――. 1989. *Shake-out: Iowa Farm Families in the 1980s.* Lexington: University Press of Kentucky.

Friedland, Williams H. 2002. "Agriculture and Rurality: Beginning the Final Separation?" *Rural Sociology* 67 (3): 350–71

Gans, Herbert J. 1962. *Urban Villagers.* New York: Free Press.

Gatens, Moira. 1996. *Imaginary Bodies: Ethics, Power, and Corporeality.* London: Routledge.

Gaventa, John. 1993. "The Powerful, the Powerless, and the Experts: Knowledge Struggles in an Information Age." In *Voices of Change: Participatory Research in the United States and Canada,* ed. Peter Park, Mary Brydon-Miller, Bud Hall, and Ted Jackson, 21–40. London: Bergin and Garvey.

Gerberich, Susan G., Leon S. Robertson, Robert W. Gibson, and Colleen Renier. 1996. "An Epidemiological Study of Roadway Fatalities Related to Farm Vehicles: United States, 1988 to 1993." *Journal of Occupational and Environmental Medicine* 38 (11): 1135–40.

Gerson, Judith M., and Kathy Peiss. 1985. "Boundaries, Negotiation, Consciousness: Reconceptualizing Gender Relations." *Social Problems* 32 (4): 317–31.

Gibbons, S., M. L. Wylie, L. Echterling, J. French. 1986. "Patterns of Alcohol Use Among Rural and Small-Town Adolescents." *Adolescence* 21 (84): 887–900.

Gibson, James William. 1994. *Warrior Dreams: Violence and Manhood in Post-Vietnam America.* New York: Hill and Wang.

Giddens, Anthony. 1984. *The Constitution of Society: Outline of the Theory of Structuration.* Berkeley and Los Angeles: University of California Press.

―――. 1985. "Time, Space, and Distanciation." In *Social Relations and Spatial Structures,* ed. Derek Gregory and John Urry, 265–95. London: Macmillan.

Gillum, Richard F. 1994. "Prevalence of Cardiovascular and Pulmonary Diseases and Risk Factors by Region and Urbanization in the United States." *Journal of the National Medical Association* 86 (2): 105–12.

Gilroy, Paul. 1993. *The Black Atlantic: Modernity and Double Consciousness.* London: Verso.

Goffman, Erving. 1959. *The Presentation of Self in Everyday Life.* New York: Doubleday.

―――. 1979. *Gender Advertisements.* Cambridge: Harvard University Press.

Goldberg, Herb. 1976. *The Hazards of Being Male: Surviving the Myth of Masculine Privilege.* Plainview, N.Y.: Nash.

Goldman, Robert. 1992. *Reading Ads Socially.* London: Routledge.

Goldstein, Joshua. 2001. *Gender and War: How Gender Shapes the War System and Vice Versa.* Cambridge: Cambridge University Press.

Goodwin, C. (marketing manager for Speight's beer). 1997. Interview by Robin Law, Dunedin, 6 January.

Gordon, Donald. 1993. *Speight's: The Story of Dunedin's Historic Brewery.* Dunedin: Avon.

Gouveia, Lourdes, and Mark O. Rousseau. 1995. "Talk Is Cheap: The Value of

Language in the World Economy; Illustrations from the United States and Quebec." *Sociological Inquiry* 65 (2): 156–80.

Gramsci, Antonio. 1957. "The Southern Question." In *The Modern Prince and Other Writings*, 28–51. New York: International Publishers.

Gutmann, Matthew C. 1996. *The Meanings of Macho: Being a Man in Mexico City*. Berkeley and Los Angeles: University of California Press.

———. 1997. "The Ethnographic (G)ambit: Women and the Negotiation of Masculinity in Mexico City." *American Ethnologist* 24 (4): 833–55.

Haag, Anthony, and Franklin Chang. 1997. "The Impact of Electronic Networking on the Lesbian and Gay Community." In *Rural Gays and Lesbians: Building on the Strengths of Communities*, ed. James Smith and Ronald Mancoske, 83–94. New York: Harrington Park.

Haggard, H. Rider. 1885/1977. *King Solomon's Mines*. New York: Hart.

Halberg, Paul Tage. 1993. *Den Stolte Sliter: Skog og Landarbeiderne, 1900–1990: En Kamp for Likeverd* (The Proud Toiler: Forest and Agricultural Workers, 1900–1990: A Fight for Equality). Oslo: Norwegian United Federation of Trade Unions.

Halfacree, Keith. 1993. "Locality and Social Representation: Space, Discourse, and Alternative Definitions of the Rural." *Journal of Rural Studies* 9 (1): 23–37.

———. 1995. "Talking About Rurality: Social Representations of the Rural as Expressed by Residents of Six English Parishes" *Journal of Rural Studies* 11 (1): 1–20.

Hall, Stuart. 1993. "Encoding, Decoding." In *The Cultural Studies Reader*, ed. Simon During, 90–103. London: Routledge.

Hanke, Robert. 1992. "Redesigning Men: Hegemonic Masculinity in Transition." In *Men, Masculinity, and the Media*, ed. Steve Craig, 185–98. Newbury Park, Calif.: Sage Publications.

Hanson, Victor D. 1996. *Fields Without Dreams: Defending the Agrarian Idea*. New York: Free Press.

Harrell, W. Andrew. 1986. "Masculinity and Farming-Related Accidents." *Sex Roles* 15 (9–10): 467–78.

Harrison, James B. 1978. "Warning: The Male Sex Role May Be Dangerous to Your Health." *Journal of Social Issues* 34 (1): 65–86.

Hatch, Elvin. 1992. *Respectable Lives: Social Standing in Rural New Zealand*. Berkeley and Los Angeles: University of California Press.

Hayward, Mark D., Amy M. Pienta, and Diane K. McLaughlin. 1997. "Inequality in Men's Mortality: The Socioeconomic Status Gradient and Geographic Context." *Journal of Health and Social Behavior* 38 (4): 313–30.

Hearn, Jeff. 1987. *The Gender of Oppression: Men, Masculinity, and the Critique of Marxism*. New York: St. Martin's Press.

———. 1994. "Changing Men and Changing Managements: Social Change, Social Research, and Social Action." In *Women in Management: Current Research Issues*, ed. Marilyn J. Davidson and Ronald J. Burke, 192–209. London: Paul Chapman.

Hearn, Jeff, and David Morgan, eds. 1990. *Men, Masculinities, and Social Theory*. London: Unwin Hyman.

Hearn, Jeff, and David Collinson. 1994. "Theorizing Unities and Differences Between Men and Between Masculinities." *Theorizing Masculinities,* ed. Harry Brod and Michael Kaufmann, 97–118. London: Sage Publications.

Herbert, Melissa. 1998. *Camouflage Isn't Only for Combat: Gender, Sexuality, and Women in the Military.* New York: New York University Press.

Hessler, R. M., S. Jia, R. Madsen, and H. Pazaki. 1995. "Gender, Social Networks, and Survival Time: A 20-Year Study of the Rural Elderly." *Archives of Gerontology and Geriatrics* 21 (3): 291–306.

Hochschild, Arlie. 1989. *The Second Shift: Working Parents and the Revolution at Home.* New York: Viking.

Hodges, Ian. 1984. "Make Mine a Large One: An Anthropological Study of the Rules and Symbols of Drinking Rituals Intended to Reconstruct Social Relations Between Men in Southern New Zealand." Ph.D. diss., University of Otago, Dunedin, New Zealand.

Holcomb, Carol A. 1992. "Personal Health Practices of Couples in Rural Kansas." *Health Values* 16 (6): 36–46.

Holliday, Ruth, and John Hassard, eds. 2001. *Contested Bodies.* London: Routledge.

Hollway, Wendy. 1996. "Masters and Men in the Transition from Factory Hands to Sentimental Workers." In *Men as Managers, Managers as Men: Critical Perspectives on Men, Masculinities, and Managements,* ed. David L. Collinson and Jeff Hearn, 25–42. London: Sage Publications.

Honeyfield, James. 1997. "Red-blooded Blood Brothers: Representations of Place and Hard Man Masculinity in Television Advertisements for Beer." Master's thesis, Department of Geography, University of Waikato, Hamilton, New Zealand.

Horwitz, Tony. 1998. *Confederates in the Attic: Dispatches from the Unfinished Civil War.* New York: Pantheon Books.

Howard, John. 1995. "The Library, the Park, and the Pervert: Public Space and Homosexual Encounters in Post–World War II Atlanta." *Radical History Review* 62 (spring): 166–87.

———. 1999. *Men Like That: A Southern Queer History.* Chicago: University of Chicago Press.

Hoyt, Danny R., Rand D. Conger, Jill G. Valde, and Karen Weihs. 1997. "Psychological Distress and Help Seeking in Rural America." *American Journal of Community Psychology* 25 (4): 449–70.

Hubbard, Phil. 2000. "Desire/Disgust: Mapping the Moral Contours of Heterosexuality." *Progress in Human Geography* 24 (2): 191–217.

———. 2002. "Sexing the Self: Geographies of Engagement and Encounter." *Social and Cultural Geography* 3 (4): 365–82.

Hubbard, Phil, and Tessa Sanders. 2003. "Making Space for Sex Work: Female Street Prostitution and the Production of Urban Space." *International Journal of Urban and Regional Research* 27 (1): 75–89.

Hughes, Annie. 1997. "Rurality and Cultures of Womanhood: Domestic Identities and Moral Order in Rural Life." In *Contested Countryside Cultures: Otherness, Marginalisation, and Rurality,* ed. Paul Cloke and Jo Little. London: Routledge.

Hwang, H. C., L. Stallones, and T. J. Keefe. 1997. "Childhood Injury Deaths: Rural and Urban Differences, Colorado 1980–88." *Injury Prevention* 3 (1): 35–7.

Jackman, Mary. 1994. *The Velvet Glove.* Berkeley and Los Angeles: University of California Press.

Jackson, Peter. 1991. "The Cultural Politics of Masculinity: Towards a Social Geography." *Transactions of the Institute of British Geographers* 16 (2): 199–213.

Jacobs, Jane. 1996. *Edge of Empire: Postcolonialism and the City.* London: Routledge.

James, Bev, and Kay Saville-Smith. 1994. *Gender, Culture, and Power.* 2d ed. Auckland: Oxford University Press.

Jellison, Katherine. 1993. *Entitled to Power: Farm Women and Technology, 1913–1963.* Chapel Hill: University of North Carolina Press.

Jensen, Kai. 1996. *Whole Men: The Masculine Tradition in New Zealand Literature.* Auckland: Auckland University Press.

Jobes, Patrick C. 1997. "Gender Competition and the Preservation of Community in the Allocation of Administrative Positions in Small Rural Towns in Montana: A Research Note." *Rural Sociology* 62 (3): 315–34.

Johansson, Ella. 1989. "Beautiful Men, Fine Women, and Good Work People: Gender and Skill in Northern Sweden, 1850–1950." *Gender and History* 1 (2): 200–212.

Johnson, Sally. 1997. "Theorizing Language and Masculinity: A Feminist Perspective." In *Language and Masculinity,* ed. Sally Johnson and Ulrike H. Meinhof, 8–26. Cambridge, Mass.: Blackwell.

Jones, Owain. 1995. "Lay Discourses of the Rural: Developments and Implications for Rural Studies." *Journal of Rural Studies* 11 (1): 35–49.

Joyce, Patrick. 1980. *Work, Society, and Politics: The Culture of the Factory in Later Victorian England.* New Brunswick: Rutgers University Press.

Junas, Daniel. 1995. "The Rise of Citizen Militias: Angry White Guys with Guns." In *Eyes Right: Challenging the Right Wing Backlash,* ed. Chip Berlet. Boston: South End Press.

Kaldal, Ingar. 1998. "Kvinnelig og Mannlig i Skogsbygdas Arbeidsliv: Slik det Fortelles i Tida etter 1930 i Trysil og Nord-Värmland" (Feminine and Masculine in the Working Life of Forest Communities: As It Is Told After 1930 in Trysil and Nord-Värmland). *Heimen* 35 (4): 243–52.

Kale, Madhavi. 1996. "Review of *The Black Atlantic:* Modernity and Double Consciousness." *Social History* 21:252–56.

Kanter, Rosabeth Moss. 1977. *Men and Women of the Corporation.* New York: Basic Books.

Kaufman, Michael, ed. 1987. *Beyond Patriarchy: Essays by Men on Pleasure, Power, and Change.* Toronto: Oxford University Press.

Keen, Sam. 1991. *Fire in the Belly: On Being a Man.* New York: Bantam Books.

Kellner, Douglas. 1995. "Cultural Studies, Multiculturalism, and Media Culture." In *Gender, Race, and Class in Media,* ed. Gail Dines and Jean Humez, 5–17. Thousand Oaks, Calif.: Sage Publications.

Kenrick, K. N.d. "Developing a Corporate Sponsorship Strategy to Reach Your Target Audience." In *Collected Papers, Fourth Annual Corporate Sponsorship and Events Marketing Conference.* [Obtainable from Robin Law.]

Kerfoot, Deborah, and David Knights. 1993. "Management, Masculinity, and Ma-
    nipulation: From Paternalism to Corporate Strategy in Financial Services in
    Britain." *Journal of Management Studies* 30 (4): 659–67.
———. 1998. "Managing Masculinity in Contemporary Organizational Life." *Or-
    ganization* 5 (1): 7–26.
Kessler, Suzanne J., and Wendy McKenna. 1978. *Gender: An Ethnomethodological
    Approach*. Chicago: University of Chicago Press.
Kimmel, Michael, ed. 1987. *Changing Men: New Directions in Research on Men and
    Masculinity*. Beverly Hills, Calif.: Sage Publications.
———. 1992. "Foreword." In *Men, Masculinity, and the Media*, ed. Steve Craig, xii.
    London: Sage Publications.
———. 1996. *Manhood in America: A Cultural History*. New York: Free Press.
King, Richard. 1995. "Review of *The Black Atlantic*: Modernity and Double Con-
    sciousness." *Ethnic and Racial Studies* 18:659–60.
Kinsey, Alfred, Wardell Pomeroy, and Clyde Martin. 1948. *Sexual Behavior in the
    Human Male*. Philadelphia: W. B. Saunders.
Kinsey, Alfred, Wardell Pomeroy, Clyde Martin, and Paul Gebhard. 1953. *Sexual
    Behavior in the Human Female*. Philadelphia: W. B. Saunders.
Kirby, Jack T. 1987. *Rural Worlds Lost: The American South, 1920–1960*. Baton
    Rouge: Louisiana State University Press.
Knobloch, Freida. 1996. *The Culture of Wilderness: Agriculture as Colonization in the
    American West*. Chapel Hill: University of North Carolina Press.
Knuttila, Murray. 1994. *"That Man Partridge": E. A. Partridge, His Thoughts and
    Times*. Regina: Canadian Plains Research Center.
Kraack, Anna. 1996. "Mates on the Piss." Honors diss., Department of Anthropol-
    ogy, University of Otago, Dunedin, New Zealand.
———. 1999. "It Takes Two to Tango: The Place of Women in the Construction
    of Hegemonic Masculinity in a Student Pub." In *Masculinities in Aotearoa/
    New Zealand*, ed. Robin Law, Hugh Campbell, and John Dolan. Palmerston
    North: Dunmore Press.
Kramer, Jerry-Lee. 1995. "Bachelor Farmers and Spinsters: Gay and Lesbian Iden-
    tities and Communities in Rural North Dakota." In *Mapping Desire: Geogra-
    phies of Sexualities*, ed. David Bell and Gill Valentine, 200–213. London:
    Routledge.
Krannich, Richard S., E. Helen Berry, and Thomas Greider. 1989. "Fear of Crime
    in Rapidly Changing Rural Communities: A Longitudinal Analysis." *Rural
    Sociology* 54 (2): 195–212.
Krogstad, Gunleif. 1998. "Skogsarbeider og Langrennsløper som Felles Identitet"
    (Forest Worker and Cross-Country Skier as Common Identity). *Heimen* 35
    (4): 261–68.
Kummel, Gerhard. 2002. "When Boy Meets Girl: The 'Feminization' of the Mili-
    tary; An Introduction Also to Be Read as a Postscript." *Current Sociology* 50
    (5): 615–40.
Kvande, Elin. 1999. "Paradoxes of Gender and Organisations." Ph.D. diss., Trond-
    heim: Norwegian University of Technology and Science.

Lake, Marilyn. 1986. "The Politics of Respectability: Identifying the Masculinist Context." *Historical Studies Australia and New Zealand* 22 (86): 116–31.

Lamy, Philip. 1996. *Millennium Rage: White Supremacists and the Doomsday Prophecy.* New York: Plenum Press.

Law, Robin. 1997. "Masculinity, Place, and Beer Advertising in New Zealand: The Southern Man Campaign." *New Zealand Geographer* 53 (2): 22–28.

Law, Robin, Hugh Campbell, and John Dolan, eds. 1999. *Masculinities in Aotearoa/ New Zealand.* Palmerston North: Dunmore Press.

Law, Robin, Hugh Campbell, and Ruth Schick. 1999. "Introduction." In *Masculinities in Aotearoa/New Zealand,* ed. Robin Law, Hugh Campbell, and John Dolan. Palmerston North: Dunmore Press.

Lawson, Henry. 1974. *The World of Henry Lawson,* ed. W. Stone. Sydney: Lansdowne Press.

Lawson, Tony. 1981. "Paternalism and Labour Market Segmentation Theory." In *The Dynamics of Labor Market Segmentation,* ed. Frank Wilkinson, 47–66. London: Academic Press.

Levine, Donald. 1995. *The Visions of the Sociological Tradition.* Chicago: University of Chicago Press.

Lewis, Gareth J. 1979. *Rural Communities: A Social Geography.* North Pomfret, Vt.: David and Charles, Inc.

Lewis, Jon. 1997. *The Handbook of the SAS and Elite Forces: How the Professionals Fight and Win.* London: Magpie.

Lewis, Neil. 2000. "The Climbing Body: Nature and the Experience of Modernity." In *Bodies of Nature,* ed. Phil Macnaghten and John Urry, 58–80 (special issue of *Body and Society* 6 [3–4]).

Leyshon, M. 2005. "'No Place for a Girl': Rural Youth, Pubs, and the Performance of Masculinity." In *Critical Perspectives on Gender and Rurality,* ed. Jo Little and Carol Morris. London: Ashgate.

Lidestav, Gun. 1998. "Women as Non-Industrial Private Forest Landowners in Sweden." *Scandinavian Journal of Forest Research* 13:66–73.

Liepins, Ruth. 1998a. "Fields of Action: Australian Women's Agricultural Activism in the 1990s." *Rural Sociology* 63 (1): 128–56.

———. 1998b. "The Gendering of Farming and Agricultural Politics: A Matter of Discourse and Power." *Australian Geographer* 29 (3): 371–88.

———. 2000. "Making Men: The Construction and Representation of Agriculture-based Masculinities in Australia and New Zealand." *Rural Sociology* 65 (4): 605–20.

Linn, J. Gary, and Baqar A. Husaini. 1987. "Determinants of Psychological Depression and Coping Behaviors of Tennessee Farm Residents." *Journal of Community Psychology* 15:503–12.

Linzer, Lori (Anti-Defamation League researcher). 1999. Telephone interview by Abby L. Ferber, 16 July.

*Lion Nathan Annual Reports.* (1992–1995). Reports for 1991 to 1994.

Little, Jo. 1987. "Gender Relations in Rural Areas: The Importance of Women's Domestic Role." *Journal of Rural Studies* 3 (4): 335–42.

———. 1999. "Otherness, Representation, and the Cultural Construction of Rurality." *Progress in Human Geography* 23 (3): 437–42.

———. 2002a. *Gender and Rural Geography.* Harlow, UK: Prentice-Hall.

———. 2002b. "Rural Geography: Rural Gender Identity and the Performance of Masculinity and Femininity in the Countryside." *Progress in Human Geography* 26 (5): 665–70.

———. 2003. "'Riding the Rural Love Train': Heterosexuality and the Rural Community." *Sociologia Ruralis* 43 (4): 401–17.

Little, Jo, and Patricia Austin. 1996. "Women and the Rural Idyll." *Journal of Rural Studies* 12 (2): 101–11.

Little, Jo, and Owain Jones. 2000. "Masculinity, Gender, and Rural Policy." *Rural Sociology* 65 (4): 621–39.

Livingstone, David W., and Meg Luxton. 1989. "Gender Consciousness at Work: Modification of the Male Breadwinner Norm Among Steelworkers and Their Spouses." *Canadian Review of Sociology and Anthropology* 26 (2): 240–67.

Lobao, Linda M., and Katherine Meyer. 1995a. "Economic Decline, Gender, and Labor Flexibility in Family-Based Enterprises: Midwestern Farming in the 1980s." *Social Forces* 74 (2): 575–608.

———. 1995b. "Restructuring the Rural Farm Economy: Midwestern Women's and Men's Work Roles during the Farm Crisis Period." *Economic Development Quarterly* 9 (1): 60–73.

Loffreda, Beth. 2000. *Losing Matt Shepard: Life and Politics in the Aftermath of Anti-Gay Murder.* New York: Columbia University Press.

Long, Kathleen A. 1993. "The Concept of Health: Rural Perspectives." *Nursing Clinics of North America* 28 (1): 123–30.

Longhurst, Robyn. 1997. "(Dis)embodied Geographies." *Progress in Human Geographies* 21 (4): 486–501.

———. 2000. "'Corporeographies' of Pregnancy: 'Bikini Babes.'" *Environment and Planning D: Society and Space* 18:453–72.

———. 2001. *Bodies: Exploring Fluid Boundaries.* London: Routledge.

Longhurst, Robyn, and Carly Wilson. 1999. "Heartland Wainuiomata: Rurality to Suburbs, Black Singlets to Naughty Lingerie." In *Masculinities in Aotearoa/New Zealand,* ed. Robin Law, Hugh Campbell, and John Dolan, 215–28. Palmerston North: Dunmore Press.

Loomis, Charles P., and Alan Beegle. 1950. *Rural Social Systems: A Textbook in Rural Sociology and Anthropology.* New York: Prentice-Hall.

Lorber, Judith. 1994. *Paradoxes of Gender.* New Haven: Yale University Press.

Lovelock, Kirsten. 1999. "Men and Machines: Manufacturing Work Sites in Mataura, Southland." In *Masculinities in Aotearoa/New Zealand,* ed. Robin Law, Hugh Campbell, and John Dolan, 121–34. Palmerston North: Dunmore Press.

Lukowiak, Ken. 1993. *A Soldier's Song: True Stories from the Falklands.* London: Phoenix.

———. 2000. *Marijuana Time: Join the Army, See the World, Meet Interesting People, and Smoke All Their Dope.* London: Orion.

Mac an Ghaill, Máirtín, ed. 1996. *Understanding Masculinities*. Buckingham: Open University Press.

MacKenzie, John M. 1987. "The Imperial Pioneer and the British Masculine Stereotype in Late Victorian and Edwardian Times." In *Manliness and Morality*, ed. Julian A. Mangan and James Walvin, 176–98. Manchester: Manchester University Press.

Macnaghten, Phil, and John Urry. 2000a. "Bodies in the Woods." *Body and Society* 6 (3–4): 166–82.

———. 2000b. *Contested Natures*. London: Sage Publications.

Maio, R. F., P. E. Green, M. P. Becker, R. E. Burney, and C. Compton. 1992. "Rural Motor Vehicle Crash Mortality: The Role of Crash Severity and Medical Resources." *Accident Analysis and Prevention* 24 (6): 631–42.

Mancoske, Ronald. 1997. "Rural HIV/AIDS Social Services for Gays and Lesbians." In *Rural Gays and Lesbians: Building on the Strengths of Communities*, ed. James Smith and Ronald Mancoske, 37–52. New York: Harrington Park.

Margolis, Maxine L. 1984. *Mothers and Such: Views of American Women and Why They Changed*. Berkeley and Los Angeles: University of California Press.

Marlenga, B. 1995. "The Health Beliefs and Skin Cancer Prevention Practices of Wisconsin Dairy Farmers." *Oncology Nursing Forum* 22 (4): 681–86.

Marrs, Texe. 1993. *Big Sister Is Watching You: Hillary Clinton and the White House Feminists Who Now Control America and Tell the President What to Do*. Austin: Living Truth Publishers.

Marsden, Terry, Philip Lowe, and Sarah Whatmore, eds. 1990. *Rural Restructuring: Global Processes and Their Responses*. London: David Fulton Publishers.

Massey, Doreen. 1994. *Space, Place, and Gender*. Minneapolis: University of Minnesota Press.

———. 1995. "The Conceptualisation of Place." In *A Place in the World: Places, Culture, and Globalisation*, ed. Doreen Massey and Pat Jess, 45–86. Milton Keynes: Open University Press.

Mazzochi, J., and L. E. Rhinegaard. "Rambo, Gnomes, and the New World Order: The Emerging Politics of Populism." Portland, Ore.: Coalition for Human Dignity.

McCausland, R. 1979. *Unto the Hills: Methven and Districts 100th Centennial, 1879–1979*. Ashburton: Methven and Districts Centennial Committee.

McClelland, J. W., W. Demark-Wahnefried, R. D. Mustian, A. T. Cowan, and M. K. Campbell. 1998. "Fruit and Vegetable Consumption of Rural African Americans: Baseline Survey Results of the Black Churches United for Better Health 5 a Day Project." *Nutrition and Cancer* 30 (2): 148–57.

McDowell, Linda. 1999. *Gender, Identity, and Place: Understanding Feminist Geographies*. Cambridge: Polity Press.

McKnight, R. H., C. A. Koetke, and J. R. Mays. 1995. "Smokeless Tobacco Use Among Adults in Kentucky: 1994." *Journal of the Kentucky Medical Association* 93 (10): 459–64.

McMillen, Sally G. 1992. *Southern Women: Black and White in the Old South*. Arlington Heights, Ill.: Harlan Davidson.

McNab, Andy. 1993. *Bravo Two Zero*. London: Corgi.

McNall, Scott G., and Sally A. McNall. 1983. *Plains Families: Exploring Sociology Through Social History*. New York: St. Martin's Press.

Meares, Alison. 1997. "Making the Transition from Conventional to Sustainable Agriculture: Gender, Social Movement Participation, and Quality of Life on the Family Farm." *Rural Sociology* 62 (1): 21–47.

Messerschmidt, James W. 1993. *Masculinities and Crime: Critique and Reconceptualization of Theory*. Lanham, Md.: Rowman and Littlefield.

Messner, Michael A. 1997. *Politics of Masculinities: Men in Movements*. Thousand Oaks, Calif.: Sage Publications.

Messner, Michael A., and Donald F. Sabo. 1994. *Sex, Violence, and Power in Sports: Rethinking Masculinity*. Freedom, Calif.: Crossing Press.

Milbourne, Paul, ed. 1997. *Revealing Rural Others: Representation, Power, and Identity in the British Countryside*. London: Pinter.

Mills, Sara. 1997. *Discourse*. London: Routledge.

Mohanty, Chandra, Anna Russo, and Lourdes Torres, eds. 1991. *Third World Women and the Politics of Feminism*. Bloomington: Indiana University Press.

Monroe, A. C., T. C. Ricketts, and L. A. Savitz. 1992. "Cancer in Rural Versus Urban Populations: A Review." *Journal of Rural Health* 8 (3): 212–20.

Mooney, Patrick H. 1988. *My Own Boss? Class, Rationality, and the Family Farm*. Boulder: Westview Press.

Moore, Henrietta. 1994. *A Passion for Difference*. Bloomington: Indiana University Press.

Morgan, David H. J. 1992. *Discovering Men*. London: Routledge.

———. 1994. "Theatre of War: Combat, the Military, and Masculinities." In *Theorizing Masculinities*, ed. Harry Brod and Michael Kaufman, 165–82. London: Sage Publications.

———. 1996. "The Gender of Bureaucracy." In *Men as Managers, Managers as Men: Critical Perspectives on Men, Masculinities, and Managements*, ed. David L. Collinson and Jeff Hearn, 43–60. London: Sage Publications.

Mormont, Marc. 1990. "Who Is Rural? Or, How to Be Rural: Towards a Sociology of the Rural." In *Rural Restructuring: Global Processes and Their Responses*, ed. Terry Marsden, Philip Lowe, and Sarah Whatmore. London: David Fulton Publishers.

Morrell, Robert. 2001. *From Boys to Gentlemen: Settler Masculinity in Colonial Natal, 1880–1920*. Pretoria: University of South Africa Press.

Morris, Carolyn. 2003. "Station Wives in New Zealand: Narrating Continuity in the High Country." Ph.D. diss., Department of Anthropology, University of Auckland.

Morris, L. 1985. "Renegotiation of the Domestic Division of Labour in the Context of Male Redundancy." In *Restructuring Capital: Recession and Reorganisation in Industrial Society*, ed. H. Newby, J. Bujira, P. Littlewood, G. Rees, and T. Rees, 221–43. London: Macmillan.

Moses, Elfin, and Janet Buckner. 1980. "The Special Problems of Rural Gay Clients." *Human Services in the Rural Environment* 5 (5): 22–7.

Muldoon, J. T., M. Schootman, and R. F. Morton. 1996. "Utilization of Cancer Early Detection Services Among Farm and Rural Nonfarm Adults in Iowa." *Journal of Rural Health* 12 (4 supp.): 321–31.

Mullins, Eustace. N.d. *Vigilante Justice*. 28.

Murdoch, Jonathan, and Andrew Pratt. 1993. "Rural Studies: Modernism, Post-modernism, and the 'Post-rural'." *Journal of Rural Studies* 9 (4): 411–27.

———. 1994. "Rural Studies of Power and the Power of Rural Studies: A Reply to Philo." *Journal of Rural Studies* 10 (1): 83–87.

Nash, Catherine. 1993. "Remapping and Renaming: New Cartographies of Identity, Gender, and Landscape in Ireland." *Feminist Review* 44:39–57.

National Cancer Institute. 1991. *Oral Cancers: Research Report*. Bethesda, Md.: National Cancer Institute.

National Safety Council. 1992. *Accident Facts, 1992 Edition*. Itasca, Ill.: National Safety Council.

———. 1994. *Accident Facts, 1994 Edition*. Itasca, Ill.: National Safety Council.

Nelson, D. E., S. L. Tomar, P. Mowery, and P. Z. Siegel. 1996. "Trends in Smokeless Tobacco Use Among Men in Four States, 1988 Through 1993." *American Journal of Public Health* 86 (9): 1300–1303.

Nelson, Margaret K., and Joan Smith. 1999. *Working Hard and Making Do: Surviving Small-Town America*. Berkeley and Los Angeles: University of California Press.

Neruda, Pablo. 1978. *Memoirs*. London: Penguin Books.

Netting, Robert. M. 1993. *Smallholders, Householders: Farm Families and the Ecology of Intensive, Sustainable Agriculture*. Stanford: Stanford University Press.

Newsinger, John. 1997. *Dangerous Men: The SAS and Popular Culture*. London: Pluto Press.

Ní Laoire, Caitríona. 1997. "Migration, Power, and Identity: Lifepath Formation Among Irish Rural Youth." Ph.D. diss., University of Liverpool.

———. 1999. "Gender Issues in Irish Rural Outmigration." In *Migration and Gender in the Developed World*, ed. Paul Boyle and Keith Halfacree, 223–37. London: Routledge.

———. 2001. "A Matter of Life and Death: Men, Masculinities, and Staying 'Behind' in Rural Ireland." *Sociologia Ruralis* 41 (2): 220–36.

———. 2002. "Young Farmers, Masculinities, and Change in Rural Ireland." *Irish Geography* 35 (1): 16–27.

O'Matz, Megan. 1996. "More Hate Crimes Blamed on Juveniles." *The Morning Call* (23 October).

Ortner, Sherry. 1996. "Making Gender: Toward a Feminist, Minority, Postcolonial, Subaltern, etc. Theory of Practice." In *Making Gender: The Politics and Erotics of Culture*, ed. Sherry Ortner. Boston: Beacon Press.

Osterud, Nancy G. 1991. *Bonds of Community: The Lives of Farm Women in Nineteenth-Century New York*. Ithaca: Cornell University Press.

*Otago Daily Times*. 1996a. 15 October, p. 23.

*Otago Daily Times*. 1996b. 26 October, p. 20.

Ownby, Ted. 1991. *Subduing Satan: Religion, Recreation, and Manhood in the Rural South*. Chapel Hill: University of North Carolina Press.

Pahl, Ray. 1964. *Urbs in Rure: The Metropolitan Fringe in Hertfordshire*. Geographical Papers no. 2. London: London School of Economics.

———. 1984. *Divisions of Labour*. Oxford: Basil Blackwell.

Parkes, James C. 1996. "Et in Arcadia . . . Homo: Sexuality and the Gay Sensibility in the Art of Derek Jarman." In *Derek Jarman: A Portrait*, ed. Roger Wollen, 137–46. London: Thames and Hudson.

Paterson, A. B. 1956. *Collected Verse*. Sydney: Angus and Robertson.

Pawson, Eric. 1996. "Brands and the Big Brewers." In *Changing Places: New Zealand in the Nineties*, ed. Richard Le Heron and Eric Pawson, 68–70. Auckland: Longman Paul.

Pearson, T. A., and C. Lewis. 1998. "Rural Epidemiology: Insights from a Rural Population Laboratory." *American Journal of Epidemiology* 148 (1): 949–57.

Perchuk, Andrew, and Helaine Posner, eds. 1995. *The Masculine Masquerade: Masculinity and Representation*. Cambridge: MIT Press.

Perrine, M. W., J. C. Mundt, and R. I. Weiner. 1994. "When Alcohol and Water Don't Mix: Diving Under the Influence." *Journal of Studies on Alcohol* 55 (5): 517–24.

Perry, Linda A., Lynn H. Turner, and Helen M. Sterk, eds. 1992. *Constructing and Reconstructing Gender: The Links Among Communication, Language, and Gender*. Albany: State University of New York Press.

Perry, Nick. 1994. *The Dominion of Signs: Television, Advertising, and Other New Zealand Fictions*. Auckland: Auckland University Press.

Peter, Gregory, Michael M. Bell, Susan Jarnagin, and Donna Bauer. 1996. "Coming Back Across the Fence: Sustainable Agriculture, Masculinity, and the Dialectics of Gender." Paper presented at meeting of the Rural Sociological Society (August).

———. 2000. "Coming Back Across the Fence: Masculinity and the Transition to Sustainable Agriculture." *Rural Sociology* 65 (2): 215–33.

Pfeil, Fred. 1995. *White Guys: Studies in Postmodern Domination and Difference*. London: Verso.

Phillips, Jock. 1987. *A Man's Country? The Image of the Pakeha Male: A History*. Auckland: Penguin Books.

Phillips, Richard, Diane Watt, and David Shuttleton, eds. 2000. *De-Centring Sexualities: Politics and Representations Beyond the Metropolis*. London: Routledge.

Philo, Chris. 1992. "Neglected Rural Geographies: A Review." *Journal of Rural Studies* 8 (2): 193–207.

———. 1993. "Postmodern Rural Geography? A Reply to Murdoch and Pratt." *Journal of Rural Studies* 9 (4): 429–36.

Pierce, William. 1978. *The Turner Diaries*. Hillsboro, Va.: National Vanguard Books.

Pope, S. K., P. D. Smith, J. B. Wayne, and K. J. Kelleher. 1994. "Gender Differences in Rural Adolescent Drinking Patterns." *Journal of Adolescent Health* 15 (5): 359–65.

Posner, B. M., A. Jette, C. Smigelski, D. Miller, and P. Mitchell. 1994. "Nutritional Risk in New England Elders." *Journal of Gerontology* 49 (3): 123–32.

Potok, Mark (Southern Poverty Law Center researcher). 1999. Telephone interview by Abby L. Ferber, 21 July.

————. 2002. Telephone interview by Abby L. Ferber, 23 December.

Poullard, Jonathan, and Anthony D'Augelli. 1989. "AIDS Fears and Homophobia Among Volunteers in an AIDS Prevention Program." *Journal of Rural Community Psychology* 10 (1): 29–39.

Pratt, Andrew. 1996. "Discourses of Rurality: Loose Talk or Social Struggle." *Journal of Rural Studies* 12(1): 68–79.

Proulx, Annie. 1999. "Brokeback Mountain." In Annie Proulx, *Close Range: Wyoming Stories*. London: Fourth Estate.

Pyke, Karen D. 1996. "Class-Based Masculinities: The Interdependence of Gender, Class, and Interpersonal Power." *Gender and Society* 10 (5): 527–49.

Quam-Wickham, Nancy. 1999. "Rereading Man's Conquest of Nature: Skill, Myths, and the Historical Construction of Masculinity in the Western Extractive Industries." *Men and Masculinities* 2 (2): 135–51.

*Racial Loyalty*. 1991. 72:3.

Raimondo, Meredith. 2001. "'Corralling the Virus': Migratory Sexualities and the 'Spread of AIDS' in the United States." Paper presented at the Queering Geographies of Globalization conference, Center for Lesbian and Gay Studies, City University of New York, 27 February.

Ramsey, Jack. 1996. *SAS: The Soldier's Story*. London: Macmillan.

Rand, Kristen. 1996. *Gun Shows in America*. Washington, D.C.: Violence Policy Center.

Retzloff, Tim. 1997. "Cars and Bars: Assembling Gay Men in Postwar Flint, Michigan." In *Creating a Place for Ourselves: Lesbian, Gay, and Bisexual Community Histories*, ed. Brett Beemyn, 226–52. London: Routledge.

Reynolds, Larry T. 1990. *Interactionism: Exposition and Critique*. Dix Hills: General Hall.

Rice, Tom W., and Diane L. Coates. 1995. "Gender Role Attitudes in the Southern United States." *Gender and Society* 9 (6): 744–56.

Rich, Adrienne. 1979. *On Lies, Secrets, and Silence*. New York: W. W. Norton.

————. 1980. "Compulsory Heterosexuality and Lesbian Experience." *Signs* 5:631–60.

————. 1986. "Towards a Politics of Location." In *Blood, Bread, and Poetry: Selected Prose, 1979–1985*, ed. Adrienne Rich. London: Verso.

Richardson, Diane, ed. 1996. *Theorising Heterosexuality: Telling It Straight*. Buckingham: Open University Press.

Roper, Michael. 1994. *Masculinity and the British Organization Man Since 1945*. Oxford: Oxford University Press.

Roper, Michael, and John Tosh. 1991. *Manful Assertions: Masculinities in Britain Since 1800*. London: Routledge.

Rose, Gillian. 1993. *Feminism and Geography: The Limits of Geographical Knowledge*. Cambridge: Polity Press.

Rosenblatt, Paul. 1990. *Farming Is in Our Blood: Farm Families in Economic Crisis*. Ames: Iowa State University Press.

Rosenman, K. D., J. Gardiner, G. M. Swanson, P. Mullan, and Z. Zhu. 1995. "Use of Skin-Cancer Prevention Strategies Among Farmers and Their Spouses." *American Journal of Preventive Medicine* 11 (5): 342–47.

Rounds, Kathleen. 1988. "AIDS in Rural Areas: Challenges to Providing Care." *Social Work* 33 (3): 218–29.

Rubin, Lillian B. 1976. *Worlds of Pain: Life in the Working-Class Family.* New York: Basic Books.

Russell, M. 1999. "The Geography of Student Drinking in Dunedin." B.A. honors diss., University of Otago, Dunedin, New Zealand.

Ryan, Chris. 1995. *The One That Got Away.* London: Ted Smart.

Ryan, Mary P. 1981. *Cradle of the Middle Class: The Family in Oneida County, New York, 1790–1865.* Cambridge: Cambridge University Press.

Sabo, Don, and David F. Gordon, eds. 1995. *Men's Health and Illness: Gender, Power, and the Body.* Thousand Oaks, Calif.: Sage Publications.

Salamon, Sonya. 1992. *Prairie Patrimony: Family, Farming, and Community in the Midwest.* Chapel Hill: University of North Carolina Press.

Salamon, Sonya, Kathleen M. Gengenbacher, and Dwight J. Penas. 1986. "Family Factors Affecting the Intergenerational Succession to Farming." *Human Organization* 45 (1): 24–33.

Salamon, Sonya, Richard L. Farnsworth, Donald G. Bullock, and Raji Yusuf. 1997. "Family Factors Affecting Adoption of Sustainable Farming Systems." *Journal of Soil and Water Conservation* 52 (2): 265–71.

Salehi, S. O., and N. C. Elder. 1995. "Prevalence of Cigarette and Smokeless Tobacco Use Among Students in Rural Oregon." *Family Medicine* 27 (2): 122–25.

Sarten, T. 1996. "It's a Hard Road Finding the Perfect Woman." *Critic* 15 (31 July): 6.

Sarvela, P. D., and E. J. McClendon. 1988. "Indicators of Rural Youth Drug Use." *Journal of Youth and Adolescence* 17 (4): 335–47.

Sarvela, P. D., C. E. Cronk, and F. R. Isberner. 1997. "A Secondary Analysis of Smoking Among Rural and Urban Youth Using the MTF Data Set." *Journal of School Health* 67 (9): 372–75.

Saugeres, Lise. 2002a. "The Cultural Representation of the Farming Landscape: Masculinity, Power, and Nature." *Journal of Rural Studies* 18 (4): 373–84.

———. 2002b. "Of Tractors and Men: Masculinity, Technology, and Power in a French Farming Community." *Sociologia Ruralis* 42 (2): 143–59.

Savran, David. 1998. *Taking It Like A Man: White Masculinity, Masochism, and Contemporary American Culture.* Princeton: Princeton University Press.

Schootman, M., L. J. Fuortes, C. Zwerling, M. A. Albanese, and C. A. Watson. 1993. "Safety Behavior Among Iowa Junior High and High School Students." *American Journal of Public Health* 83 (11): 1628–30.

Sedgwick, Eve K. 1985. *Between Men: English Literature and Male Homosocial Desire.* New York: Columbia University Press.

Segal, Lynne. 1990. *Slow Motion: Changing Masculinities, Changing Men.* New Brunswick: Rutgers University Press.

Seidman, Steven. 1994. *Contested Knowledge: Social Theory in the Postmodern Era.* Oxford: Blackwell Press.

Serrano, Richard. 1990. "Civil Suit Seeks to Bring Down Metzger Empire." *Los Angeles Times* (18 February).

Services Sound and Vision Corporation. 1995. *Room to Manoeuvre*. Publicity video C.1871.

Short, John. 1991. *Imagined Country: Society, Culture, and Environment*. London: Routledge.

Shuttleton, David. 2000. "The Queer Politics of Gay Pastoral." In *De-Centring Sexualities: Politics and Representations Beyond the Metropolis*, ed. Richard Phillips, Diane Watt, and David Shuttleton, 125–46. London: Routledge.

*Skogeieren* (The Forest Owner). 1976, 1986, and 1996 [all 40 issues]; 1999, issue 11.

Smith, James. 1997. "Working Within Larger Systems: Rural Lesbians and Gays." In *Rural Gays and Lesbians: Building on the Strengths of Communities*, ed. James Smith and Ronald Mancoske, 13–21. New York: Harrington Park Press.

Smith, James, and Ronald Mancoske, eds. 1997. *Rural Gays and Lesbians: Building on the Strengths of Communities*. New York: Harrington Park Press.

Smith, Margaret, and David Crossley. 1975. *The Way Out*. Melbourne: Lansdowne Press.

Smith, Mark H., Roger T. Anderson, Douglas D. Bradham, and Charles F. Longino. 1995. "Rural and Urban Differences in Mortality Among Americans 55 Years and Older: Analysis of the National Longitudinal Mortality Study." *Journal of Rural Health* 11 (4): 274–85.

Snipp, C. Matthew. 1996. "Understanding Race and Ethnicity in Rural America." *Rural Sociology* 61 (1): 125–42.

Sokolosky, M. C., J. E. Prescott, S. L. Collins, and G. A. Timberlake. 1993. "Safety Belt Use and Hospital Charge Differences Among Motor Vehicle Crash Victims." *West Virginia Medical Journal* 89 (8): 328–30.

Sorensen, E. S. 1994. "Daily Stressors and Coping Responses: A Comparison of Rural and Suburban Children." *Public Health Nursing* 11 (1): 24–31.

Southern Poverty Law Center. 1997. *False Patriots: The Threat of Antigovernment Extremists*. Montgomery, Ala.: Southern Poverty Law Center.

———. 1999. *Intelligence Report*. Montgomery, Ala.: Southern Poverty Law Center.

Spence, Cameron. 1997. *Sabre Squadron*. Harmondsworth: Penguin Books.

———. 1998. *All Necessary Measures*. Harmondsworth: Penguin Books.

Spurlin, William. 2000. "Remapping Same-Sex Desire: Queer Writing and Culture in the American Heartland." In *De-Centring Sexualities: Politics and Representations Beyond the Metropolis*, ed. Richard Phillips, Diane Watt, and David Shuttleton, 182–98. London: Routledge.

Stamm, B. Hudnall, ed. 2003. *Rural Behavioral Health Care: An Interdisciplinary Guide*. Washington, D.C.: American Psychological Association.

Staples, William G. 1987. "Technology, Control, and the Social Organization of Work at a British Hardware Firm, 1791–1891. *American Journal of Sociology* 93 (1): 62–88.

Stern, Kenneth S. 1996. *A Force upon the Plain: The American Militia Movement and the Politics of Hate*. New York: Simon and Schuster.

Stewart, Tricia. 2001. *Calender Girl*. London: Sidgwick and Jackson.

Stock, Carol McNichol. 1996. *Rural Radicals: Righteous Rage in the American Grain.* Ithaca: Cornell University Press.

Stølen, Kristi Anne. 1995. "The Gentle Exercise of Male Power in Rural Argentina." *Identities: Global Studies in Culture and Power* 2 (4): 385–406.

Strachan, Hew. 1997. *The Politics of the British Army.* Oxford: Oxford University Press.

Strate, Lance. 1992. "Beer Commercials: A Manual on Masculinity." In *Men, Masculinity, and the Media,* ed. Steve Craig. Newbury Park, Calif.: Sage Publications.

Strupstad, Liv Marit. 1991. *Den Tause Skogeier* (The Silent Forest Owner), report 43. Bø i Telemark: Telemark Research Foundations.

Stueland, D., S. H. Mickel, D. A. Cleveland, R. R. Rothfusz, T. Zoch, and P. Stamas. 1995. "The Relationship of Farm Residency Status to Demographic and Service Characteristics of Agricultural Injury Victims in Central Wisconsin." *Journal of Rural Health* 11 (2): 98–105.

Thomas, Jennifer C., and Paul Mohai. 1995. "Racial, Gender, and Professional Diversification in the Forest Service from 1983 to 1992." *Policy Studies Journal* 23 (2): 296–309.

Thompson, Mark. 1987. *Gay Spirit: Myth and Meaning.* New York: St. Martin's Press.

Tivers, Jacqueline. 1999. "'The Home of the British Army': The Iconic Construction of Military Defence Landscapes." *Landscape Research* 24 (3): 303–19.

Tom of Finland. 1992. *Tom of Finland.* Cologne: Taschen.

Tönnies, Ferdinand. 1887/1957. *Gemeinschaft und Gesellschaft.* New York: Harper and Row.

United States Preventive Services Task Force. 1996. *Guide to Clinical Preventive Services,* 2d ed. Baltimore: Williams and Wilkins.

Valentine, Gill. 1993. "(Hetero)sexing Space: Lesbian Perceptions and Experiences of Everyday Spaces." *Environment and Planning D: Society and Space* 11 (4): 395–413.

———. 1997. "Making Space: Lesbian Separatist Communities in the United States." In *Contested Countryside Cultures: Otherness, Marginalisation, and Rurality,* ed. Paul Cloke and Jo Little, 109–22. London: Routledge.

Vance, Carole S. 1995. "Social Construction Theory and Sexuality." In *Constructing Masculinity,* ed. Maurice Berger, Brian Wallis, and Simon Watson, 37–48. New York: Routledge.

Van Dijk, Teun. 1997. "The Study of Discourse." In *Discourse as Social Interaction,* ed. Teun van Dijk, 10–34. London: Sage Publications.

Van Lieshout, Maurice. 1995. "Leather Nights in the Woods: Homosexual Encounters in a Dutch Highway Rest Area." *Journal of Homosexuality* 29:19–39.

Van Maanan, John. 1988. "Confessional Tales." In John Van Maanan, *Tales of the Field: On Writing Ethnography,* 73–103. Chicago: University of Chicago Press.

Verbrugge, L. M., and D. L. Wingard. 1987. "Sex Differentials in Health and Mortality." *Women and Health* 12 (2): 103–45.

Villa, Mariann. 1999. "Born to Be Farmers? Changing Expectations in Norwegian Farmers' Life Courses." *Sociologia Ruralis* 39 (3): 328–42.

Virgil [Publius Vergilius Maro]. 2002. "Virgil: The *Georgics*." Trans. A. S. Kline [a new translation of Virgil's *Georgics*, his four books on farming]. Online: http://www.tkline.freeserve.co.uk/VirgilGeorgicsII.htm.

Walter, Gerry. 1997. "Images of Success: How Illinois Farmers Define the Successful Farmer." *Rural Sociology* 62 (1): 48–68.

Walter, Gerry, and Suzanne Wilson. 1996. "Silent Partners: Women in Farm Magazine Success Stories, 1934–1991." *Rural Sociology* 61 (2): 227–48.

Warner, Keith, and Lynn England. 1995. "A Technological Science Perspective for Sociology." *Rural Sociology* 60:607–22.

Weber, Max. 1978. *Economy and Society: An Outline of Interpretive Sociology*, ed. Geunther Roth and Claus Wittich. Berkeley and Los Angeles: University of California Press.

Weiler, R. M. 1997. "Adolescents' Perceptions of Health Concerns: An Exploratory Study Among Rural Midwestern Youth." *Health Education and Behavior* 24 (3): 287–99.

Weir, John. 1996. "Going In." In *Anti-Gay*, ed. Mark Simpson, 26–34. London: Cassell.

Weis, Lois. 1993. "White Male Working-Class Youth: An Exploration of Relative Privilege and Loss." In *Beyond Silenced Voices: Class, Race, and Gender in United States Schools*, ed. Lois Weis and Michelle Fine. Albany: State University of New York Press.

"Welfare Reform for Farmers." 2003. Editorial, *New York Times*, 10 November, A22.

West, Candace, and Don H. Zimmerman. 1987. "Doing Gender." *Gender and Society* 1 (2): 125–51.

———. 1991. "Doing Gender." In *The Social Construction of Gender*, ed. Judith Lorber and Susan A. Farell, 13–37. Newbury Park, Calif.: Sage Publications.

Weston, Kath. 1995. "Get Thee to a Big City: Sexual Imaginary and the Great Gay Migration." *GLQ* 2 (3): 253–77.

Wetherington, Michael V. 1994. *The New South Comes to Wiregrass Georgia, 1865–1910*. Knoxville: University of Tennessee Press.

Whatmore, Sarah, Terry Marsden, and Philip Lowe, eds. 1994. *Gender and Rurality*. London: David Fulton.

Wilkie, Jane R. 1993. "Changes in United States Men's Attitudes Toward the Family Provider Role, 1972–1989." *Gender and Society* 7 (2): 261–79.

Willems, James P., J. Terry Saunders, Dawn E. Hunt, and John B. Schorling. 1997. "Prevalence of Coronary Heart Disease Risk Factors Among Rural Blacks: A Community-Based Study." *Southern Medical Journal* 90 (8): 814–20.

Williams, Brackette. 1995. "Review of *The Black Atlantic*: Modernity and Double Consciousness." *Social Identities* 1:175–92.

Williams, Ted. 2004. "Sportsmen for Bush: Wise Up!" *Progressive Populist* 10 (1): 6–7.

Williamson, Judith. 1978. *Decoding Advertisements: Ideology and Meaning in Advertising*. London: Marion Boyars.

Willits, Fern K., Robert C. Bealer, and Vincent L. Timbers. 1990. "Popular Images of 'Rurality': Data from a Pennsylvania Survey." *Rural Sociology* 55 (4): 559–78.

Wilson, Angelia. 2000. *Below the Belt: Sexuality, Religion, and the American South.* London: Cassell.

Women and Geography Study Group. 1997. *Feminist Geographies: Explorations in Diversity and Difference.* London: Longman.

Woodward, Rachel. 1996. *Green or Khaki Spaces? The Relationships Between the Armed Forces and the Countryside.* Working paper 19. Newcastle: Centre for Rural Economy.

———. 1998. "'It's a Man's Life!': Soldiers, Masculinity, and the Countryside." *Gender, Place and Culture* 5 (3): 277–300.

———. 1999. "Gunning for Rural England: The Politics of the Promotion of Military Land Use in the Northumberland National Park." *Journal of Rural Studies* 15 (1): 17–33.

———. 2000. "Warrior Heroes and Little Green Men: Soldiers, Military Training, and Construction of Rural Masculinities." *Rural Sociology* 65:640–57.

———. 2001. "Khaki Conservation: An Examination of Military Environmentalist Discourses in the British Army." *Journal of Rural Studies* 17 (2): 201–17.

———. 2003. "Locating Military Masculinities: The Role of Space and Place in the Formation of Gender Identities in the Armed Forces. In *Military Masculinities: Identity and the State,* ed. Paul Higate, 43–56. Westport, Conn.: Praeger.

———. 2004. *Military Geographies.* Oxford: Blackwell.

Woodward, Rachel, and Patricia Winter. 2002. Interview of senior British army officer by Trish Winter, Tri-Service Equal Opportunities Training Centre, UK, summer.

———. 2004. "Discourses of Gender in the Contemporary British Army." *Armed Forces and Society* 30 (2): 279–302.

———. 2006. "The Limits to Diversity: Gender, Women and the British Army." *Gender, Work, and Organization* 13 (1). Woolf, Steven H., Steven Jonas, and Robert S. Lawrence, eds. 1996. *Health Promotion and Disease Prevention in Clinical Practice.* Baltimore: Williams and Wilkins.

Wright, Gerard. 1999. "Gay Grief in Cowboy County." *The Guardian,* 27 March, 3.

Wright, Les, ed. 2000. *The Bear Book II: Further Readings in the History and Evolution of a Gay Male Subculture.* New York: Haworth.

Young, Thomas J. 1990. "Violent Hate Groups in Rural America." *International Journal of Offender Therapy and Comparative Criminology* 34 (1): 15–21.

Yuval-Davis, Nira. 1997. *Gender and Nation.* London: Sage Publications.

# Index

RURAL STUDIES SERIES

*Leif Jensen, General Editor*
*Diane K. McLaughlin and Carolyn E. Sachs, Deputy Editors*

The Estuary's Gift: An Atlantic Coast Cultural Biography
*David Griffith*

Sociology in Government: The Galpin-Taylor Years in the U.S.
Department of Agriculture, 1919–1953
*Olaf F. Larson and Julie N. Zimmerman*
*Assisted by Edward O. Moe*

Challenges for Rural America in the Twenty-First Century
*Edited by David L. Brown and Louis Swanson*

A Taste of the Country: A Collection of Calvin Beale's Writings
*Peter A. Morrison*

Farming for Us All: Practical Agriculture and the Cultivation
of Sustainability
*Michael Mayerfeld Bell*

Together at the Table: Sustainability and Sustenance in the American
Agrifood System
*Patricia Allen*